2 CORINTHIANS

Text copyright © Aída Besançon Spencer 2001

The author asserts the moral right to be
identified as the author of this work

Published by
BRF, First Floor, Elsfield Hall,
15–17 Elsfield Way, Oxford OX2 8EP
ISBN 1 84101 073 1

First edition 2001
10 9 8 7 6 5 4 3 2 1 0

Acknowledgments
Unless otherwise stated, scripture quotations are taken from
The New Revised Standard Version of the Bible, copyright ©
1989, 1995 by the Division of Christian Education of the
National Council of the Churches of Christ in the United States
of America, and are used by permission. All rights reserved.

Scripture quotations taken from the *Holy Bible, New International
Version*, copyright © 1973, 1978, 1984 by International Bible
Society. Used by permission of Hodder & Stoughton Limited. All
rights reserved. 'NIV' is a registered trademark of International
Bible Society. UK trademark number 1448790.

Revised English Bible with the Apocrypha copyright © 1989 by
Oxford University Press and Cambridge University Press.

Extracts from the Authorized Version of the Bible (The King
James Bible), the rights in which are vested in the Crown, are
reproduced by permission of the Crown's Patentee, Cambridge
University Press.

A catalogue record for this book is
available from the British Library

Printed and bound in Great Britain
by Omnia Books Ltd, Glasgow

2 CORINTHIANS

THE PEOPLE'S BIBLE COMMENTARY

AÍDA BESANÇON SPENCER

A BIBLE COMMENTARY FOR EVERY DAY

Dedicated to
the Reverend Doctor William David Spencer,
co-worker with me for my joy,
whom I love dearly

Introducing the
People's Bible Commentary
SERIES

Congratulations! You are embarking on a voyage of discovery—or rediscovery. You may feel you know the Bible very well; you may never have turned its pages before. You may be looking for a fresh way of approaching daily Bible study; you may be searching for useful insights to share in a study group or from a pulpit.

The People's Bible Commentary (PBC) series is designed for all those who want to study the scriptures in a way that will warm the heart as well as instructing the mind. To help you, the series distils the best of scholarly insights into the straightforward language and devotional emphasis of Bible reading notes. Explanation of background material, and discussion of the original Greek and Hebrew, will always aim to be brief.

- If you have never really studied the Bible before, the series offers a serious yet accessible way in.

- If you help to lead a church study group, or are otherwise involved in regular preaching and teaching, you can find invaluable 'snapshots' of a Bible passage through the PBC approach.

- If you are a church worker or minister, burned out on the Bible, this series could help you recover the wonder of scripture.

Using a People's Bible Commentary

The series is designed for use alongside any version of the Bible. You may have your own favourite translation, but you might like to consider trying a different one in order to gain fresh perspectives on familiar passages.

Many Bible translations come in a range of editions, including study and reference editions that have concordances, various kinds of special index, maps and marginal notes. These can all prove helpful in studying the relevant passage. The Notes section at the back of each PBC volume provides space for you to write personal reflections, points to follow up, questions and comments.

Each People's Bible Commentary can be used on a daily basis, instead of Bible reading notes. Alternatively, it can be read straight through, or used as a resource book for insight into particular verses of the biblical book.

If you have enjoyed using this commentary and would like to progress further in Bible study, you will find details of other volumes in the series listed at the back, together with information about a special offer from BRF.

While it is important to deepen understanding of a given passage, this series always aims to engage both heart and mind in the study of the Bible. The scriptures point to our Lord himself and our task is to use them to build our relationship with him. When we read, let us do so prayerfully, slowly, reverently, expecting him to speak to our hearts.

PREFACE

I enjoyed the opportunity to write this devotional commentary and appreciate Naomi Starkey of the Bible Reading Fellowship for having invited me to participate. My husband, William David Spencer, carefully edited every page and, as well, co-wrote the 1989 *Bible Study Commentary* on 2 Corinthians which was a helpful resource for this more extensive commentary. Karen Smith, pastor of discipleship at Pilgrim Church regularly prayed for the smooth completion of the work, as did the Network for Presbyterian Women in Leadership and many others. How could I succeed in studying God's message without God's help? Gordon-Conwell Theological Seminary granted me a semester's sabbatical from teaching which was essential for the time and concentration needed. And my typist Kelli Brodrecht applied particular care and diligence as she worked hard to type my manuscript. Jinyoung Seo and editors of the Bible Reading Fellowship double checked the Bible references.

Many secondary works have been helpful, but a list of some of the cited works is given at the end of the Introduction (p. 25) in case any readers want to verify any information:

At the end of the study, I wrote a poem, together with my husband, to summarize figuratively some of the key thoughts of 2 Corinthians. The poem is printed overleaf; you may want to read it now and at the end of your own studies, as a way to encapsulate the book.

Beneath the Master Gardener

The garden is devastated.
Where once were beauty and growth
are now broken stems and torn leaves.
Animals have breached the fences
and black rust lingers like crows.

The sun knows how to heal it,
if the gardener and garden give their welcome.
I bow my head beneath that grace and prune away the rust.
I mend protecting fences to grant it peace to grow.

A shadow Sabbath summons rest.
I straighten up and stretch sore muscles tendered by the work.
Luminous with life the garden glows at dusk.
Its health demands it keep the charge of Eden.

Like Eden, so many gardens lost,
overgrown or turned over to try again…
garden and gardener beneath the Master Gardener
find paradise at hand in every city yard and every country field,
tilling lives to yield lasting fruit.

Aída Besançon Spencer & William David Spencer

CONTENTS

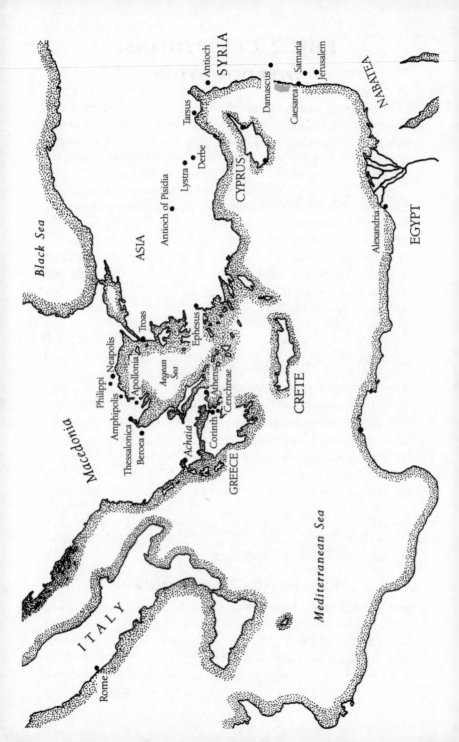

PBC 2 CORINTHIANS:
INTRODUCTION

2 Corinthians is a letter forged in the heat of difficult circumstances, where doctrine and practice integrate. The apostle Paul is a theologian, learned in doctrine, and a pastor who loves and desires the best for his people. Not a loner, he works with co-workers. His people love him and yet can be deceived and attracted to false leaders.

Because this letter is both a sensitive and a passionate communication, its transitions are subtle. Its tone changes. Nevertheless, when the church at Corinth first received this letter, not having heard from Paul for many months, they certainly did not tell the reader to stop after one sentence and they would hear more next week! I am sure they heard the whole message aloud. Later, they may have gone back to the letter and analyzed parts of it in detail: 'Read me the part about the fragrance! Read me the part about the angel of light! Read me the part about Paul's love for us!' So, too, I would recommend you begin your study of 2 Corinthians by using an easy-to-read version and reading all of it at one sitting in a quiet place where you will not be disturbed. (It takes me twenty minutes to read all of 2 Corinthians.) Then together we will go sentence by sentence through the letter in more detail. For the studies, I quote the New Revised Standard Version. Paul wrote the letter in the international language of his time, Greek, which in God's providence is still a living language today. Reading 2 Corinthians in ancient Greek is, therefore, of course, most accurate! But if you do not know Greek, the NRSV is very close to the original and clear and easy to understand today.

When Paul quotes the Old Testament, at times he does his own translation directly from the original Hebrew and at other times he quotes the Greek Septuagint version (LXX, which had been translated by a team of scholars in 250–200BC).

Who wrote 2 Corinthians?

Paul and Timothy are mentioned in the letterhead. Normally, both would be considered authors, but since 'I' is used only of Paul (2:1–13; 9:1–15; 10:1; 11:21—12:17; 13:6, 10) and Timothy is described in the third person (1:19), almost everyone agrees that Paul is the writer. Timothy is included on the letterhead as a partner in ministry, exemplifying Paul's concept of genuine leadership.

Paul is presented in 2 Corinthians as an apostle (1:1; 12:12), a Hebrew (11:22) (a descendant of Abraham and Eber) and a follower of Jesus Christ (1:2; 11:23). He has suffered greatly, been physically deprived, lived through dangerous situations and been imprisoned. He is well educated (11:6; Acts 26:24), passionate, bold and honest, but he does not want to frighten away his listeners. His skilful writing is admired even by opponents (10:10).

Every early Christian who mentions Paul sees him as a model. Clement of Rome, considering Paul part of his own generation and inspired by 2 Corinthians 11:23–25, writes:

> *Through jealousy and strife Paul showed the way to the prize of endurance; seven times he was in bonds, he was exiled, he was stoned, he was a herald both in the East and in the West, he gained the noble fame of his faith, he taught righteousness to all the world, and when he had reached the limits of the West he gave his testimony before the rulers, and thus passed from the world and was taken up into the Holy Place—the greatest example of endurance.* (1 Clement v. 5–7)

Ignatius, who wanted to follow in Paul's footprints, describes Paul to a later group of Ephesians as 'sanctified, who gained a good report, who was right blessed' (xii.2). Polycarp describes Paul as 'blessed and glorious', a man who 'taught accurately and steadfastly the word of truth, and also when he was absent wrote letters to you, from the study of which you will be able to build yourselves up into the faith given you; which is the mother of us all' (*Philippians* iii.2–3). In contrast, Paul saw himself as an example to sinners, that Christ Jesus came to save, of whom Paul was the foremost: 'I was formerly a blasphemer, a persecutor, and a man of violence. But I received mercy because I had acted ignorantly in unbelief, and the grace of our Lord overflowed for me with the faith and love that are in Christ Jesus' (1 Timothy 1:13–14). Paul is a great example of a marvellous human transformation.

He enters the Bible as a young man (probably in his mid-twenties) who stood by approvingly, guarding the outer coats of the witnesses who were stoning Stephen (Acts 7:58—8:1). He was so stirred by this event, he himself set about to destroy the Church, extending its first major persecution over 130 miles to Damascus. On that road, Paul discovered that instead of promoting the living God, he had been persecuting the promised Messiah, Jesus (Acts 9:5), and that he had been chosen by God to proclaim Jesus' name even if he had to suffer to do so (Acts 9:15—16). Some fourteen years later, Paul (Saul is his Jewish name), with co-worker Barnabas, was called to a special work (Acts 13:2). He had sojourned in Damascus, Jerusalem, Tarsus and Arabia (Galatians 1:17—2:1), but not until now did God consider Paul ready to be sent out from Antioch, his home church.

Paul was converted around AD33–35 during the reign of Roman Emperor Tiberius (AD14–37). Acts recounts his missionary journeys, which lasted several decades and ended in imprisonment in Rome (around AD59–61/62). Acts leaves Paul in Rome, under house arrest, still proclaiming Jesus as the promised Messiah (28:16, 30–31). Paul expected to be released (Acts 25:25; 26:32; Philippians 2:24). 2 Timothy and early church tradition testify to a second imprisonment, when Emperor Nero began to persecute Christians in AD64–68 (2 Timothy 4:6–7). This second imprisonment resulted in Paul's execution, around AD67–68 (Eusebius, *History* ii.25; iii.1).

Paul lived about 33 years as a Jew transformed by his relationship with Jesus the Messiah and, consequently, was used by God to transform thousands of other people by his exemplary life and his God-breathed writings (2 Timothy 3:16).

Who are Paul's co-workers?

In 2 Corinthians, Timothy, Silvanus and Titus are mentioned by name (1:1, 19; 12:18). When Paul uses the first person plural 'we' in 2 Corinthians, he tends to refer to his ministering team as together modelling the principles of genuine Christian service: the hardships *we* suffered (for example, 1:3–12; 7:5–6); 'our competence is from God' (3:1–18); 'we have wronged no one' (7:2; 10:3–7; 11:12); 'we are not commending ourselves' (5:12). 'I hope you will find out that we have not failed' (13:6) shows that Paul writes 2 Corinthians with his co-workers in mind. What makes each of these co-workers unique?

Timothy

Timothy works with Paul, providing a living model of Paul's teachings. His name is included not only in the 2 Corinthians heading, but in those of Philippians, Colossians, 1 and 2 Thessalonians and Philemon. Timothy is described by Paul as 'our brother' (2 Corinthians

1:1; Colossians 1:1; Philemon 1), Paul's spiritual child (Philippians 2:22; 2 Timothy 1:2), a minister (1 Timothy 4:6), a slave (*doulos*) of Christ Jesus (Philippians 1:1), a co-worker (Romans 16:21; 1 Corinthians 3:9; 1 Thessalonians 3:2) and evangelist (2 Timothy 4:5).

The son of a Jewish Christian mother and Gentile father (Acts 16:1), Timothy lived in Lystra, where he may have become a Christian when Paul passed through on his first missionary journey (Acts 14:6–7). All the Christians in his home town had spoken well of Timothy, and Paul wanted him to join his pastoral team. But to avoid the opposition of the Jews to having a hellenized Jew for a preaching companion, Paul had Timothy circumcised (Acts 16:3). Paul left Timothy in Beroea and Thessalonica to establish the Thessalonians in the faith (Acts 17:14). Timothy's job was to exhort and explain the part that afflictions have in the faith, and was apparently successful, for he was able to bring Paul good news about the Thessalonians' faith (1 Thessalonians 3:2–7). With the Corinthians, Timothy reminds them of the ways of Paul and serves, himself, as a model (1 Corinthians 4:16–17). Paul himself urges the Philippians to live according to the pattern that both he and Timothy gave them (Philippians 3:17). Timothy visits Paul in prison in Rome, serving his spiritual parent Paul, as Paul serves Christ.

Silvanus (also called Silas)

When Timothy joined Paul at Lystra, Silas (Latin 'Silvanus') was already travelling with Paul. As a leader among the Christians in Jerusalem, Silas was sent with Paul and Barnabas to confirm the Jerusalem Council's positive decision about the Gentiles (Acts 15:22). As a prophet, he encouraged and strengthened the new believers at Antioch (Acts 15:32). When Paul and Barnabas could not agree about John Mark, Paul invited Silas to join him on his second missionary journey (Acts 15:40). Silas, along with Paul, was imprisoned in Philippi after Paul commanded the evil spirit to depart from the fortune-telling woman. Silas was together with Paul 'praying and singing hymns' in the innermost cell (Acts 16:19–25).

When Paul was attacked in Thessalonica, the crowds also looked for Silas. Both of them were sent on to Beroea for their own protection. Silas, along with Timothy, stayed behind to teach the new believers in Beroea (Acts 17:5, 10, 14), but later they joined Paul in Corinth (Acts 18:5). Paul alludes to their preaching and writing ministry in Corinth in his letter (2 Corinthians 1:19). They also wrote to the new Christians in Thessalonica while at Corinth (1 Thessalonians 1:1; 2 Thessalonians 1:1). Finally, years later (around AD64–68), Peter sent Silas with his letter (1 Peter), again both to encourage and to reinforce the written message with a living presence. Peter calls him a 'faithful brother' (1 Peter 5:12). Silas was a Christian who could be trusted.

Titus

Titus must have been quite a diplomat. He is the first person to intercede in difficult situations. Many times Paul urged him to go on his behalf to Corinth (2 Corinthians 8:6, 17; 12:18). Paul could expect that the highly sensitive Corinthians would not feel exploited by Titus. He also would intercede for the Corinthians (2 Corinthians 7:7, 15). An encourager (Titus 2:15), he also may have had organizational gifts and gifts of service (Titus 3:12–13). Titus was a Gentile who became a follower of Jesus. He accompanied Paul and Barnabas with the earlier collection for the Christians in Jerusalem (Acts 11:30; Galatians 2:1–3), as he did with the current collection (2 Corinthians 8:6). He also stayed at Crete to 'put in order what remained to be done' and 'appoint elders in every town' (Titus 1:5). Titus had to silence the circumcision party (Titus 1:10–12), an explosive task for a Gentile Christian who once had been a second-class Gentile God-fearer.

Paul abounds with affection when he writes of 'brother' Titus (2 Corinthians 2:13). He calls him his 'loyal child' (Titus 1:4), his 'partner and co-worker' (2 Corinthians 8:23). The last we hear of Titus is that he has accompanied Paul to Rome and then left for Dalmatia (2 Timothy 4:10). The early Church esteemed Titus and Timothy, calling them the first bishops appointed to the churches of Crete and Ephesus (Eusebius, *History of the Church* iii:4).

Paul worked with many co-workers, partners in ministry. As an apostle, a witness to the living Lord, Paul laid the foundation (1 Corinthians 3:10; Ephesians 2:20; 2 Corinthians 10:14). Silas, as a prophet, would receive and speak forth God's message. Timothy, as an evangelist, would preach, baptize and instruct people in the basics of faith. Titus, as an encourager, would advocate and work on reconciliation between warring parties.

Why is Achaia included?

Today 'Greece' includes both the ancient provinces of Macedonia and Achaia. But when Paul wrote 2 Corinthians, 'Greece' included only Achaia (Acts 20:2). The city-states in Achaia had earlier united to try to defeat King Philip II of Macedon. By 150BC Corinth had become the capital of the league of cities in Achaia. When this Achaian League refused to disband, the Romans, led by consul Lucius Mummius, burned the city of Corinth in 146BC. In 44BC, because of its strategic position, Julius Caesar decreed the refounding of Corinth as a military precaution.

Why does Paul address 2 Corinthians to include 'all the saints throughout Achaia' (1:1)? Some of the issues with which Paul will deal are especially relevant to the entire province. The issue of collecting money for the poor Christians in Jerusalem is a matter for all the churches (9:2). Paul does speak directly to the Corinthians (1:23; 6:11). Only the Corinthians appear to be in revolt against Paul's leadership. Paul did not want the 'super-apostles' to leave Corinth and wreak the same havoc in another city. Paul appears aware that his letters, infused with God's prophetic message, have a larger audience, as he writes to the Colossians: 'And when this letter has been read among you, have it read also in the church of the Laodiceans; and see that you read also the letter from Laodicea' (Colossians 4:16).

When did these events occur?

Acts 18:2 tells us that, about AD49, Emperor Claudius issued a decree against Jewish Christians. As a result, Aquila and Priscilla transferred from Italy to Corinth. Then Silas and Timothy arrived from Macedonia. Now Paul could preach full-time. For a year and six months he stirred up the city with the startling message of Jesus (Acts 18:5). Finally, some enraged Jews dragged Paul before proconsul Lucius Junius Gallio (summer of AD51), placing Paul in Corinth around AD50–51. Acts 18:18 tells us he stayed about three months after his aborted trial, until late autumn 51/early 52, when he returned to Antioch.

Thus, Paul wrote 2 Corinthians after leaving Corinth in the autumn of 52 but before he collected the financial gift for the believers in Jerusalem (Acts 20:2–3). About five years later he was arrested in Jerusalem (around AD57).

Paul writes at least three letters to the Corinthians between the two visits recorded in Acts. The first letter, in God's sovereignty, has not been preserved. Paul sends Titus with a letter about not associating with immoral Christians (1 Corinthians 5:9–10). Paul follows Titus' presentation of the letter with several visits by Timothy and Erastus (1 Corinthians 4:17; 16:10; Acts 19:22). Paul then receives news from Chloe's household about the Corinthians quarrelling (1 Corinthians 1:11) and a letter with questions, personally delivered by Stephana(s), Fortunatus and Achaicus (1 Corinthians 16:17). Paul writes his second letter (1 Corinthians in our canon) in the spring (around AD56) from Ephesus (1 Corinthians 16:8, 19), during his three years ministering in Ephesus (Acts 19:8, 10, 22).

Titus and Timothy return from Corinth to Ephesus. Paul himself makes a quick trip to Corinth, which ends up quite 'painful' (2 Corinthians 2:1–8; 1 Corinthians 4:19). This trip is not mentioned in Acts. Paul follows this second visit with a letter 'out of much distress and anguish of heart and with many tears' to let the Corinthians know of his 'abundant love' (2 Corinthians 2:3–9; 7:8–12) and foreshadows his 'third' visit in 2 Corinthians (12:14; 13:1). Titus personally brings this letter to determine the Corinthians' spiritual state and to remind them of the collection (2:13; 7:6–15). Some scholars think the letter of 'tears' was 1 Corinthians; however, I do not think this description well fits the tone and topic-by-topic discussion of 1 Corinthians. Other scholars think that 2 Corinthians 10—13 were originally the letter of 'tears'. However, papyrus 46, our earliest document (29–144 years older than the original), includes all 2 Corinthians' 13 chapters together, which is one of many good arguments for the unity of 2 Corinthians.

Paul had prearranged to meet Titus at the seaport town of Troas, in Asia, across from Macedonia (2 Corinthians 2:13; Acts 20:1). When Titus does not return, Paul in distress takes a boat across the Aegean Sea to Neapolis, a seaport town in Macedonia. They meet somewhere in Macedonia, where Paul discovers that, though Titus has had some success with the Corinthians (2 Corinthians 7:5–6), their submission to Paul's leadership has worsened. Paul writes 2 Corinthians in AD56 from Macedonia (9:2, 4–5). He has already received generous donations from the churches in Macedonia (8:2). Paul sends 2 Corinthians with Titus and others to prepare the Corinthians for the final collection and his third visit (8:6, 17–24; 13:1–10).

This next visit to Corinth appears to have gone well. He recounts,

'Macedonia and Achaia have been pleased to share their resources with the poor among the saints at Jerusalem' (Romans 15:26). Romans was written soon after this third visit to Corinth. Clement, later in the first century, praises the Corinthians for their virtue, godliness, hospitality, obedience, humility and unity, qualities they did not have in AD56, even though again they have problems with disunity. According to Hegesippus, Corinth continued in orthodox doctrine until Primus became bishop (after 100) (Eusebius, *History* iv.22).

What was Corinth like?

Imposing Corinth stood as the hub of a three-city complex, straddling the south-west end of the tiny isthmus that connects the southern part of the Greek peninsula to the mainland. About two miles north was Lechaeum, and over six miles east was Cenchreae, home of Phoebe (Romans 16:1–2).

In 44BC, Corinth was renamed 'Colonia Laus Julia Corinthiensis', rebuilt by a colony of freed Italians, Roman army veterans, Greeks, Egyptian merchants, Phoenicians, Phrygians, Jews and other Asians. Latin became its official language, and under Augustus Caesar, Julius Caesar's adopted son, it flourished.

Into this mix a fully integrated church of Gentiles and Jews was planted. To the former Paul would write, 'You know that when you were pagans, you were enticed and led astray to idols' (1 Corinthians 12:2). To both Gentile and Jew he counselled, 'Circumcision is nothing, and uncircumcision is nothing; but obeying the commandments of God is everything' (1 Corinthians 7:19). This brand new city lacked an aristocracy, so money and power ruled. Within less than twenty years of its refounding, Corinth became the capital of the province of Achaia and the administrative seat of the Roman government's proconsul for southern and central Greece. Thus, by the time Paul arrived, Corinth had grown to be one of the largest cities in the Roman Empire.

Because the southern tip of Greece around the horn of Cape Malea was extremely dangerous, almost all trade and travel from the east to the west had to be done through Corinth. Corinth collected the imperial duties, becoming a major banking and commercial centre. Its crafts were renowned. Its pottery was beautiful; its bronze world-famous. Strabo wrote, 'The city of the Corinthians, then, was always great and wealthy, and it was well equipped with men skilled both in the affairs of state and in the craftsman's arts' (*Geography* 8.6.23). Further, the Isthmian games, second only to the Olympics, were celebrated every two years, going back under Corinth's control some time between 7BC and AD3.

Yet Corinth was infested with pagan temples. Towering over the city, perched on the sheer cliffs of the grey limestone of the mountain Acrocorinth, reclined one of Corinth's temples of Aphrodite, goddess of love. Over one thousand temple slaves or prostitutes once served the holy brothel of Aphrodite, and though the number may have lessened by the time Paul visited, decadence still characterized Corinth's religious rites. Temples abounded to Demeter, the Great Mother, Isis, Serapis, Asclepius, Apollo, Tyche, Hermes and the Pantheon—the many gods. Paul, Aquila and Priscilla probably had their store in the newly opened shop area on the Lechaeum Road, in the shadow of Apollo's sanctuary near the smaller meat market.

The Jews of the congregation, whose synagogue was also on the Lechaeum Road, initially resisted Paul, becoming abusive (Acts 18:6). But Crispus, the synagogue ruler, and his entire household believed. When the enraged synagogue members dragged Paul before proconsul Gallio, who summarily rejected their suit and tossed them out of court, they turned on Sosthenes, the synagogue ruler, and beat him in front of the court (Acts 18:17). (Paul later ministered in Ephesus with a Christian Sosthenes who may well have been this very same beaten synagogue ruler—see 1 Corinthians 1:1.)

What were the Corinthians like?

Corinth boasted of its intellectual activity, but it paled beside Athens and Alexandria. The church at Corinth, too, loved prophecy and knowledge, preferring speech over love (1 Corinthians 1:5; 13:8–9; 14:2; 2 Corinthians 8:7), but, like the city, the church pursued knowledge avidly but not wisely. As a result, members lorded it over one another and fell out in disputes, taking each other to court (1 Corinthians 1:10; 6:1; 11:18; 2 Corinthians 13:1, 11).

Corinth was a town of the *nouveau riche*: it had no real roots. What Paul highlights in the church was true of the city as well: 'your present abundance' (2 Corinthians 8:14). This sudden influx of wealth in a rootless boom town made Corinth like one vast drunken sailor, all at once rich with pay, squandering its swiftly gotten gains on pleasure. Indeed, Corinth was the most immoral city in Greece, perhaps in the entire Roman empire. As early as the days of the satirist Aristophanes (about 450–385BC), Corinth had been working on its immoral reputation. He coined the verb *corinthiazomai* ('to live like a Corinthian'), meaning 'to practise fornication'.

What kind of people would be produced by such a city? Paul reminds the church of Corinth of what they had been—sexually immoral, drunken thieves, steeped in idol worship: 'But you were washed, you were sanctified, you were justified in the name of the Lord Jesus Christ and in the Spirit of our God' (1 Corinthians 6:11). Residual sins such as incest (ch. 5) and sexual immorality (6:9–18; 2 Corinthians 12:21) had to be brought to attention and eradicated in the Corinthian church. Managing to be both immoral and ascetic (1 Corinthians 7:1; 2 Corinthians 2:6–7), the Corinthians only lacked moderation!

The Corinthians also were stingy. They were more likely to flaunt their newly gained wealth than share it (1 Corinthians 11:21–22). Like most miserly people, they wanted their preachers, Barnabas and Paul, to earn their own living and to minister *gratis* (1 Corinthians 9:6–18). Yet, when Paul received financial support from Macedonia, the Corinthians became jealous and suspicious that somehow Paul was taking advantage of them (2 Corinthians 7:2)! Though he had the right, Paul did not charge the Corinthians for his services to them, scrupulously avoiding the accusation of being a 'peddler' of God's word (2 Corinthians 2:17; 11:7–9).

Not all bad, the Corinthians could be loyal (1 Corinthians 11:2; 2 Corinthians 7:15), maintaining Paul's teachings. They did have a zeal for Paul and were grieved by his letter, wanting his approval (2 Corinthians 7:9), but they were fickle and unreliable. Paul was not certain of their total obedience (2 Corinthians 2:9). To Paul they were children in Christ (1 Corinthians 3:1; 2 Corinthians 6:13), still questioning such foundational doctrines as the resurrection of the dead (1 Corinthians 15:12).

That God could love the Corinthians, and Paul could persevere, despite continual disappointments, to love and serve them, is such a comforting thought for us all. For Paul assured the errant Corinthians again and again that he loved them (2 Corinthians 2:2–4; 7:3; 11:11; 12:15), deriving pride and joy from them (1 Corinthians 4:15; 2 Corinthians 7:3–16; 9:2).

He forgives all their failings because he regards them as a father does a child. Indeed, he is their spiritual father (Acts 18:1–18; 2 Corinthians 10:14; 11:2; 12:14), and because of his parental love he can be hurt by their lack of devotion and harsh criticism (2 Corinthians 10:1; 11:5). Made vulnerable by his love for them, Paul wants their commendation for all his struggle and suffering on their behalf (2 Corinthians 3:1; 12:11). And he dreads the potential disappointment both he and the Corinthians may experience in one another when they meet (2 Corinthians 12:20–21). He is deeply disturbed by their lack of faith (2 Corinthians 11:1–3; 13:5), imploring them urgently to follow his example, as he follows the example of Christ (1 Corinthians 11:1).

Overview of letter

Paul constructs a chronological schema and inserts along the way theological truths that each event teaches. 2 Corinthians is like a slide or video show of a journey through the Mediterranean countries, which is periodically halted to explain what was happening in the participant's mind at each place.

1 In 1:3–11, Paul speaks of the troubles in Asia and what they teach about comfort and suffering.

2 In 1:12—2:11, Paul outlines his plans to enter Macedonia.

3 In 2:12—7:4, Paul has now moved on to Troas, a port between two land masses.

4 In 7:5—8:15, Paul has crossed the Aegean Sea into Macedonia and found Titus. In the midst of difficulties, Paul receives good news from Titus about the Corinthians (7:5–16) and the Macedonians (8:1–15).

5 When Paul envisions future travel south to the province of Achaia (8:16—9:15), he discusses the collection.

6 In 10:1–2, Paul envisions his entrance into Corinth itself. His tone changes as he thinks of the distressful abandonment of his leadership. Now, focusing on Corinth, he confronts his opponents directly (10:1—12:18).

7 All the different themes in the letter occur again in the conclusion (12:19—13:14).

Like a jewel whose many facets are studied, the theme of suffering and grace is reflected in different lights: whom it benefits; how decisions change; how confidence can persist in difficulties; how repentance is worth the pain; how people work together with God's provision; and how genuine leadership, by God's grace, persists in suffering.

The contents of 2 Corinthians may be outlined as follows:

Purpose: Paul defends his and his co-workers' leadership style as an honourable one (according to God's grace, not worldly wisdom) in order that the Corinthians may not be misled.

1   Introductory greetings (1:1–2).

2   Paul's defence: we behave sincerely with pure motives in God's grace (1:3—2:17).

   a) Paul's team experiences afflictions in Asia (1:3–11).
   b) Paul's planning was sincere (1:12—2:17).

3   Paul's explanation: our competence comes from God (3:1—5:21).

   a) God's covenant written on living hearts causes frankness (3:1–18).
   b) God's mercy encourages Paul in hard times (4:1—5:10).
   c) Corinthians should be proud of Paul and his team (5:11–21).

4   Paul's warning: do not accept God's grace in vain (6:1—9:15).

   a) Paul's plea: make room for us in your hearts (6:1—7:3).
   b) Paul has confidence in the Corinthians (7:4—9:15).

5   Paul's warning: change or be disciplined (10:1—13:11).

   a) Paul defends his team's actions as not worldly (10:1—11:11).
   b) Paul explains his style of work (11:12—12:18).
   c) Paul summarizes his defence (12:19—13:11).

6   Paul gives final greetings (13:12–14).

Suggestions for further reading

Philip Wesley Comfort, *The Quest for the Original Text of the New Testament*, Baker, 1992.

Philip Edgcumbe Hughes, *Paul's Second Epistle to the Corinthians*, Eerdmans, 1962.

Henry George Liddell and Robert Scott, *A Greek-English Lexicon, 9th ed.,* Clarendon, 1968.

Alfred Plummer, *A Critical and Exegetical Commentary on the Second Epistle of St Paul to the Corinthians*, T & T Clark, 1915.

A.T. Robertson, *A Grammar of the Greek New Testament in the Light of Historical Research*, Broadman, 1934.

A.T. Robertson, *Word Pictures in the New Testament iv,* Baker, 1931.

Aída Besançon Spencer, *Paul's Literary Style: A Stylistic and Historical Comparison of II Corinthians 11:16—12:13, Romans 8:9–39, and Philippians 3:2—4:13*, University Press of America, 1998.

Aída Besançon Spencer, '2 Corinthians', *Study Bible for Women: The New Testament*, Eds. Catherine Clark Kroeger, Mary Evans & Elaine Storkey, Baker, 1995.

Aída Besançon Spencer and William David Spencer, *Bible Study Commentary*, Zondervan, 1989.

Ceslas Spicq, *Theological Lexicon of the New Testament*, trans., ed. James D. Ernest, Hendrickson, 1994.

Joseph Henry Thayer, *Thayer's Greek-English Lexicon of the New Testament*, National Foundation for Christian Education, 1889.

Bruce W. Winter, 'The Entries and Ethics of Orators and Paul (1 Thessalonians 2:1–12)', *Tyndale Bulletin 44*, May 1993, 55–74.

TEACHINGS *in the* MIDST *of a* LETTERHEAD

Letter writing was a popular genre of communication in ancient times, as it still is today. Students from primary school to university level were taught how to write letters. Demetrius thought that a letter was the form of composition which most reveals the writer's character (*On Style*, 227). A letter began with the name of the writer(s) and possibly a title ('Paul, an apostle of Christ Jesus by the will of God, and Timothy our brother'), followed with the name(s) of the recipients(s) ('To the church of God that is in Corinth, including all the saints throughout Achaia'), and ending with a greeting ('Grace to you and peace from God our Father and the Lord Jesus Christ'). Often the letter itself began with a prayer, wish or thanksgiving. 2 Corinthians 1:1–2, in effect, is a letterhead.

An apostle and a brother write

Paul describes himself with one word, 'apostle'. An 'apostle' is an individual sent forth as an envoy of a person or a group with specific orders. For example, the different churches 'sent forth' someone to represent them with their collection for the churches in Jerusalem (8:23). Paul is also an 'apostle', but he is an apostle 'of Christ Jesus', in accordance with God's will. Christ Jesus 'sent forth' Paul when he called him on the road to Damascus. Paul, like the other apostles of Jesus, was appointed to bear witness to the resurrected Jesus (Acts 1:21–22; 26:16; 1 Corinthians 9:1). Supernatural works and suffering confirmed Paul's witness (2 Corinthians 12:12; Acts 2:43). In 2 Corinthians Paul's main intent is to defend himself as a genuine apostle in contrast to the more flamboyant false 'super-apostles' (11:5, 13).

Timothy, as well as Titus (2:13), Silas and others, are called 'brother(s)' in order to highlight the familial aspect of the church (compare John 19:26–27). 'Brother or sister' may also be a title showing a certain responsibility in Christian ministry (for example, 8:23).

For the Greco-Romans, secular 'church' was comprised of voting adult citizens with ultimate authority to make important decisions, similar to a town council meeting. Jesus, too, uses 'church' to signify a final authoritative group of believers (Matthew 18:17). For all Christians, the 'Church' is the gathering of men, women and children who belong to God. One part of this Church is living in Corinth and in the province of Achaia. In the same way, even today, the Church continues to be the gathering of people who belong to God but who dwell in specific places around the world.

Grace and peace come from God

Paul uses the noun form 'grace', instead of the more usual form 'greeting' (as in Acts 23:26; James 1:1), and has the identical greeting in most of his letters (1 Corinthians 1:3; Romans 1:7b; Galatians 1:3; Ephesians 1:2; Philippians 1:2; Philemon 1:3). In 2 Corinthians, especially, grace will become a key principle of genuine godly leadership (1:12). 'Grace' is 'gift'. It has the same root as 'joy'.

Paul always wants good things for his readers. 'Grace' is a common Greco-Roman word which reminds the readers of the new covenant, while 'peace' is a common Hebrew word (for example, Luke 10:5; Exodus 4:18) which reminds the readers of the first, or old, covenant. 'Peace' literally refers to being physically safe and unharmed (Joshua 9:15). Peacemakers seek the well-being of others and of themselves, live justly and bring peace and reconciliation between people at war (for example, Psalm 34:13–14). Perfect grace and peace come from God. Thus, Paul's greeting is also a prayer.

'Lord' is a term used of God the Father and now also of Jesus. For a Jew to call Jesus 'Lord'—that is, equal to God—is a momentous act. 'Lord' was an ancient title for someone a slave was compelled to obey (Romans 6:16). The difference for Christians is that God gives people the freedom to choose. Their wills are not superseded as they were by slave traders (1 Timothy 1:10). While some people sold themselves into slavery, possibly for a time, in order to benefit educationally and economically, God invites all people to benefit for eternity—educationally, economically and in every other way—by willingly taking on Jesus as Lord (2 Corinthians 4:5; Romans 10:9–10).

PRAYER

As I read and study 2 Corinthians, may I learn more about your grace and peace and lordship in my life and in the church at large.

PRAISING GOD

Frequently Paul begins a letter by thanking God for some special trait the readers have (1 Corinthians 1:4–7; Philippians 1:3–7; Colossians 1:3–6; 1 Thessalonians 1:2–10; 2 Thessalonians 1:3–4) but in 2 Corinthians Paul begins by praising God (as he does in Ephesians 1:3), because the readers have few positive traits.

Eulogies are for the living God

First, Paul highlights that God is 'blessed'. Many a devout Jew would similarly praise God, saying, 'Blessed is he that...' and adding an appropriate phrase such as 'Blessed is he that made the Great Sea' or 'Blessed is he, the good and the doer of good' or 'Blessed is he, the true Judge'. Thus, Zechariah, a devout Jew, begins his prophecy: 'Blessed be the Lord God of Israel' (Luke 1:68). To 'bless' is to give a good word or to celebrate someone with praises. Who is more worthy of praise than God? God is worth celebrating because God is God, and therefore unique. God is also the 'Father' of Jesus, not in a sexual way, as a human begets a child, or as, in Greek myth, Zeus and Hera begot Ares, Hephaestus and Hebe. Rather, God is the 'Father' of Jesus in that God-the-Trinity caused one person of the Trinity to be born as a human, Jesus (Luke 1:35; John 1:14; Philippians 2:5–7).

When Paul calls God the Father of Jesus, he is highlighting the equality of Jesus with God (John 5:18). Paul probably also alludes to the very common ancient practice in which 'father–son' indicated the giving of all inheritance rights to a 'son'. For instance, the Roman Emperor Gaius promised that he would appoint himself to be 'father' to his cousin Tiberius Gemellus—not simply a guardian, tutor or teacher—thereby stating that Tiberius would share ruling power with him (Philo, *Embassy to Gaius* iv). Similarly, God told David he would be to him 'as a father', signifying that David's inheritance and covenant line would be guaranteed (2 Samuel 7:13–16). That promise was fulfilled in David's descendant Jesus, to whom, of course, are continued in full measure all inheritance rights (Hebrews 1:5–8).

God the merciful advocate

God is to be celebrated also because God is the 'Father' or source of godly characteristics. Paul highlights two words of equal importance: 'mercies' and 'consolation'. 'Mercies' (*oiktirmos* in Greek) comes from the root idea of 'ah!' (*oi*), an exclamation of pain, grief, pity, astonishment. Here Paul uses the plural ('mercies') because he does not describe a one-time event but an ongoing characteristic. God is always ready to respond to humans in pity and, moreover, God is the source of pity. Paul wants the Corinthians to have mercy on him and therefore sympathetically understand why he did not recently visit them (1:23) and why Paul and his co-workers are genuine leaders (11:29). God's 'mercies' is not a frequently used word, but Paul uses it at key places. It is the basis for his appeal to the Romans to present their bodies as a living sacrifice (Romans 12:1) and to the Philippians to complete his joy (Philippians 2:1–2). In other words, God's mercy does not mean ignoring injustice. Rather, God has pity toward those unjustly treated. Thus, Paul can be sure of God's mercy toward him in the midst of his own difficult situation.

The suggestion in this passage that believers should be merciful as God is merciful is made explicit elsewhere. Paul exhorts the Colossians to put on 'mercies' as if they were clothing (Colossians 3:12). And where did Paul learn this? Jesus himself exhorted, 'Be merciful, just as your Father is merciful' (Luke 6:36).

'Consolation' is the second characteristic of God that Paul highlights. Like 'mercies', it is an aspect of God's love. Paul uses the noun and verb forms of this word ten times in 1:3–7 and 28 times throughout 2 Corinthians. 'Consolation', also translated 'comfort' and 'encouragement', literally means 'to call to one's side' or 'send for'. Sometimes it was used to signify summoning your friends to attend you in a trial, to call them as witnesses. Sometimes it was used of prayer. God is an advocate to whom we can always appeal for help. 'Consolation' is here modified by 'all' to indicate that God's 'consolation' knows no limit.

Thus, Paul begins his letter by praising the always merciful and unlimited advocate, God.

PRAYER

Do not, O Lord, withhold your mercy from me;
let your steadfast love and your faithfulness keep me safe for ever.

Psalm 40:11

ADVANCING GOD'S MISSION
despite TROUBLES

Paul's reason for thanking God gives, in microcosm, the principle behind the entire letter. Christians should not be evaluated as successful by the extent to which they do *not* suffer, because even suffering can be used to advance God's mission. Paul describes God as being full of 'consolation' because God's nature will become a source and a model of consolation for Paul and his co-workers and for the Corinthians and their relationships throughout the entire letter.

God the ceaseless advocate

After having described God by two characteristics ('mercies' and 'consolation', 1:3), Paul develops the latter characteristic ('consolation') by making more specific its context and result. God is the one consoling us (v. 4). God is the one who, not just once but continually, stands at our side defending us and helping us. In what context does God advocate for us? If God is our advocate, then affliction is our prosecutor. 'Affliction' or 'troubles' literally refers to 'pressure' or 'crushing'. For example, Jesus had to preach from a boat so that the crowd of people would not 'crush' him (Mark 3:9). The physical sensation of something pressing down on something else is similar to people discriminating against others ('oppressing' them) or causing some other difficulty ('affliction').

Paul uses 'affliction' many times in 2 Corinthians as a general term to describe the external and internal difficulties that exert pressure on a person—physical hardships (6:4–5), economic need (8:2, 13) and mental anguish about unreconciled relationships or about a person's welfare (2:4; 7:4–6). Such external difficulties can include famine, labour pains, slavery, persecution and imprisonment (Acts 7:10–11; 11:19; 20:23; Ephesians 3:13; John 16:21). Jesus warned his followers that difficulties were sure to come: 'Servants are not greater than their master. If they persecuted me, they will persecute you' (John 15:20).

Receiving help enables help

As Paul and his co-workers find themselves in the midst of these difficulties, they discover that God is there advocating for them. What is the result of God's actions? Paul and his co-workers become 'able to console' another group of humans, the ones who also are in the midst of difficulties. All these groups of people have a certain sympathy of mind. They have been in the same situation, in 'affliction'. Paul and his co-workers have been consoled by God and have learned how helpful it is to be consoled, and now they can transfer this help to others. Not only must we 'do to others' as we 'would have them do' to us (Matthew 7:12), but we can also 'do to others' *because* others 'have done to us'. Those who receive compassion can themselves go on to give compassion.

Paul writes up his thoughts in a chiastic, not a parallel, manner because he wants to show the interconnection of actions and how they begin and end with God. Imitating the Greek letter *chi*, a chiasm presents a comparison in a ABBA order, not a parallel (ABAB) order, as in 'food (A) for the stomach (B) and the stomach (B) for food (A)' (1 Corinthians 6:13). Paul's argument begins in 2 Corinthians 1:4 with God ('who'), then continues with humans ('us'), adds humans ('those') and concludes with 'God'. Humans have genuine responsibilities, but those responsibilities should be discharged in the atmosphere of God's sovereignty. Paul is describing a vital relationship between God and humans, showing how, from something negative, something positive can arise. Suffering is not something the Corinthians view in a positive manner. In 1 Corinthians 4:8–16, Paul has already had to begin to deal with the church's desire to live only a life of comfort.

Christianity is not simply a religion that works during times of ease. It works also during times of difficulty.

MEDITATION

Have you ever been able to help someone because you had received help from God? Today, prayerfully observe others with whom you have contact to see if you can 'console' them or find someone else who may be able to console them because they have been through the same situation.

BALANCING CONSOLATION *with* SUFFERINGS

How does this process work, whereby we are encouraged in difficulties by the encouragement we receive from God (1:4)? Imagine a see-saw or an old-fashioned scale. On one side are sufferings, which weigh that side down. Comfort will counterbalance the other side. Advocacy from God will always counterbalance sufferings.

Make sure you suffer well

Paul does not encourage all sufferings here. He specifies 'the sufferings of Christ' (v. 5). 'Sufferings' (*pathema*) comes from the root *pathos*. It can refer to any incident, good or bad, which happens to someone; or to emotion, passion or sensation, of either pleasure or pain. Here, Paul uses *pathema* as parallel in thought to 'we are being afflicted' (v. 6): therefore, he clearly uses it in a negative sense. When he modifies 'sufferings' with 'of Christ', he is further specifying that these are negative incidents which occur because someone has done an action for Christ's sake. Someone who had not wanted to serve Christ would not have had to undergo these negative experiences. Paul will list in detail, later in 2 Corinthians, many of the negative incidents he has had to suffer (see 4:8–9; 6:4–10; 11:23–33; 12:10). However, this very same word (*pathema*) is used in 2 Timothy 3:11 to describe the effort the unbelieving Jewish leaders from Antioch and Iconium exerted to kill Paul, eventually succeeding in winning over the crowd in Lystra to stone him (Acts 14:19). While Acts gives us the visual view of what happened, 2 Corinthians gives us the internal perspective. Paul had been preaching about Jesus. Because he was so effective, some unbelievers responded in anger (Acts 14:1–2).

If Christ is the reason for the sufferings, Christ is also the antidote. Paul highlights that 'through Christ' consolation increases. How can Christ work today in the believer's life? Since 'the Lord is the Spirit' (3:17), the Lord is present everywhere.

It is all for you

After Paul has explained the effect of this balancing between suffering and consolation on his team ('us', 'our'), he describes how it affects others. To do actions for Christ (v. 5) is to act also for others' well-being (v. 6). When Paul and his co-workers are pressured ('being afflicted'), it is not because they are overworking for their own personal advancement. They are 'advocating' for others, rescuing people from certain destruction ('salvation'). If, in contrast, they themselves receive help ('consoled'), even this they use to help others. What kind of 'consolation' are they writing about? It is the kind won from the university of adversity!

One winter we discovered in our garden a pansy that had survived months of freezing weather. Its petite purple face had looked out at a bleak winter. So, too, this 'consolation' is one that endures through the winds of persecution. It has 'remained behind' or 'patiently endured'. To us, this flower that had survived became special. Instead of a 'pansy', we rechristened it an 'ever bloom'. So, too, this 'consolation' through Christ and of Christ, that survives through difficulties, ever blooms.

Paul's progression of thought is again chiastic, showing the circular or communal aspect of suffering and consolation. From discussing his team's own suffering and consolation ('us', v. 5) on behalf of the Corinthians ('your... same', v. 6), he returns to his team's own sufferings ('we are also suffering'). When we suffer, we can easily feel alone and forsaken. But people who persevere will find that they are not the only ones who have ever suffered for Christ's sake. Indeed, they will find themselves observing the suffering of those who led them to faith. This community of suffering may introduce a new type of mutual love and understanding. Paul concludes verses 4 and 6 with a brief clause, which in itself is full of pathos pointing back to Paul and his co-workers: 'we ourselves are consoled by God', 'we are also suffering'—remember us. In microcosm that is Paul's message to the Corinthians.

PRAYER

Help me to recognize the sufferings for your sake that I have undergone and that I should endure. Advocate for me, Lord, as I advocate for others. Help me to persist until your return and to discover believers who are persisting through sufferings similar to my own.

HOPE *in* PARTNERSHIP

How on earth can Paul and his co-workers have an 'unshaken' hope for the Corinthians? Does not Paul urge the Corinthians 'not to accept the grace of God in vain' (6:1) and to 'make room' in their hearts for them (7:2)?

Hope is a goal

Hope is not simply a daydream wish we make on an idle afternoon. 'Hope' can refer to a goal we have. For instance, since Paul and his co-workers look forward to the full and glorious manifestation of the new covenant as their 'goal' or 'hope', therefore they are bold (3:11–12). They also have a goal that as the Corinthians' faith increases, Paul and his team will be able to do more among them (10:15). Therefore, Paul and Timothy's goal for the Corinthians would be their 'hope'. What is their goal? They seek the Corinthians' 'consolation and salvation' (1:6).

When our goal is God or something promised by God (1:10), that goal is sure. The Corinthians themselves are not Paul's hope here (not 'our hope is you') but Paul's team has hope 'for' the Corinthians ('our hope' is 'for you').

Further, Paul and his co-workers are not slightly sure about their goal. Their hope is 'unshaken'. It is firm, steadfast, constant. Their hope is as secure as an anchor's hold on a sailing vessel (Hebrews 6:19), or the warranty of a reputable store for its product, or an oath confirming a decision (Hebrews 6:16). It is 'in effect', as a will comes into effect when someone dies (Hebrews 9:17). The hope of Paul and Timothy is firm because they 'firmly' endured through their sufferings (2 Corinthians 1:6).

Why will they not deviate from their hope? Why will they not pray that the Corinthians never have to give up anything for Christ's sake? Because they know something. Paul's explanation of what they know comprises a summary of all he has presented so far. He begins by presenting again the balance between sufferings and comfort. In 1:5 he compared sufferings and comfort by using 'to be abundant'. 'To be abundant' means to be over and above a fixed number. It is as if someone were filling up a glass with water and never turning off the tap, so the water keeps pouring in, lapping over the sides of the glass. When the crowd of over 5000 finished eating the five loaves of bread and two fish, twelve baskets of bread were 'left over' (Matthew 14:20). Thus, Paul metaphorically describes suffering and consolation as if they too overfill a glass measure (1:5). He compares them with a numerical image. But, in verse 7, he compares them with an interpersonal image, 'you share'.

Partnership is sharing in common

'Partner' was used in ancient times, as today, for financial joint ownership of a business. For instance, James and John were 'partners' with Simon in a fishing business (Luke 5:10). Their fishing equipment was all common property. Later, Paul will write about a financial partnership when discussing the Corinthian gift (2 Corinthians 8:4). The gift itself will even be called a 'sharing' (9:13). Thus, to be a partner is to have common shares in a business. In verse 7 Paul writes metaphorically. If the Corinthians share in common with other believers who are suffering, since standing up for Christ is more important than feeling comfortable, then they will also share in common the advocacy (or 'consolation') from God and other believers. They will have a full share in the Christian community.

Paul and his team have no doubts that the Corinthians will be consoled if they suffer on Christ's behalf. The early Church has left us many records of people who were partners in suffering and consolation. The early historian Eusebius quotes Clement's account of the death of Peter and his wife. Peter saw his wife led out to death during the reign of Emperor Nero. He interpreted it as her returning 'home' to God's presence. His 'consolation' or appeal to her was, 'My dear, remember the Lord.' Clement concludes: 'Such was the marriage of the blessed, and their consummate feeling towards their dearest' (*Church History* iii.30).

MEDITATION

*Do you know of people who are having difficulties
because of their desire to serve Christ? How can you become a
partner with them? Consider asking them if you can pray for them
and how you might otherwise support them.*

GOD *the* RESCUER

Paul now gives a more developed illustration of the partnership of sufferings and consolation, from Asia, the province from which he wrote 1 Corinthians and the centre of his ministry for the last three years.

Paul addresses the Corinthians as 'brothers and sisters' (*adelphos*). In this letter Paul calls his readers 'brothers and sisters' only three times (v. 8; 8:1; 13:11), as compared to 21 times in 1 Corinthians. What a contrast! It is a reminder of the near-ruptured relationship between the Corinthians and Paul's team. Nevertheless, even in the midst of their difficulties, they are still related. 'Brothers and sisters' is a tender expression of Paul's love.

Relatives should be concerned

Should Paul have kept the Corinthians 'blissfully ignorant' of their troubles, in the same way that some people might not tell other family members of the illness of a relative, so that they might not be disturbed by the unpleasantness of mortality? No, the Corinthians need to know about God's activity in the world, that God brings victory through difficulties.

What did happen in Asia? Probably these events occurred after the writing of 1 Corinthians. Acts 18:23—20:1 describes Paul's ministry in Asia. Paul and his team were publicly maligned by some Jews (Acts 19:9). They were also attacked by an angry Gentile mob (Acts 19:23–40), who were furious over the economic and religious ramifications of Paul's ministry. Later in 2 Corinthians, Paul will specify more concretely all the troubles he has endured (11:23–33). Although, in Acts, Luke the historian does not describe Paul's feelings as his team experienced these difficulties while in the midst of helping people, here in 2 Corinthians we can hear Paul's reactions (vv. 8–9).

Relatives should appeal to God

Paul does not describe what happened simply to let off steam, and certainly not to brag about all they went through. God can prevent believers from having difficulties (Luke 4:11). Probably many times we have failed to thank God for catastrophes avoided because we could not have known a catastrophe was imminent. Paul describes their most momentous difficulties so the Corinthians might learn that, when difficulties occur, God's power is exhibited in their midst.

When all looks bleak and a solution humanly impossible, then God, as if out of nowhere, rescues the believer. God 'raises' the dead (v. 9). God certainly did raise Jesus (1 Thessalonians 1:9–10) and Paul (2 Corinthians 11:23–25). The participle form (God is 'the one raising the dead') highlights that God's power is not simply in the past, but is continually at work. To reiterate this point, Paul restates it: God 'rescued' (past tense), 'will continue to rescue' (future tense) and again 'will rescue' (future tense) (v. 10).

'Rescue' (hruomai) has a root idea of dragging something toward oneself with force (eruo). Indeed, asking God to rescue someone forcibly from their enemies is a major theme in the Psalms. In the New Testament, God protects (drags to God's self) or sets a believer free from death (2 Peter 2:7), powerlessness over sin (Romans 7:23–24) and the evil one (Colossians 1:13). Jesus taught his disciples to ask God to rescue them from evil (Matthew 6:13) and Paul repeatedly requests this kind of prayer (Romans 15:30–31; 2 Thessalonians 3:2). Near the end of his life Paul claims that God continually rescued him from persecutions (2 Timothy 3:11; 4:18). How were Paul and his co-workers rescued in Ephesus? In one instance, Paul simply left and found another place to teach (Acts 19:9). In another instance, the Gentile magistrate exhorted the crowd to use the official courts for complaints and not to take matters into their own hands (Acts 19:35–41). But Paul perceived that God was delivering through these events.

What is the place of humans in God's work? What can believers do to assist other believers being persecuted in other countries? They can 'join in helping' or 'serve together' by praying for their needs (v. 11). For example, praying Corinthians would be a blessing to Paul and his team, instigating prayers of thanksgiving because all ended well. Thanking God is one way to testify of God's work in the world. When we depend on God, sufferings can indeed end in consolation (1:7).

PRAYER

In you, O Lord, I seek refuge; do not let me ever be put to shame;
in your righteousness deliver me... Be a rock of refuge for me,
a strong fortress to save me.

Psalm 31:1–2

The HEART of the LETTER

In this one sentence (v. 12) is a microcosm of the whole letter.

'Frankness and godly sincerity' will be developed in the next larger section (3:1—5:21). Paul and his associates are frank and holy because they are ministers of a new spiritual covenant. 'Earthly wisdom' refers to the super-apostles and those who follow them, who will be directly described in the last section of the letter (10:1—13:11). 'All the more toward you' suggests the middle section of the letter where Paul entreats the Corinthians not to accept God's grace in vain (6:1—9:15). 'Boast' and 'grace of God' are also important themes in the letter.

Boasting is bearing testimony

How can Paul and Timothy 'boast'? In early Greek comedy the boastful *alazon* was a stock character—a charlatan who achieved his ends by shameless false pretension, deception through exaggeration. Moreover, has not Paul said that boasting is now 'excluded' (Romans 3:27)? When Paul employs the word 'boast' in 2 Corinthians 1:12, it is a synonym for 'testimony'. He is about to explain what Paul and Timothy know to be true: boasting in itself is not wrong. What we must evaluate is the object of our boasting. Boasting should not be about our being justified by our actions, because they will never be good enough (Romans 3:27). Boasting should not take credit for other people's achievements, since that would be untruthful (2 Corinthians 10:13–17). Boasting also should not be about actions displeasing to God (11:12–13, 18).

The Corinthians themselves had problems with improper boasting. They were taking credit for gifts from God (1 Corinthians 3:21; 4:7) and flaunting immorality rather than repenting of it (5:6). In 2 Corinthians, Paul will reinterpret 'boasting'.

'Conscience' (*suneidesis*) is related to the verb 'to see together with others' (*suneidon*). Thus, it means literally 'joint-knowledge', 'knowledge shared with another' or 'communication'. The apostle Paul is the New Testament writer who most frequently uses the word 'conscience'. In Acts, he refers to his clear conscience before the Sanhedrin and Felix (23:1; 24:16), and in later writings accentuates the importance of a good conscience and sincere faith as key bases for love and orthodoxy (1 Timothy 1:5, 19–20; 3:9). In 2 Corinthians 1:12 Paul uses 'conscience' in the singular but he refers to the plural 'our', indicating joint-knowledge between Paul and his co-workers. All of them agree in their testimony.

Behaviour has standards

To what do Paul and his co-workers testify? Their behaviour among the Corinthians and toward all people has met certain standards.

The first standard is 'with frankness and godly sincerity'. The NRSV has a footnote explaining that instead of 'frankness', 'other ancient authorities read *holiness*'. Along with REB and NIV, I have selected 'holiness' as preferable over 'frankness' because the oldest excellent authorities read 'holiness' or 'moral purity'. To be holy is to be set apart to or by God. 'Godly sincerity' (*eilikrineia*) can also be used of unmixed or pure metals without alloy, or of bread without yeast (1 Corinthians 5:8). Paul will repeat *eilikrineia* in 2:17 to describe those speakers who do not sell their speeches for monetary profit. Thus, Paul uses two words for purity to highlight that their behaviour toward the Corinthians is not deceptive. It is very, very pure.

The second standard is negative. They did not act by 'earthly' or, literally, 'fleshly' wisdom. 'Flesh' can be a neutral term for our mortal self or skin (for example, 2 Corinthians 4:11; 7:5; 12:7), as 'world' is neutral here. But here 'fleshly' is clearly negative. Paul and his associates have themselves been accused of acting in a 'fleshly' or wrong way (10:2). Paul has to persuade his readers that, yes, they are mortal, but no, they are not ungodly (10:3). And, instead, the pretentious, self-centred, comfort-seeking leaders they adulate are 'fleshly' or 'earthly' in God's sight (11:18–29). The contrast to 'earthly wisdom' is the 'grace of God'. 'Grace' is God's loving generosity. When God rescues dedicated followers from the natural end result of difficulties (1:10), then God's grace has become manifest.

MEDITATION

Do you think you act in holiness and purity by God's grace?
Do you support those who do? What can you do to further
this type of behaviour?

WHY WRITE?

At Corinth, some people accused Paul of frightening them with his letters since they 'are weighty and strong' (10:10). Paul first introduces the topic of his writing here as an illustration of how genuine holiness affects the way people communicate. Paul and his associates write intending to be clear, not obscure.

Believers should read and review

Paul uses a play upon words which sound alike ('read' and 'understand'). The same root word, 'know' (*ginosko*) has two prefixes (*ana*, 'on' or 'up', and *epi*, 'upon'). In the first verb, one 'knows' by 'reading up' (*anaginosko*). In the second verb, one 'knows' by observing, by having one's eyes rest upon an object (*epiginosko*). It's the difference between a quick morsel (a 'read') and a thorough five-course meal, a thoughtful study ('review'). For example, the Ethiopian official was reading (*anaginosko*) the book of Isaiah (Acts 8:30), but not understanding it. To 'understand' (*epiginosko*) is a deeper apprehension. It can refer simply to recognizing someone, as the crowds recognized Jesus as the man who could heal (Matthew 14:35). But it can also refer to being able to perceive someone's unexpressed thoughts (Mark 2:8) as God fully understands what every human thinks (1 Corinthians 13:12). The knowledge between the persons of the Trinity entails such a complete apprehension (Matthew 11:27). Perceiving genuine leaders by their actions, as opposed to false, destructive ones, entails such knowledge (7:15–16).

Paul and Timothy want both types of knowing. They want the Corinthians to be able to have superficial comprehension of their words and they hope they can also attain a deeper understanding. Sometimes, listeners become impressed with speakers they do not fully understand because they assume that those speakers must be truly brilliant or deep. But God has no hidden agenda and those who do not aim to be clear may be muddled in thought themselves or may intend to deceive. Paul repeats, his goal is for his listeners fully to comprehend (v. 13). ('Until the end' may also be rendered 'fully'.)

Paul clearly states that the Corinthians themselves have this deeper understanding (v. 14) only 'in part'. Titus gave Paul and Timothy a mixed report about the Corinthians. They were repentant about some matters (7:7) but not others (6:13; 13:11). Thus, Paul is slowly, subtly leading up to a more direct confrontation of the leadership problem at Corinth, but leaving hints of what will later be completely disclosed.

Reviewing should lead to boasting

What is the heart of what Paul and his co-workers want the Corinthians to understand? They love them. And how is that love fleshed out? If boasting about achievements, which are really gifts, is displeasing to God, what type of boasting is acceptable? To boast in people. Paul is not describing the type of boasting where one person takes credit for all the achievements of another, which in reality destroys the independence of the other. Rather, he describes a mutual pride. In 1 Corinthians, Paul describes such boasting as the process of rejoicing when another believer is honoured (12:26). It is lack of envy (13:4). It is desiring the very best for another person. As the Corinthians' spiritual father, Paul wants to be proud of his spiritual children (7:4, 14; 8:24; 9:2–3; 12:14).

'The day of the Lord Jesus' is a common expression for the day when Jesus will return to the earth as judge (for example, 1 Corinthians 1:8; Matthew 24:37–44). That day should be one in which believers are filled with joy as they see God commend those people with whom they have laboured (1 Thessalonians 2:19). It is not self-pride but pride in others, and ultimately pride in God who has worked through ourselves and others (Romans 15:17–18).

Holiness and purity are not abstract concepts, but they affect all we do. Here they affect our goals for communication (to be heard and to be heeded) and for people (they become fully commended by Christ at the judgment day).

PRAYER

O Lord, you have searched me and known me. You know when I sit down and when I rise up; you discern my thoughts from far away... I praise you, for I am fearfully and wonderfully made. Wonderful are your works; that I know very well.

Psalm 139:1–2, 14

ONE VISIT TOO FEW

Paul paints a picture of a relational Christianity where people eagerly await a visit from a Christian brother or sister. Even plans have theological underlying principles which Paul wants to explain.

Of what was Paul 'sure' (v. 15)? He was certainly sure that some day Jesus will return to earth (1:14). But in 1:12–14, Paul's main point is that the behaviour of his team was holy, sincere, clear and relational. Paul was 'sure of' their own character. They were there wholly for the Corinthians.

Visits are times of joy

Paul explains again his travel plans which had been proposed in a previous letter sent between 1 and 2 Corinthians (2 Corinthians 2:3). Paul expected that the Corinthians would welcome his visit and they would especially welcome two visits. Calling his visits a 'double favour' (or, literally, 'double grace') does not sound modest. However, Paul and the Corinthians know that God's grace or 'favour' (1:12) may be brought by humans (v. 15). Grace can even increase as people extend thanksgiving to God for one another's blessings (4:15). 'Grace' (*charis*) in Greek is closely related to 'joy' (*chara*). Paul wanted his visit to be a time of joy, pleasure and delight, as did the Corinthians.

Normally, a traveller from Asia would go north to the seaport Troas, cross the Aegean Sea, and then descend south through Macedonia down to Achaia, because ancient boats tended to travel close to the coast and embark at night (Acts 16:10–11; 19:21; 20:1–2). But Paul had promised the Corinthians a different itinerary. He would cross the Aegean Sea directly from Ephesus to Cencheae, Corinth's port. From Corinth, he would travel north up through Macedonia and then return to Corinth to embark again from Cencheae to Ephesus.

Visits build relationships

Paul paints a vivid picture with his prepositions. 'To (*pros*) you' (v. 15) is the same root preposition as in 'face' (*prosopon*). Paul wants to see the Corinthians face to face. With today's telephones, answer machines, e-mail, chat rooms, televisions and films, we may forget how very important it is at times to speak to people face to face. We can hear better, interpret words in contexts of vocal tone and facial expressions and body language, and feel a stronger personal presence. Thus, although Paul certainly used letters and intended to be clearly understood, he also knew the importance of personal presence.

In addition, Paul wanted to go 'through' (*dia*) the Corinthians as if they would be standing on either side of a track cheering and encouraging Paul as he began his marathon race up 'into' (*eis*) Macedonia. Paul did not simply intend to reach Macedonia's border. He planned to go into the province. Then Macedonia would be his point of departure ('from', *apo*) as he returned 'to' another face-to-face encounter (*pros*) with the Corinthians. At this point, some of the Corinthians might even have 'accompanied' Paul to Judea. 'Send' forth or 'accompany' may also be rendered 'escort' (Acts 21:5). They would all go 'into' Judea, possibly bringing the collection for the poor.

Paul's travels would be longer than necessary so that he could interact more with the Corinthians. And apparently the Corinthians were eager to see Paul these extra times. They agreed with Paul that these visits would indeed be a 'favour' or 'gift'. But Paul decided not to come. And instead he came first to Macedonia (8:1; 9:2). Instead of the Corinthians being treated extra specially, they were visited last! Paul presupposed a negative response to his change of plans (v. 17), which we can assume came to his ears from his discreet messenger, Titus (7:6–7). In Greek, Paul's first question (v. 17a) anticipates a negative answer. Paul does not think he acted lightly. Later Paul will directly tell us that some people think he acted according to 'human standards' (10:2). Here he indirectly assumes such a challenge. To have 'human standards' (literally, 'fleshly' ones) in our travel plans is to say 'Yes, yes' and 'No, no' (v. 17).

Paul and his co-workers instead aim to please God by genuinely loving others.

MEDITATION

Is there someone you might visit or invite this month who would consider your visit a gift from God? In the last month, did you give your word to someone and fail to keep it? If it might have been misinterpreted, consider clarifying your intentions.

GOD IS FAITHFUL

If Paul's promises could not be trusted, then Paul's God could not be trusted. Because God is truthful and reliable, so too God's messengers speak and act truthfully and reliably (v. 18).

God's faithfulness was at work

If God is fully reliable, Jesus, because he is indeed God's Son, is also reliable (v. 19). Paul describes Jesus as the one 'among you, through us, having been preached' (literally). The message the Corinthians had received (originally described in Acts 18:1–18) was personally imparted. Preaching was not mere words, but words incarnated through human beings. And who were those specific humans? 'I' and 'Silvanus and Timothy' (v. 19; Acts 18:5). Paul reminds the Corinthians to pause and dwell on the character and motives of each of the members of his team.

Paul has progressed from God's reliability to their reliability (v. 18) and now to Christ's reliability (v. 19). Jesus is the content of their message. God is the basis of their message (v. 18). Jesus' character has not changed. Similarly, Hebrews 13:8 says, 'Jesus Christ is the same yesterday and today and for ever'. Jesus has pure and holy motives (2 Corinthians 1:12). Jesus does not appear to say one thing but intend to do another. Rather, Jesus is the very incarnation of the cosmic 'Yes', affecting the entire state of the world (v. 19).

In what other ways is Jesus the cosmic 'Yes'? Jesus fulfilled all of God's promises. God's promise that Abraham's descendants would be heirs was fulfilled through Jesus (Romans 4:13–14 referring to Genesis 22:17–18). David's kingdom continued for ever through Jesus (Acts 13:23; 2 Samuel 7:13). God promised that the Messiah would be resurrected from the dead (Acts 13:32–33 quoting Psalm 2:7). And through Jesus, God promised that eventually the Gentiles would become members of God's covenant (Romans 15:8–12 quoting Psalm 117:1 and Isaiah 11:10). No one is more trustworthy than Jesus. That is why Paul and his co-workers conclude their prayers 'in Jesus' name' (v. 20). Jesus is the one who makes God's promises possible. He is even called 'the Amen' (Revelation 3:14)!

'Amen' is a transliterated Hebrew word, signifying 'to make firm'.

'The amen' is an ancient Jewish way for listeners to confirm something (for example, Deuteronomy 27:15–26). Paul even expected that visitors to Christian worship could affirm what was happening by such a word (1 Corinthians 14:16).

God's faithfulness is still at work

These verses can help us in several ways to understand better the nature of believers and of Jesus. For believers to act and speak in a trustworthy way is crucial because we follow a trustworthy God. Even in Old Testament times, doing what you said you would do was very important (Deuteronomy 23:21–22). Jesus reiterated the importance of carrying out our vows (Matthew 5:33–37; 7:21–23). What we say should be followed by action. Or, in reverse, when we have doubts about Jesus we should remember the Christ-like character of those who first taught us.

To be God's 'Yes' means that Jesus fulfilled all God's promises. The nature of Jesus as fully trustworthy was a key reason I became a follower of Christ. I was brought up in the church, but when I was in high school and college I began to be filled with doubt as to the historicity of Christianity's claims. In college I began more diligently studying Christianity, slowly answering more and more of my questions. I became active in a Christian fellowship. However, I never made a clear commitment to Christ until my friend (and eventual husband) asked me, 'Do you know you are saved?' I did not know for sure. But as I thought prayerfully that evening I decided, 'Who is more trustworthy than Jesus?' And on the basis of Jesus' trustworthy nature, I bridged the gap between knowing a trustworthy historical set of beliefs and a life serving Jesus, the one who makes possible God's promises.

PRAYER

Save us, O Lord our God, and gather us from among the nations,
that we may give thanks to your holy name and glory in your
praise. Blessed be the Lord, the God of Israel, from everlasting to
everlasting. And let all the people say, 'Amen.' Praise the Lord!

Psalm 106:47–48

11

The AUTHENTICATING GOD

Humans can 'say the "Amen"', or confirm matters (1:20), because God affirms humans (v. 21). Paul uses several metaphors to describe God's greatness and on that basis clarifies his actions.

God validates believers

Paul describes God with four participles: establishing, anointing, putting a seal and giving (vv. 21–22). God 'establishes' us as an ongoing activity (present participle). Since the Corinthians were disturbed about Paul's change of plans (1:17), 'establish' is an appropriate word to use (v. 21). It can refer to making good our word, and also to guaranteeing the validity of a purchase. When the Corinthians were given spiritual gifts, the gifts 'established' or 'confirmed' what they had heard about Christ (1 Corinthians 1:6–7). God is the one who keeps on validating Paul's team as they interact with the Corinthians to advance Christ's name.

'Anoint' was usually used in the Old Testament for the process of anointing a priest or ruler by touching the body with oil. By this process, a person would be set apart or consecrated for a task (Exodus 28:41; 1 Samuel 9:16). Jesus was anointed by God the Father to bring good news to the poor, not by oil, but by the Holy Spirit and power (Luke 4:18; Acts 10:38).

'Anoint' indicates that Paul and his co-workers were consecrated by God as part of God's new priesthood of all believers (1 Peter 2:5), consecrated to work among the Corinthians. God treats Paul and his co-workers as a valid set of messengers ('establish')—just as if they had received the symbol of oil ('anoint'), the public consecration to their task.

'Establish' and 'anoint' are one pair, followed now by a second pair of words ('put a seal' and 'give first instalment'). Seals would authenticate documents or certify that an object had been examined. When Jesus' body was placed in the tomb, it was sealed so that no one could open the tomb without everyone knowing (Matthew 27:64, 66). Today in the USA, officials will mark a letter with a seal to indicate that they saw the person sitting in their presence sign it. Thus, metaphorically, God the Father 'sealed' Jesus, thereby indicating that

Jesus is truly God's unique heir and worth living for (John 6:27). Paul and his co-workers were also 'sealed' by God to indicate that they have been examined by God and found to be genuine (v. 22).

Because they were genuine, God has given them the Holy Spirit to be present permanently and internally ('in our hearts'). A 'first instalment' was money deposited by the purchaser and forfeited if the purchase was not completed. For example, one ancient first-century writer sent a mouse-catcher a 'first instalment' or 'earnest-money' of eight drachmae to catch mice on someone else's behalf. In the same way today, people send non-refundable registration money to colleges. God, too, gives believers a down-payment of proof that God's promises of an eternal inheritance are forthcoming (Ephesians 1:13–14). That down-payment is the Holy Spirit (see also 2 Corinthians 5:5). Believers do not need cards or letters (3:1) to indicate their faith; the Holy Spirit shines out to others and inwardly to themselves.

Love serves others

Therefore, God serves as witness to Paul's calling and intentions (v. 23). Paul did not change his plans because he made light of the Corinthians (1:17), but rather because he wanted to 'spare' them. 'Spare' can mean not destroying people in war or having consideration for people. A visit by Paul to Corinth would have resulted in discipline for actions displeasing to God (13:10). Paul wanted to give the Corinthians opportunities to repent and change (2:3; 12:21). Thus, Paul's 'Yes' (1:19) to the Corinthians was to act always to further their faith and joy, even if that entailed a change of plans.

If Paul and his co-workers had simply wanted to flaunt their authority, they would have come. Leadership which 'lords it over' others is not what Jesus wants from his followers (v. 24). Paul fulfils Jesus' command by using the words 'co-workers' or 'workers with you'. Christians should not choose favourites, as if leaders are in a competition. Rather, all serving Christians are working together for the increased joy of those they serve (v. 24). Paul and his team are co-workers in the joint enterprise with the Corinthians, helping them to mature in their faith, since the Corinthians made a commitment to begin it.

MEDITATION

Have you ever felt the Holy Spirit's presence?
When, and to what task(s), did God anoint you?

CO-WORKERS *of* JOY

Paul goes back explicitly (v. 1) to the topic he discussed earlier—the plans which he explained in a letter (1:17). He never intended to be unclear (1:13) and he did not make light of his promise to visit. It was for their sake that he did not go (1:23). Now, Paul will explain what it means to be co-workers of joy (1:24).

Co-workers want to be joyful

Co-workers of joy are concerned that the person with whom they serve should be joyful. If the Corinthians were disciplined without fair warning, they would not have had the opportunity for joy. Truly holy persons are always moved by their effect on others. Notice here that Paul, not the whole team, decided not to visit again (v. 1). Titus did decide to go (7:7). Paul did not want 'another painful visit'.

How many people become Christians expecting therefore to have only blessings, happiness, pleasure, and no pain? As a matter of fact, half of the total New Testament uses of 'pain' occur in this one letter! 'Pain' can refer to literal physical pain, such as the pain a woman can feel in labour (John 16:21). It can also refer to psychological distress, sometimes temporarily felt physically as a knot in the stomach. The 'pain' can be simply a deeply felt regret, as when King Herod regretted his daughter's request for John the Baptist's head (Matthew 14:8–9), or when the disciples heard Jesus would die (John 16:6, 20; Matthew 17:23; Luke 22:45). But, most often in 2 Corinthians, 'pain' refers to difficulties in relationships. Paul's last visit had resulted in the Corinthians being grieved in spirit. They had felt no pleasure in Paul's visit. (This visit is not recorded in Acts, but occurred after the first visit in Acts 18:1, and before the third visit in 20:2.)

Neither did Paul feel any pleasure in grieving them! He demonstrates a tenderness and gentleness of feeling because he wants to be cheered up by them too (v. 2). Thus, Paul visited them and then, instead of visiting them again, he wrote to them (v. 3). Paul expects that the Corinthians and he will make each other joyful. But because the Corinthians were still behaving in ways that were displeasing to God, Paul would have to reprimand them.

When I was in college, I studied under a social worker who

exhorted us to remember that we would serve people who might be carrying out criminal or anti-social behaviour. We should, as social workers, accept all of them. But because we *accepted* them, this did not mean we should *approve* of all their behaviour. A difference exists between acceptance and approval. Similarly, Paul even more than 'accepts' the Corinthians—he *loves* them—but he does not approve of all they do. As he told them earlier, love 'does not rejoice in wrong-doing, but rejoices in the truth' (1 Corinthians 13:6). Paul rejoices, therefore, when other Christians become more Christ-like (Philippians 2:2; Romans 16:19; Colossians 2:5; 1 Thessalonians 3:9). He rejoices when believers make the right choices (2 Corinthians 7:7–9).

Joy pleases God

Yet Paul has high expectations for the Corinthians. As their co-worker of joy (1:24), he expects—he is even 'confident'—that they will have the same goal, 'joy' (v. 3). What makes Paul joyful or delighted? Not only does he rejoice in seeing others make godly moral choices, but he also rejoices in the company and safety of other believers such as Titus and Timothy (7:13; 1 Corinthians 16:17; 2 Timothy 1:4). He rejoices in advancing God's reign even if it entails difficulties (8:2; Philippians 1:18; Colossians 1:24; 1 Thessalonians 1:6) because joy itself comes from God (Romans 15:13; Galatians 5:22). People are so important to Paul that he personifies them as the quality of joy itself (Philippians 4:1; 1 Thessalonians 2:19–20). So, what common goal do he and the Corinthians have, according to Paul? What is Paul's joy and their joy? Joy is the Corinthians making the right choices, God-pleasing ones, based on their relationship with God and with Paul, Timothy and Silas, God's genuine messengers to them (1:19).

Paul and his team are co-workers of joy—desiring others to become joyful, concerned for their own joy, but, most of all, helping people to make choices which will bring joy because they please the source of all joy, God.

PRAYER

Help me to be a co-worker of joy with others.

The WHY AFFECTS the HOW

Paul refers to an earlier letter, which some think is 1 Corinthians, but others (myself included) think is a letter written after 1 Corinthians but before 2 Corinthians.

How Paul writes

Paul describes how and why he wrote the letter. His description of how he wrote it uses two phrases: 'out of much distress and anguish of heart' and 'with many tears' (v. 4). 'Distress' (*thlipsis*) literally refers to 'pressure' or 'a pressing together', while 'anguish' (*sunoche*) literally refers to 'holding together' or 'contraction'. Paul's inmost self (his 'heart') felt as if it was pressing together and greatly constricted because of his concern for the Corinthians. It was a concern that flowed from Paul's overflowing love for them. No wonder he cried silently as he wrote. Tears may be shed as an expression of compassion and desire that others repent. These are the types of tears God will gently wipe off at the beginning of the new heaven and earth (Revelation 21:4), but in the meantime these types of tears are wonderful models for us of genuinely felt concern for others.

Why Paul writes

Paul is definitely writing an apologetic for a previous letter. He has already explained that he and his team intend in writing to be clear (1:13). But now he further explains his intentions in writing. He did not intend to cause them pain, but he does want them to know of his abundant love (v. 4). An 'abundant' love is one that is more than enough. It is precious spring water measured into a cup, filling it up, and running over the top. Paul has love to spare for the Corinthians.

Apparently some Corinthians thought Paul had inflicted pain on them. Paul, rather, thinks that they are the ones inflicting pain, not he. The Corinthians lacked balance or moderation. About a year earlier, the church had not only allowed but had even boasted about a son's freedom to have sexual relations with his father's wife (1 Corinthians 5:1–2). But now they have not forgiven someone else who has repented of sin (v. 7). From disciplining someone who needed some curbs, the Corinthians went on to excessive fault-finding. Instead of expressing 'abundant' love (v. 4), they overwhelmed someone with 'excessive' or 'abundant' 'sorrow' (v. 7). The pain they gave was more than enough; so now they needed to 'forgive and console'.

'Forgive' is the verb form of 'grace', a key idea in 2 Corinthians. God's grace contrasts with earthly wisdom (1:12). God's grace is generous, life-affirming (8:1–2, 9; 9:8), always sufficient (12:9). God's grace needs to flow out to this individual through the means of these particular humans' consolation. The Corinthians need to 'advocate' for (v. 7) this person, no longer simply find fault. Paul himself appeals to the Corinthians, advocating for this person (v. 8).

Two thousand years later, we still do not know this person's name or sin. Paul intended only the persons involved to know these details for the sake of confidentiality. Possibly, the original letter was not preserved in order to keep confidential this maligned person. We of posterity have been given as much information as is necessary for our sanctification, not as much as is needed for our curiosity.

One word that has occurred twice in these verses is 'love'. 'Love' is much used in our times, but what can we learn about it from this passage? Love is concern for others' spiritual growth. Affecting action, it should be part of ministry to others. This concern for others can be deeply felt and also expressed in writing. No one need be stingy with love because its source is unlimited in God (13:11).

Paul does not overtly define 'love' in this letter because he has already defined it (in 1 Corinthians 13:4–7). Love is accompanied by gentleness (1 Corinthians 4:21) and is greater than knowledge, which the Corinthians especially admired (1 Corinthians 8:1). Love is the greatest of all enduring Christian virtues (1 Corinthians 13:1–3, 13). Paul had concluded 1 Corinthians (16:14) with an exhortation to live lives in love, and, indeed, in 2 Corinthians Paul and his co-workers model what love means in their own lives.

MEDITATION

Are you concerned about someone's spiritual growth?
How can you demonstrate your love for that person
without inflicting on them unnecessary pain?

TESTED CHARACTER IS FORGIVING

Paul frequently moves in this letter from a subtle to a more direct discussion of the same problem. In 1:13 Paul 'writes' because of the lack of a full understanding between him and the Corinthians, but now he more directly 'writes' because he wants to know whether the Corinthians are fully obedient (v. 9). At the conclusion of the letter he most directly 'writes' to allow them time for repentance (13:10).

Paul wants to see tested character

What is the purpose of Paul's letter? Paul wants to 'test' them or, literally, to 'know your character' ('know the proof', v. 9, KJV). 'Character' (*dokime*) is 'tried or approved character', an important concept for Paul (four of six uses occur in 2 Corinthians). 'Character' is what a person has after enduring sufferings (8:2; Romans 5:3–4). It results in generosity (8:2; 9:13). Timothy himself is an example of someone with a 'tried character' because he sought Jesus' interests, not his own, while serving with Paul like a son with a father (Philippians 2:21–22). A related word, *dokimasia* ('examination'), referred to the scrutiny of elected magistrates, to see if they fulfilled the legal requirements of full citizenship. The Hebrews in the desert scrutinized God despite the fact that they had seen God at work for forty years (Hebrews 3:9). This kind of scrutiny is appropriate for new believers, but not for people who have already seen God's marvellous acts. Similarly, the Corinthians, we will discover later, are asking again for what Paul has already shown them, that 'Christ is speaking' in Paul (13:3). But Paul counters by examining them, not to revisit proven truths, but to challenge them to Christ-like behaviour. Will they be 'obedient' in affirming, forgiving and consoling the overly accused person in their midst (2:7–9)?

Character is obedient to grace

'Obedience' (*hupekoos*) is a word built on the root idea of 'hearing' (*akoe*). The verb form refers properly to someone like Rhoda who, at a knock on the door, comes to listen to discover who wants admittance (Acts 12:13). To 'listen' to a command is to obey. The Corinthians 'obeyed' when they welcomed Titus (7:15). But Paul thought their obedience was incomplete at this time (10:6). Obedience is a choice, not something that one is forced to do. The choice comes at the point of hearing. Hearing then affects action.

Of course, who or what we obey is crucial. Obedience in itself is not praiseworthy. That was the message of the film *The Remains of the Day*. The butler implicitly served the master of the house without questioning his master's purposes. Thus, Paul warns his readers, they will be slaves of whom they obey (Romans 6:16–17). Paul wants his readers to obey Christ (v. 9; 10:5), who himself had been obedient to fulfil his purpose on earth (Philippians 2:8). Paul simply reminds the Corinthians of what obedience to Christ entails in this particular situation.

Even though Paul wants the Corinthians to hearken to what he exhorts (v. 9), yet he also brings out that they have the authority to represent Paul in this action of forgiveness, or extending God's grace. If they think Paul has been too lenient, Paul reminds them that their extending grace to this one person will benefit themselves and ultimately represent Christ. 'The presence of Christ' is literally 'the face of Christ' (v. 10). The Church as Christ's body on earth functions to enact Christ's decisions on earth. Jesus himself had taught that decisions to forgive people were reaffirmed in heaven (Matthew 18:18). But, of course, the Church only becomes Christ's 'face' when it is obedient to Christ.

How do the Corinthians benefit by extending God's grace to the person who received too much pain (2:7, 10)? Someone who does not forgive, or extend grace to, another will eventually be 'outwitted' by Satan (v. 11). Satan will 'take advantage' of them. 'Outwit' or 'take advantage' (*pleonekteo*) comes from the root 'to have more' (*pleon* and *echo*). Satan always wants more. As C.S. Lewis stated so vividly in the preface to *The Screwtape Letters*, Satan has a ravenous hunger and wants to 'suck the weaker into itself and permanently gorge its own being on the weaker's outraged individuality'. Satan, the adversary, who opposes the grace and freedom of believers, is in reality behind such lack of forgiveness.

PRAYER

'Forgive us our sins, for we ourselves forgive everyone indebted to us. And do not bring us to the time of trial.'

Luke 11:4

An OPEN DOOR *for* LOVE

Paul now describes his visit to the city of Troas (v. 12), a seaport town in Asia across from Macedonia. This locale, this place between places, reminds Paul of theological truths of transition and change, such as the two covenants (ch. 3), the paradox of glory and mortality (chs. 4; 6), and the old versus the new creation (ch. 5).

A door opens for opportunities

Paul is still showing how his behaviour toward the Corinthians is motivated by his great love for them. All his behaviour is motivated by love. He had gone into Troas for the express purpose of preaching the good news of Christ (v. 12). 'A door was opened for me' indicates that the place and opportunity to preach were under God's sovereignty, not something Paul by himself sought out. The place and opportunity were 'in the Lord', which means they were not chosen as a selfish opportunity but in following God's will.

Often Paul would preach at a synagogue, since ancient Jewish worship leaders would invite visitors to speak a word to the congregation after the scripture readings (see, for example, Acts 13:15). At Ephesus he taught daily in the lecture hall of Tyrannus (Acts 19:9). Paul does not mention any further specifics about the place in Troas, since it is not relevant to this communication.

Often, Christians today use an 'open door' as a test by which to decide whether God wants them to take a certain action. An 'open door' is an opportunity. But for Paul it was often a situation that had more hardships, as in Ephesus where 'a wide door for effective work has opened to me, and there are many adversaries' (1 Corinthians 16:9). At Troas, Paul had this 'open door' yet he did not avail himself of it, but sailed over to Macedonia. Paul's action teaches us today that we cannot allow 'open door' opportunities to be our ultimate criteria for decisions. More important than opportunities are relationships.

Love is greater than opportunities

Paul's spirit had no 'rest' because he did not find Titus at Troas. Apparently, Titus and Paul had agreed on meeting again at this city. Paul would have been travelling in Asia, north from Ephesus to Troas, while Titus would have been travelling in Macedonia, south to Achaia and returning north again to Macedonia, sailing back to Troas. Troas is where Paul first had a vision of a man in Macedonian attire pleading for him to help them (Acts 16:8–9). It was again a meeting place for various Christian groups on the way to Jerusalem (Acts 20:5–6). Paul even left clothes and his library at Troas when he went to prison years later (2 Timothy 4:13). A church met in Troas, and it was here months later where Paul spoke until past midnight, causing youthful Eutychus to fall asleep and drop off a window-ledge, almost to his permanent death (Acts 20:7–12).

Troas, 'one of the notable' cities of the ancient world, was about ten miles south of ancient Troy. It was watered by the 'many-fountained' Mount Ida, which had a great number of rivers flowing from it (*Geography* xiii.1.26, 43, 47).

Paul describes Titus as 'my brother'. Such an appellation was not a casual term, but indicated Paul's great love for Titus. Paul may never have married, but through his worship of Jesus the Messiah he adopted a new family. Therefore, he now had new brothers and sisters, mothers and fathers, and children. Titus was his 'brother' and a colleague in ministry. Greater in importance to Paul than any possible new converts were his 'brothers and sisters' in the Lord, Titus and the Corinthians (1:8; 2:13). Paul's concern for his co-worker and the new believers at Corinth was more important than potential believers and keeping to his original goal—to preach at Troas. How different Paul was from some Christians who seek only new converts and have little interest in the well-being of other believers! Titus had gone to the Corinthians to determine their spiritual state (7:7) and to prepare them for the forthcoming gathering of funds for the famine-affected Christians in Judea (8:6). When Paul saw that Titus had not returned and no one had word of him, he 'said farewell', leaving others to minister at Troas, and crossed the sea into Macedonia trying to find Titus and news of the Corinthians.

MEDITATION

What does 'open door' mean for you? If having an 'open door' is not the ultimate criterion for making decisions, what criteria should you use according to verses 12–13?

THANKS *to a* VICTORIOUS GOD

If the Corinthians complained about Paul's fickleness in his plans to visit Corinth, the Asians might also have complained of his 'irresponsibility' at Troas. Paul will explain the rationale for his action at Troas in chapter 3, but since he is taking us on a journey of his spirit, he breaks forth into a triumphant benediction in 2:14–17. The benediction presages the news Paul will share in 7:6–7, that God 'consoled [Paul and Timothy] by the arrival of Titus, and not only by his coming, but also by the consolation' the Corinthians had given him.

God is the triumphant general

Paul alludes to the image of a triumphant general (v. 14). After a victorious battle, the spoils, captives, general and army would all parade into the city that had won the fight. Tablets would be carried that listed the spoils and pictured the different battles. After the captives, but before the victorious general in his chariot, incense bearers would walk, releasing fragrant odours, somewhat as, in the recent past, ticker tape used to be thrown out of windows on to parading soldiers. The victors would also sacrifice in thanksgiving to gods before and after the parade. For example, the Roman historian Appian describes the triumphant procession of General Scipio:

Trumpeters led the advance and wagons laden with spoils. Towers were borne along representing the captured cities, and pictures showing the exploits of the war; then gold and silver coin and bullion, and whatever else they had captured of that kind: then came the crowns that had been given to the general as a reward for his bravery by cities, by allies, or by the army itself. White oxen came next, and after them elephants and the captive Carthaginian and Numidian chiefs. Lictors clad in purple tunics preceded the general; also a chorus of harpists and pipers, in imitation of an Etruscan procession, wearing belts and golden crowns, and they march in regular order, keeping step with song and dance... Next came a number of incense bearers, and after them the general himself on a chariot embellished with various designs, wearing a crown of gold and precious stones... Then followed those who had served him in the war as secretaries, aides, and armour-bearers. After these came the army arranged in squadrons and cohorts... When Scipio arrived at the Capitol the procession came to an end, and he entertained his friends at a banquet in the temple, according to custom. (Roman History *viii, 'The Punic Wars' 9:66*)

In Paul's analogy, God is the general. Paul and his co-workers are the army. Even though they felt as if they had received the death sentence (1:9), they ended up living, and being the victors. This God in whom all promises are 'Yes' is also the general who always wins, no matter how bleak the prospect of victory may seem. People do defect from the army, but those who remain will always be on the winning side.

Christians are the sweet fragrance

Spices were carried by the incense bearers, so they would 'spread in every place the fragrance'. But Paul develops the image further. Not only are Christians the army, they are the very 'aroma' itself (v. 15). The fragrance would drift back to the general and the army, and sideways to the spectators. 'Fragrance' (vv. 14, 16) may refer to any odour, whether foul or fragrant. 'Aroma' (v. 15) is always a sweet smell or bouquet, especially of sacrifices. 'To God' Paul and his co-workers were always a sweet aroma. Why? Because they represented 'Christ'. They were the sweet fragrance of incense or of living sacrifices. This aroma did two things simultaneously. To people being saved, it caused them to receive more life. To those perishing (the captives), it caused them to get that much closer to death. The aroma worked as a catalyst furthering a process that had already begun in others.

Paul teaches us that we cannot measure the effectiveness of our work by people's responses. Responses are determined by people's own will, their own desire to repent or not to repent. But we can measure our effectiveness by whether what we say and do indeed accurately represent Christ and the message revealed by God. In other words, we must ask, 'Is our fragrance from Christ? Have we given life to the living, and death to the dying, rather than vice versa?'

PRAYER

O Lord of hosts, may we be a smell of sweetness continually pleasing in your sight, wafting forth from your own offering upon the altar.

Allusion to Genesis 8:20–21

SPEAKING TRUTHFULLY

Paul concludes his extended metaphor describing Christians as incense bearers (2:14–16a) with a rhetorical question, an exclamation in reality: 'Who is sufficient for these things?' (v. 16b). How can we be equipped with adequate power to be a 'constant fragrance' representing God? Only God can make us competent, Paul will answer (3:5–6). But in chapter 2 he presents another image, of what Paul and his team are not (v. 17), as opposed to what they are (vv. 14–16).

Christians are not hustlers

In 1:24 Paul had explained that he and his co-workers do not 'lord it over' the Corinthians' faith. Now Paul adds in 2:17 that they do not 'peddle' God's word. A 'peddler' was a retail-dealer such as a small shopkeeper, secondhand dealer and especially a tavern-keeper. (A small retail-dealer is cited in contrast to a considerable merchant who imports goods in Ecclesiasticus 26:29.) Peddlers had the reputation, in ancient times, of falsifying merchandise. Along with Israel's other sins (loving bribes, not pleading for orphans and widows), Isaiah lists wine merchants who dilute wine by mixing in water, falsifying their product in order to enlarge their profits (Isaiah 1:22). Paul is not against receiving financial recompense for spiritual service (1 Corinthians 9:11). However, he is against falsifying or adulterating God's teachings in order to get excessive financial gain from teaching or preaching.

Genuine Christian leadership is neither dictatorial (1:24) nor exploitative (v. 17). Paul did not accept money from the Corinthians for his own ministry—although he did from the Philippians (Philippians 4:15)—because he wanted to contrast his ministry with that of the dictatorial and exploitative 'super-apostles' (11:8–9, 20; 12:13).

Christians speak out of purity

In contrast to tavern-keepers who mixed water into wine to dilute it, Paul and his co-workers acted 'as persons of sincerity' (v. 17). The source of their actions was 'sincere' or, literally, 'without mixture', 'pure'. Genuine preachers act out of pure motives. They are holy and truthful (1:12; 1 Corinthians 5:8; Philippians 1:10–11). Why are their actions pure? Their actions are pure because their source is pure —Almighty God.

Paul describes both their very being ('we are') and their words ('we speak'). Words are important. Their words are described by three parallel phrases in Greek: 'sent from God' ('out of God'), 'standing in [God's] presence' ('opposite God') and 'in Christ'. 'From' has the basic meaning that one had been in a place before departing, as Jesus had been leaving from within the Jordan River before the Holy Spirit descended (Mark 1:10). Paul's first point is that their words and their mission come right from God. 'Standing in presence' literally refers to being 'opposite from', as Jesus directed his disciples to find a donkey in the village 'opposite' or 'ahead' of them (Matthew 21:2). Paul's second point is that what they say is done consciously before God as their witness.

'In' has the basic idea of being inside a place, as the church dwelled 'in Corinth' (1:1). Paul's third point is that their words are daily emanating from Christ's presence. 'From', 'before', and 'in' describe their multi-dimensional relationship to God. Paul will reiterate this same point in the conclusion of his letter (12:19). Genuine preachers receive their message from God, aim to please God and live in Christ's presence. Therefore, they are free to love others, not to exploit them. Their message will not always be well received by all people, but it will always be well received by the sender, God (2:15–16).

The true source of our message and the extent to which we represent that message accurately are key criteria for measuring effectiveness in day-to-day living and, more specifically, in Christian service. Sometimes politicians are accused of changing their policies in order to get into office. Paul, in contrast, defends his policies as unchangeable because they come from God, even if Paul's actions might change to implement those policies appropriately among different people (1:23).

MEDITATION

What might be the main temptations to keep you from presenting and living out God's truth?

LIVING LETTERS

In chapters 1 and 2, Paul defends himself and his associates as having behaved with pure motives, while in chapters 3—5 he shows that their competence to lead comes from God.

Letters of recommendation

Paul uses in verses 1–2 the technical phrase 'letters of recommendation'. Ancient letters of recommendation would ask a favour for the person introduced ('Welcome [Phoebe] in the Lord as is fitting for the saints, and help her in whatever she may require from you') and cite reasons why the recipient should grant the favours requested ('for she has been a benefactor of [or leader over] many and of myself as well') (Romans 16:2). Paul's letter to Philemon, Apphia, Archippus and the church in their home might also be considered a letter of recommendation, a lengthier one recommending that they welcome back Onesimus in the same manner that they would welcome Paul (Philemon v. 17).

In the first century, letters of introduction or recommendation were customarily carried by the person concerned. Government officials had their own couriers who would run swiftly from city to city. Sometimes couriers with important messages would place signs on their chests so that they could run unhindered.

Paul's question certainly suggests that the Corinthians were in contact with some people who did have letters of introduction (v. 1). Since the false apostles (ch. 11) were highlighting their own earthly status, most likely they would flaunt introductory letters for themselves. The Corinthians were so impressed with their letters that they were apparently suggesting that Paul and his co-workers obtain some. But Paul and his team did not need a letter of recommendation to the Corinthians or from them, because they already had one.

Living letters of recommendation

So dedicated was Paul to developing the Christian maturity of the people with whom he served (his 'letter of recommendation') that he refused to preach at Troas and left for Macedonia. The couriers or messengers are Paul and Timothy. They are running with a message from, and going back to, their heavenly ruler ('sent from God and standing in [God's] presence', 2:17). That message or letter is the Corinthians themselves! The couriers have only one letter (v. 2) because, although the Corinthians may want to divide into many factions, in God's sight they are one, a community of interdependent people, one sanctuary for the presence of God (1 Corinthians 6:19; 12:1–27). The message is not simply placed on Paul and his co-workers' chests, but it is inscribed on the hearts of these messengers by God (v. 3). Paul and his associates have great affection for the Corinthians. This letter is visible to everyone, even as Paul's letters are meant to be understood fully (1:13). The Corinthians' faces are engraved on the mail couriers' chests. The letter is from Christ, written with the ink of the Spirit of the living God (v. 3).

Another image that might fit the extended metaphor in verses 1–3 comes from Exodus 32:15–19. Since Paul will be alluding to the old covenant shortly (3:7), here he may be suggesting that he and Timothy are messengers like Moses. As Moses carried two tablets of stone down from Sinai mountain, so, too, Paul and Timothy carry a 'tablet'. They carry only one 'tablet', the Corinthians. As with the lettering on Moses' tablets, Paul's and Timothy's 'tablet' can be seen by everyone. The difference is that the message Paul and Timothy carry is engraved by the Spirit on their hearts, not on stone tablets. The writing is still the writing of God, but this new message cannot be thrown and broken at the foot of any mountain.

Paul is explaining how his and his team's concern and love cannot be broken. It cannot be hidden. It is 'known and read by all' (v. 2). It cannot be destroyed. Their love is so great that it marks their bodies. The Corinthians are a part of Paul's very self: as he will say, 'our heart is wide open' (6:11). The Corinthians themselves are proof of Christ's commission to Paul, the apostle, and of Christ's work among them.

When we go about our work for Christ, we too need to remember that our effect on people is what counts. Our goal is to have living letters of recommendation. Our measure of success is whether we have spoken (and lived) true to God's word.

MEDITATION

Who do you know who might be your living letter of
recommendation? How were you Christ's courier in their lives?

The EMPOWERING GOD

Paul had raised a question in 2:16 which he has yet to answer fully: 'Who is sufficient for these things?' Who can represent Christ so well that only other people's desire to repent or not to repent affects the communication (2:15)? Who can love people so much that, if necessary, they will ignore opportunities to speak publicly on Christ's behalf (2:13)? Who can love people so much that they will not use God's word for their own financial and ambitious benefit (2:17)? Who can equip someone to be a minister of a new, spiritual covenant (v. 6)? Paul and his team are 'confident' they can do all those things, creating out of their hearers living letters of recommendation (3:3), because God's empowerment makes them confident.

God gives competence

'Competence' is a major theme of verses 5–6. For cultures in which 'how to' books are bestsellers, these verses should be quite engaging. 'Competent' can refer to having sufficient money (Matthew 28:12), lights (Acts 20:8), people (Mark 10:46), and pigs (Luke 8:32). In these examples, 'sufficient' is 'many'. 'Sufficient' can also carry a sense of 'too much'. The punishment of the offender in their midst by the Corinthian Christian majority is now too much (2:6). When applied to people, 'competent' basically has the idea of being equipped to perform a duty. Paul will ask Timothy to find people who have the gift or competency to teach (2 Timothy 2:2). But for some tasks, no one is equipped. John the Baptist declares that he does not have merit enough to perform a slave's duty when it comes to carrying Jesus' sandals (Matthew 3:11). Paul declares that he does not have merit enough to be called an apostle (1 Corinthians 15:9). Similarly, he explains that no human beings could be equipped from their own inner strength to serve as ministers of this new spiritual covenant (v. 5).

Only God can equip someone. Only God can be the source. This is what God had predicted over 600 years earlier. Tired of the Israelites breaking their part of the covenant, God would put the law 'within' people and 'write it on their hearts' and 'be their God', and they would be God's people. God would forgive their iniquity and remember their sin no more (Jeremiah 31:33–34, quoted in Hebrews 8:8–12).

Only the Spirit can empower this spiritual covenant (v. 6). The new covenant begins with the permanent reconciliation between God and humans, accomplished by Jesus dying on behalf of human sin (Matthew 26:28). When people enter the new covenant, their obedience does not flow from external enforcement, but from an internal desire to please and an internal understanding (Jeremiah 31:33–34). The Holy Spirit is now a permanent presence.

The law condemns

Why is a new covenant necessary, according to Paul? 'The letter kills, but the Spirit gives life' (v. 6). The 'letter' literally refers to letters written down (Galatians 6:11). It could also refer to having one's 'letters' or being well educated (Acts 26:24). In verse 6, 'letter' represents the way the first covenant was communicated. It was written down (3:7).

How does it 'kill'? Paul uses two different verbs for death: 'kill' (*apokteino*, v. 6) and 'perish' (*apollumi*, 2:15). 'Perish' describes people who are 'lost', their lives gradually going further and further away from God. Only God can decide if someone has become so 'lost' that their life and body will be destroyed utterly by being relegated to Gehenna (Matthew 10:28). *Apokteino* can refer to judges who can choose to 'condemn' a criminal 'to death'. The judges do not kill the criminal, but they make a decision which results in their death. For instance, King Herod wanted to condemn John the Baptist to death because John had told Herod not to commit adultery (Matthew 14:4–5). Some of the religious leaders also sought to condemn Jesus to death because they did not like his teachings (Matthew 26:1–4). Thus, Paul explains that God's written covenant ends up 'condemning' people 'to death' (v. 6). The law condemns because it does not justify people (Galatians 3:10–14), but it simply indicates what people must do to please God (Romans 7:11).

Therefore, we must all learn what pleases God, but we can never do that unless we are enabled by God's Spirit.

PRAYER

Please equip me to have the power to become a servant of your new, spiritual covenant.

GOOD IS NOT BEST

When the Corinthians questioned Paul's integrity, Paul understood that they had questioned the integrity of the God he represented (1:17–21). If the Corinthians question the nature of his team's effectiveness as leaders, then they have also questioned the nature of the message or covenant they proclaim. Why would Paul raise this defence of the new covenant if he did not suspect that the Corinthians were living according to another covenant? Paul now describes the two covenants and explains why the new one gives them such hope (3:12).

Agreements can serve

Paul contrasts two 'ministries', one of 'death' (v. 7) and one of the 'Spirit' (v. 8). Paul uses the more common word 'covenant' earlier (3:6). God established 'covenants' with humans as early as Noah and his descendants (Genesis 9:9–17). These are personal compacts, agreements, arrangements that serve.

'Ministry' refers to serving and paying for food and drink, the food and drink itself and taking care of physical and emotional needs. It can also refer to the servant of a ruler, similar to today's minister in government. For example, Paul explains that rulers are God's 'servants' for people's good (Romans 13:4). Metaphorically, Paul and his co-workers 'served' ('prepared') God by delivering his letter (3:3). In verse 7, even 'death' is personified (described with human attributes) as a servant of God.

Expanding on the argument in 3:6b, 'death' (v. 7) is not evil, but, rather, is the result of the condemnation of a judge. To the Hebrews, the ten commandments represented such ruling justice (Exodus 34:1). They were considered so holy that God had them stored inside the Ark of the Covenant in the Holy of Holies (Deuteronomy 10:5). Paul will also call the written covenant a 'ministry of condemnation' (v. 9). 'Condemnation' has to do with judging. A judge gives a sentence against a defendant, which might be a sentence of death if the defendant is declared 'guilty', as when the chief priests and scribes sentenced (or 'condemned') Jesus to death (Matthew 20:18; Mark 14:64).

But the 'ministry' of the Spirit (v. 8) continues the positive and personal connotations of service. As opposed to 'condemnation', it ends in 'justification' (v. 9). 'Justification' or 'justice' is also rendered by a judge when freeing a defendant who is declared 'not guilty' and therefore given life (3:6). The 'ministry' or service of the Spirit delivers a freeing letter of reprieve from Christ (3:3) because Christ is the one who 'died for all' (5:15).

Agreements are weighty

Both covenants have glory. 'Glory' could simply mean 'opinion, judgment' (in the Bible always a good opinion); but here it refers to 'splendour, brightness, weight', the brightness around God's presence. For instance, God's glory, 'like a devouring fire', covered the cloud over Mount Sinai (Exodus 24:16–17), and the Lord appeared to Moses in a flame of fire out of a bush that was burning but never got burnt up (Exodus 3:2). Similarly, the new covenant came with fire-like tongues (Acts 2:3). In order to describe the glory of the written covenant, Paul explains that simply the residue of being in God's presence was so bright that Moses' skin shone, causing Aaron and all the Israelites to be afraid (v. 7; Exodus 34:29–30).

Paul then compares the glory of the two covenants in three ways—time, nature and length. The first covenant 'came' (past tense), but the second covenant 'will come' (future tense) (vv. 7–8). The past glory was great, but the future glory will be greater. This future glory will be hinted at in 3:18, where not merely one person, Moses, shines, but all believers will shine with God's glory. Second, Paul compares the glory of judgment ('condemnation') with the abounding glory of 'justification'. Third, he compares their length of existence (v. 11). 'Set aside' means to 'leave unemployed' or 'idle'. The written covenant is slowly being 'laid off', like a hard, able worker whose work hours are reduced as retirement approaches. The second covenant, in contrast, is the replacement ('the permanent', v. 11). Thus, the glorious written covenant seems to have no glory when compared to the second and more glorious covenant (v. 10).

MEDITATION

List ways in which God's new covenant has
demonstrated glory in your life.

HAVING PERSISTENT BOLDNESS

Verse 12 begins with a word meaning 'since, then' or 'therefore'. Paul will not leave his discussion of covenants in the theoretical realm. All his theology is applied. Because of the future, justifying, permanent glory of the Spirit's covenant (3:7–11), the behaviour of Paul's team is affected. What is their hope? Their hope is to experience a greater and permanent glory and a full righteousness.

A bank offering boldness

How do they then act? (Literally, what do they 'use'?) 'Act' or 'use' in Greek properly means to receive a loan or borrow. Thus, Paul and his team have a 'bank' that gives them unlimited credit, not in drachmas but in 'boldness'. 'Boldness' refers to speaking freely and without concealment, openly and visibly. It includes the idea of the 'boldness' (Acts 4:31) for which Paul asked and which he received when he was in prison in Rome (Ephesians 6:19–20; Acts 28:31). Therefore, it is a synonym for boasting and love without premature condemnation (7:3–4). It also includes the idea of speaking publicly (Colossians 2:15; Mark 8:32; John 7:26; 18:20) and directly (Philemon 8–9; John 10:24; 11:14).

A bank never bankrupt

Paul earlier described how Moses' face shone as he carried the ten commandments down Mount Sinai (3:7; Exodus 34:29). This was evidence for the glory of the written covenant. Now Paul continues describing the same incident as proof of the temporary nature of that covenant. Paul makes an analogy. In the same way as the glory on Moses' face was temporary, so too the written covenant's glory was temporary.

When Moses descended with his skin shining, the people were afraid. We might have expected Moses to veil himself while he presented God's words so that the Israelites would not be afraid. But Moses placed a veil or covering over his face *after* he had finished speaking with the people of Israel (Exodus 34:30–35). According to Paul, he placed this veil over his face so that the people could not see the end of the glory. He did not want them to see that the radiance was temporary (v. 13).

Why did Moses cover his face? Was he being deceitful? Neither Paul nor the Old Testament records suggest that. Moses did not want the people to see that the radiance came to an end, because then they may have questioned his authority. They had already made a golden calf. Moses had already broken the first set of tablets. Seeing his face shine created a fear in the people—a right, if basic, reaction to God. This fear may be all that Moses had to use to spur the people on to worship the one living God.

Thus, Moses' action was concealed, private and not bold. Paul and his associates, in contrast, do not have to veil their faces, or their message, because the glory of the covenant they profess is ever increasing, not decreasing and disappearing. This conclusion enlightens and affirms several of Paul's points so far. He and his co-workers aim to be understood (1:13). Their plans are not secret (1:17). Their motives and actions are pure (2:17). 'Boldness', with its denotations of clarity, publicness and unashamedness, summarizes well the type of ministry they have.

Paul in this letter writes an apologetic for his team's open ministry style. His colleagues Peter and John were also renowned for their lack of concealment. Even though Peter lacked university level education, the religious leaders of his time were amazed at his ability to speak freely and confidently (Acts 4:13, 17–20).

Many early Christians were bold in the midst of persecution. During the reign of the Roman Emperor Marcus Aurelius (AD161–179), persecution flared up in Gaul. A servant, Blandina, 'was filled with such power that' despite the continual torture 'the blessed woman, like a noble athlete, kept gaining in vigour in her confession' (Eusebius, *Church History* v. 1.18–19).

PRAYER

Grant to your servants to speak your word with all boldness,
while you stretch out your hand to heal, and signs and wonders are
performed through the name of your holy servant Jesus.

Acts 4:29–30

In CHRIST STONE TURNS to FLESH

Paul has made several figurative applications from the same incident —Moses regularly covering his face (Exodus 34:29–35). First, the glory of that covenant was temporary (3:7, 13). Second, because Moses did not allow the people to see the truth that the glory was temporary, the viewers became like the viewed: the people of Israel ended up, as it were, having a covering over their own faces. For Moses, it was a literal covering; for the people of Israel, it became a figurative covering. Or we can see it in another way. Moses himself became a symbol of all the people. What he did, they all did. The great irony is that Moses himself ended up obscuring his own writings (v. 15). The promises in the Pentateuch for a permanent covenant of the Spirit were obscured.

Flesh can become stone

The eyes see so that the mind can apprehend. Moses did not want the people to gaze upon the disappearing glory (3:13). Instead, what did they fix their eyes on? Their gaze became limited to a covenant chiselled on stone, and they themselves ended up turning into stone. 'Hardened' (v. 14) is related to the noun *poros*, a marble stone used in building. The verb, used in the construction and medical fields, means to 'petrify', as when a stone or bone callus forms. Like lime-stone turning into marble, the Israelites' minds turned to stone by fixation on the wrong object.

Hardening can be a positive biblical image, such as the tongue of the righteous being 'hardened' like 'choice silver' (Proverbs 10:20), firm, resolute and valuable. However, hardening is usually a negative biblical idea. Hardening of the arteries may be caused by too much cholesterol. Hardening of the mind is caused by too much unbelief, not giving God the credit for working before our own eyes. When people fail to see God at work once, they fail to see God at work later; and eventually, like the effect of cataracts, the eyes get misty or the brain gets less clear. For example, the disciples did not understand that Jesus could give them what they needed to eat, so they became terrified when Jesus walked on water (Mark 6:52; 8:14–17). By not perceiving correctly, their hearts were becoming 'hardened'. The saddest state of all is when God then affirms what a person has de-cided to do, as when God hardens people's minds temporarily while they receive the repercussions of their own actions (Isaiah 6:10–12).

Stone can become flesh again

This condition of 'hardened minds' need not continue. Christ can 'set' it 'aside' (v. 14). 'Set aside' has been used by Paul twice already. The glory of the written covenant (3:7, 11) is, as it were, laid off or unemployed. Paul uses it to refer to something which cancels out something else, such as an earlier argument (Galatians 3:17). He also uses it to describe something which will become totally inoperative, such as the body (1 Corinthians 6:13) or the gifts of prophecy, tongues and knowledge (1 Corinthians 13:8, 10). It can also refer to an action, or person, or covenant which no longer has power but still continues on in its less powerful mode, such as the rulers of the world or death (1 Corinthians 2:6; 15:24, 26), or the law (Ephesians 2:15). The 'old' covenant is still around in its decreasing glorious state.

The proof that 'hardened' minds need not remain a permanent state is reiterated in verse 16. Humans are responsible to 'turn to' the Lord. They cannot lift off the veil themselves because the evil one has cemented it on (4:4), but they can turn to the Lord, who then lifts off the veil.

In Paul's own preaching he met fellow Jews who exemplified both conditions. When he preached in Corinth that Jesus was the Messiah, some people 'opposed and reviled him', becoming so upset by him that they eventually brought him before the Roman proconsul Gallio (Acts 18:5–6, 12–13). Others, like Crispus, the ruler of the syna-gogue, and his whole household, on the other hand, became believ-ers (Acts 18:8). Or, in Antioch in Pisidia, after the reading of the Old Testament during the synagogue service, Paul was invited to preach. Many Jews wanted to hear more (Acts 13:15–16, 43).

MEDITATION

Was your mind ever hardened to the gospel?
How did it become open?

The LIBERATING SPIRIT of CHRIST

This verse appears to come from nowhere, but Paul is explaining how turning to the Lord, having the veil over one's heart lifted (3:15–16), is related to the Spirit's covenant.

Beyond the veil

Paul writes with several levels of meaning that do not contradict one another.

- When people turn toward the Lord (3:16), they discover that they are facing the Spirit. That is because the Spirit is the person of the Trinity who is actively administrating this new covenant (3:8). The Spirit writes Christ's letter and gives life (3:6) and justification (3:3, 6, 9). Christ is the one who died for all (5:14), but the Spirit communicates Christ's death to people's lives.

- Naturally, the presence of the Spirit is a reminder to the reader of this new spiritual, life-giving, holiness-giving covenant.

- In 3:3 the distinctiveness of the Trinity is described. The letter is 'of Christ', written by 'the Spirit of the living God'. In verse 17, the unity of God is stated. The Spirit, also being God, is the Lord, or Christ; but also the Spirit is a messenger of the Lord or Christ. Sometimes we Gentiles want to treat God more as three Gods than as one God. A passage such as this one reminds us of the unity of the Godhead, as Paul will do again in 4:4, identifying Christ with God. The whole letter ends in presenting the three equal persons of the Trinity (13:13).

The truth that the Holy Spirit will be communicating about Christ is not new. Jesus himself warned his disciples that after his death and resurrection, the believers would receive the Holy Spirit as a permanent presence, who would glorify Christ, declare and remind people of Christ's words, convict of sin and righteousness, and give life (John 6:63; 7:38–39; 14:16; 16:7–15). Paul had highlighted his teaching about the Holy Spirit in his first letter, since the Corinthians themselves had been blessed by the Spirit with many gifts (1 Corinthians 1:5).

Christ's Spirit emancipates

The second half of verse 17 can be rendered (as in NRSV) as 'Where the Spirit of the Lord is, there is freedom' or (as in Alfred Plummer's 1915 commentary on 2 Corinthians) as 'He who possesses the Spirit of Christ has liberty'. My own preference is the latter. Referring back to 3:15–16, Paul's point is that when we turn to the Lord, we then are filled by or 'have' the Lord's Spirit, who then gives us freedom.

What kind of freedom does Paul have in mind here? Literally, freedom is a political concept, such as when a human is free—belonging to no other person, having rights of inheritance and marriage, and having freedom of choice in occupation, mobility and property—as opposed to a slave, whose relative freedom is determined by another's decision. Paul encourages slaves to become legally free when possible (1 Corinthians 7:21). But in this passage Paul discusses the spiritual concept of freedom, which Jesus had foreshadowed in his teachings (John 8:31–36; Luke 4:18; Isaiah 61:1).

This freedom of the mind, first of all, is a freedom to perceive how Moses' written covenant foreshadows a more glorious covenant (3:14). It is a freedom, second, to speak and act freely and without concealment (3:12). Third, it is a freedom to lead others without fear of an impermanent glory, without the need to keep people fearful so that they will continue to serve the one living God, and without the need to ask for external signs such as letters or veils (3:1, 13). Fourth, this freedom has the qualities of permanence, because the Spirit is always present (3:11), and of justification, not condemnation, because Christ is communicated through it (3:3, 9).

Of course, this freedom given by the Spirit is not freedom to do things contrary to God's holiness, because it is freedom that comes from a covenant of justification or righteousness (3:9). It is freedom to behold Christ, whom we see through the agency of the Spirit (3:17–18).

PRAYER

Create in me a clean heart, O God, and put a new and right spirit within me. Do not cast me away from your presence, and do not take your Holy Spirit from me. Restore to me the joy of your salvation, and sustain in me a willing spirit.

Psalm 51:10–12

The TRANSFORMING MIRROR

Paul contrasts verse 18 with verses 13–15, highlighting differences in the number of people involved, whether they are veiled or unveiled, what they see, how they see it and what they become as a result.

He begins emphatically with 'all of us' (whereas in 3:13–15 the focus had been on Moses), because now leadership is more shared. Since the covenant is written on people's hearts (3:2), no priest is necessary to represent the people (1 Peter 2:9). Now, every believer is privileged to enter into God's presence without fear.

A blaze has no curtain

Paul highlights how and what people see. *How* people see is with an 'unveiled' face. They see without a covering because they have turned to the Lord (3:16). The Greek uses the singular 'face' (KJV), not the plural 'faces' (NRSV) because the Church has one body and one head (1 Corinthians 12:27). In symmetry with Moses' individual face, the Church too has one collective face. The singular 'face' of the collective Church also implies the priesthood of all believers. Paul also stresses this sense of unity when it comes to giving (8:24). But he uses the plural 'faces' in 1:11 ('many') because he suggests there that the prayers come from 'many' individuals.

What people see is 'the glory of the Lord' (v. 18). They see what the people of Israel could not keep gazing upon because the glory was so bright (3:7); and they keep on seeing it, whereas Moses would not let the Israelites see the fading of the first covenant's brightness (3:13).

The Son reflects

The action of seeing is described 'as though reflected in a mirror', or 'beholding for ourselves in a mirror'. 'All of us' do this action for ourselves; it is not done to us (compare 3:13). The Greek has at least two different terms for 'mirror'. Both are built from the verb 'to see' (*opto*) (from which we get such words as 'optometrist'). *Katoptrizo* (v. 18) is related to *katoptron* ('mirror'). Ancient mirrors were highly polished bronze or silver, often held by hand. As an example, the women who served at the tabernacle gave their mirrors to Bezalel so that he could make them into a bronze basin and stand (Exodus 38:8). If an ancient mirror had a dim reflection, the mirror would be held lower than one's face in order to improve its ability to reflect the sun's rays and thereby clarify one's own reflection. In Paul's analogy, instead of the sun, the source of light is the Lord of the Spirit ('from' connotes source). Christ's glory, through the Spirit, external to the mirror, is reflected into it, a reminder of God's glory that appeared like a consuming fire (Exodus 24:17).

This mirror-like beholding (v. 18) contrasts with the 'gazing' that the Israelites did at Moses (3:7, 13). 'Gaze' can have a critical sense to it. For example, Paul gazed at the magician Elymas only to reprimand him (Acts 13:9–10). The crowd in Nazareth stared at Jesus, eventually to attack him (Luke 4:20–29). The council glared at Stephen before they had him killed (Acts 6:15; 7:54, 58). Peter stared with disfavour at the vision of unclean animals (Acts 11:6, 8). The word can also simply have a more neutral sense—to study someone in order to make a decision about them, as Paul stared at the crippled man to see if he had faith to be healed (Acts 14:9). Thus, Moses feared both the intense scrutiny and the potential criticism of his people (3:13).

In the new covenant, people look at the glorious face of Christ (the 'same' image), actively, becoming more glorious and Christ-like themselves, instead of staring into the chiselled covenant, becoming stone-like (3:7, 14). 'Being transformed' is a participle indicating that the change is a gradual process, in the same way that sanctification (and perishing) are gradual processes (2:15). As people (individually and collectively) keep beholding Christ's reflection, they slowly become inwardly the way God sees them outwardly, as fully righteous.

No wonder Paul and his co-workers have hope and act with great boldness (3:12)!

MEDITATION

What can you do to behold the Lord's glory? Do you ever find yourself staring instead at a less glorious covenant?

COMMENDATION *by the* TRUTH

In 2 Corinthians theology and doctrine are integrated throughout the letter. Therefore, after describing the ever more glorious new covenant that he and his co-workers preach, Paul returns again to its significance for daily living.

Not practising cunning

Paul and his co-workers are open and frank in their work because they believe in a covenant made visible to all, which never loses its glory (3:8–18). In 4:1 Paul continues writing about the openness of their work, but adds the additional ramification of this new covenant: 'we do not lose heart'. He and his co-workers do not become discouraged or tire of their work. The verb may mean not only 'lose heart' but also 'behave badly'. In that case, Paul would be saying that having received this covenant of mercy that changes his team members' inner natures to be like the character of the Lord of the covenant, they do not behave badly. This latter translation contrasts with 'the shameful things that one hides' (v. 2).

What type of behaviour is totally inconsistent with this new covenant? The 'shameful things that one hides' are described as 'to practise cunning or to falsify' (v. 2). 'Cunning' also refers to the adulteration of drugs or money. 'Falsify' also refers to adulterating incense or wine, beguiling, ensnaring, taking by craft.

Paul develops the imagery he has introduced in 2:17—'peddlers'. Unlike dishonest peddlers, Paul and his associates have not deceived the Corinthians by adding 'alloys' to their message, nor have they changed God's revelation so as to benefit themselves and unfairly attract the Corinthians. They have preached the unadulterated message that they received from God. Cunning and falsification, Paul implies, are characteristics of the ways of those who oppose him. Paul will tell the Corinthians more bluntly in 11:3 that cunning was a characteristic of the serpent which deceived Eve. Cunning also characterized the spies who tried to trick Jesus (Luke 20:22–23). Jesus saw through their duplicity and prevented the spies from trapping him. Paul, too, saw the duplicity of his opponents and was seeking to reveal the truth.

Commending themselves

Instead of living in trickery, Paul and his team 'commend' themselves (v. 2), the same verb used in 3:1. Paul will return to this theme of commendation again and again in this letter (5:12; 6:4; 7:11; 10:12, 18; 12:11). Once my husband and I were asked to reapply for jobs we already had. We were deeply insulted, because we thought we had shown our competence in the years of our work and, moreover, we had established genuine relationships with our employers. Apparently Paul, too, was deeply hurt. He had given his life for the Corinthians. Nevertheless, he did not allow his feelings to keep him from defending their ministry.

The process of commendation is modified in three ways—how, for what, and before whom it is done. Instead of falsifying words, Paul and his team commend themselves by revealing the truth. Earlier he pointed out that instead of letters of recommendation, the Corinthians themselves were their living letter, written on their own hearts (3:3). Here, he continues to state that their commendation is perceived by something inward, the conscience.

The 'conscience', literally, is 'knowledge shared with another'. Thus, when it refers to the inner awareness of right or wrongdoing, it implies the ability to have an inner conversation, as well as to possess knowledge of right and wrong (for example, Hebrews 10:2). A conscience is driven by the knowledge it has (1 Corinthians 8:7). A seared or corrupt conscience will command aberrant behaviour (1 Timothy 4:2–3). Thus, Paul has the conviction to challenge all of the consciences at Corinth for their commendation. And who could be more knowledgeable than God? Even if consciences can be misinformed or corrupted, God can never be misinformed, corrupted or false. As in 2:17, God is the ultimate witness of the genuine ministering Christian (v. 2).

PRAYER

Make me to know your ways, O Lord; teach me your paths.
Lead me in your truth, and teach me, for you are the God of my
salvation; for you I wait all day long. Be mindful of your mercy,
O Lord, and of your steadfast love, for they have been from of old.

Psalm 25:4–6

JESUS IS *the* GOD PREACHED

Paul had said that he and his team were 'the smell of death' to those who are perishing (2:15–16). One reason their message is perceived by some as 'death' is that the senses of people who have rejected God's message have been altered by 'the god of this world'—Satan. The good news seems hidden only to these people, but not because the good news is in any way a secret knowledge. The good news is delivered in an honest and clear fashion, but it cannot always be understood. Their altered senses keep them from perceiving the *shekinah* glory of Christ.

God incarnate in Jesus

Even as the Lord Christ is the Spirit (3:17–18), so, too, Christ is 'the image of God' (v. 4). Although the Greek word for 'image' is the same one used to describe humans made in the 'image' of God (Genesis 1:26; 5:1), in this context Christ's glory is unique. Christ is more than a mirror image of God. Christ is the living image or representation of God. If the 'image' of humans reflected God in the same way as the 'image' of Christ reflects God, then indeed Paul and his associates would 'preach themselves' (v. 5). But since Christ is the living image of God, humans must look to Christ to get God's glory, and therefore must preach 'Jesus Christ as Lord'.

Jesus is preached

Verse 5 is an excellent summary of the style of leadership Paul and his co-workers maintain: 'For we do not proclaim ourselves; we proclaim Jesus Christ as Lord and ourselves as your slaves for Jesus' sake.' This transition sentence both summarizes the previous chapters and introduces the section to come. So far Paul has explained that to 'proclaim ourselves' is to use deception and to distort God's word (4:2; 2:17; 1:12). To 'proclaim ourselves' is impossible if the preacher wants the listeners to receive the glory that comes from God. If indeed the preacher elevates and highlights Jesus Christ as Master, then the preacher must be the slave of others for the sake of this great Master. No matter how frequently we mouth 'servant leader' as a concept of leadership (the leader who serves others), frequently we live by 'man (sometimes woman) with a mission', 'a person set aside', 'a special person'. Respecting and appreciating leaders gets twisted into undue attention and reverence. As was once said of a famous 'devout' popular entertainer, 'He is too important a person to have to live by everyday morality' (in other words, not committing adultery). The glory that comes from Christ, which is then reflected on to the human face, can get misunderstood. The listener or the preacher can begin to think that that reflected glory is not reflected at all but a self-generated glory, or that the reflected glory is not available to all. God's glory shines in all the hearts of all the people who have turned to the Lord (3:18; 4:6).

'Slaves' of others (v. 5) is a metaphor; it is not literally true. Greville MacDonald comments in his biography of his father, the novelist George MacDonald, that churches are in 'danger of treating their minister as if he were their servant instead of Christ's' (*George MacDonald and His Wife*, George Allen & Unwin, 1924). No Christian should enslave another. However, because of the marvellous light that we receive, we are freed and we are strengthened to serve others voluntarily 'for Jesus' sake'. Paul does here say that they are the servants of the Corinthians. But his Lord is Jesus, not the Corinthians. Jesus is the Lord who sends his slaves to take care of a neighbour's problems. The slaves may be helping the neighbour, but they are under directives from their own heavenly Master. The source of the glory must always be appreciated. It is the 'glory of God in the face of Jesus Christ' (4:6).

MEDITATION

Dwell upon what Jesus Christ as Lord means in your life.

GOD ENLIGHTENS

Why do Paul and his co-workers devote themselves to preaching the Lordship of Jesus Christ? So far in this one chapter alone they have mentioned appreciation of God's mercy (4:1), the gospel as illuminating, truthful and glorious (4:2, 4), and now the marvellous character of God (v. 6).

God lights up the dark

The God that believers worship in the new covenant is not different from the God of the old covenant. The same God who created physical light simply by a command ('Let there be light', Genesis 1:3) on the first day of creation is also the God who creates spiritual 'light' within human beings who have turned to the Lord (3:16). Paul uses four different words for 'light' in this one verse (v. 6), indicating its importance. Light has been a continual image to describe God's presence, from the consuming fire and flashing mountain (Exodus 20:18; 24:17) to burning lamps at the throne (Ezekiel 1:13; Revelation 4:5). Even God's angelic messengers are described with light (Daniel 10:6; Acts 12:7).

Ancient lamps were lit by oil. A small hand-held lamp might burn for two to three hours. We might call them torches. Gideon used torches in his army (Judges 7:16). Metaphorically, the sun was called the great 'lamp' in the sky. Jesus referred to lamps in his parables— the bridesmaids who carried lamps (Matthew 25:1–8) and the lamp that was placed on a lampstand in order to light a house (Matthew 5:15–16). A great shining light was an image used to describe God's approval (Isaiah 4:2). When Jesus is 'transformed' on the mountain (same verb as in 2 Corinthians 3:18), his face shines as the sun and his clothing becomes white as the light, hearkening back to Psalm 104:2, language used only of God (Matthew 17:2).

What makes light so powerful? It can change the character of darkness. Darkness no longer becomes a place of stumbling, but a place where we can see clearly. The light of the sun keeps shining brighter, enlightening more and more (Proverbs 4:18–19). Thus, when God 'enlightens' people, their knowledge of God's glory keeps increasing and in that glory they will see Jesus' face (4:6; 3:18).

God's light is muted

Where is this magnificent light stored? In a clay pot! Here is a paradox for the Christian life. A clay pot cannot reveal what is inside. A great treasure (God's glory) is stored in a fragile container. Corinth used to have a potters' quarter one mile west of its centre. No doubt the Corinthians would have used these clay pots frequently. Lamps could be made of clay, bronze and gold. Also, precious treasures could be hidden in cheap and fragile clay containers. Although in Roman triumphal processions (2:14) gold and silver would often be exhibited 'for show', the treasure of God's glory is hidden in clay containers. Clay containers are used to show that 'this extraordinary power belongs to God and does not come from us' (v. 7). Paul and his co-workers' competency must come from God. No one can confuse the treasure and its container if the container is no treasure itself. The 'extraordinary power' of these co-workers must come from God and not be self-generated.

What are the clay containers? They are defined in 4:8–9. Paul does not here write about physical bodies. The clay containers are more specifically the life of difficulties arising from external and internal opposition to genuine Christian ministry.

PRAYER

Bless the Lord, O my soul. O Lord my God, you are very great.
You are clothed with honour and majesty, wrapped in light as with
a garment. You stretch out the heavens like a tent, you set the
beams of your chambers on the waters, you make the clouds your
chariot, you ride on the wings of the wind, you make the winds
your messengers, fire and flame your ministers.

Psalm 104:1–4

The PARADOX of CLAY & CROSS

Paul has several lists of trials in the Corinthian correspondence: 1 Corinthians 4:9–13; 2 Corinthians 4:7–10; 6:1–10; 11:18—12:10. In each of these lists Paul describes a slightly different aspect of the same topic, the lifestyle of a true Christian leader, with the same result, a list of difficulties. 1 Corinthians 4:9–13 focuses on the present low esteem in which the apostles are held. 2 Corinthians 4:7–10 focuses on why such low esteem is really necessary—to show that God is the source of power.

God breathes into clay

These lists of difficulties are written in a magnificent style reflecting the magnificence of the treasure they describe. Here in verses 8–9, Paul first lists his difficulties in a rhythmic, forceful and vivid parallelism. In parallelism, like is paired with like:

- afflicted, but not crushed

- perplexed, but not driven to despair

- persecuted, but not forsaken

- struck down, but not destroyed

Paul repeats 'but not' four times, heightening the paradoxes of the Christian life, making his list all the more rhythmic, passionate and vivid. The explanation of 4:7 has broken out into this surprising, powerful listing of exactly what is symbolized by 'clay containers'— trouble, uncertainty, persecution, attack. If the Corinthians, as we, may have been attracted to the positive imagery of light in 4:6, they too, as we, may have been shocked by Paul's contrasting negative list in verses 8–10. Paul writes with emotion and vividness because he reacts with emotion and vividness to the events he has had to experience. He does not embrace difficulties for their own sake.

The parallel phrases mirror the closeness of the concepts of affliction, perplexity, persecution and being struck down. The phrase 'but not' contrasts these concepts. God's power is manifested (4:7) when affliction (which is so close to destruction) does not degenerate into being crushed, perplexity does not degenerate into despair, persecution does not leave us forsaken, and being hurled down does not produce death. The images to which Paul alludes are quite physical—pressure, crushing, throwing. The extraordinary quality of God's power prevents the natural human result.

God makes the cross alive

Paul builds up to a climax that comes in verse 10. What personal advantage can Paul and his co-workers have if they carry their treasure in jars of clay full of difficulties? What exactly have they been carrying about? Why must they experience trouble? They carry about the death of Jesus. Here is Paul's final paradox in this list: because they carry the 'death' of Jesus in their bodies, now 'the life of Jesus' can be revealed. The perfect parallelism is broken by the addition of the pronoun 'our'. 'Our' bodies will not have revealed in them Jesus' life if Jesus' death has not been previously carried. The imagery of 'life' hearkens back to the 'light' and 'glory' of 4:6 and the 'treasure' in 4:7.

Paul leaves the reader with a vivid image in verse 10. 'Death' is personified as a dead person whom people must carry. Who wants to carry around a cold, stiff, heavy corpse? Paul uses 'carry around', not simply 'carry', to accentuate that such a burden occurs 'always' or 'at all times'. Indeed, Paul alludes to the very image Jesus used—to bear a cross—except that here the cross is no longer wood but the carpenter, Jesus, himself. That 'cross' means experiencing trouble, being uncertain, being persecuted, being thrown down. But even as God spoke and out of darkness commanded light, so the dead body we carry becomes a living body within our own body. The dead carpenter is revealed as the living Lord. And if the dead carpenter becomes the living Lord, so, too, like the carpenter, those who carry the carpenter will themselves be resurrected and receive life (4:14).

MEDITATION

Can you think of any way you experienced a difficulty for Christ's sake which did not end in its worst, expected result?

LIFE *for* JESUS' SAKE

In verse 11 Paul rephrases the content of 4:10 to highlight certain aspects. In 4:10a he emphasized the object, who or what they carry, 'the death of Jesus' (which in Greek begins the clause). This is a poignant summary of all the difficulties listed in 4:8–9. But in verse 11a Paul highlights the paradox that those who are living receive death.

Followers always follow

How frequently did Paul and his co-workers have difficulties? 'Always'. Paul and his team have taken Jesus' teachings seriously: 'If any want to become my followers, let them deny themselves and take up their cross daily and follow me' (Luke 9:23). Paul had told the Corinthians earlier, 'I die every day!' (1 Corinthians 15:31). Jesus asked his followers not to be ashamed of him and his words (Luke 9:26). But he also promised that we will save our lives, if we give them over to Jesus (Luke 9:24). This is what Paul and Timothy did. They gave their energy and time to be used by Jesus. As Jesus had warned, 'if they persecuted me, they will persecute you' (John 15:20), Paul and Timothy discovered that in a fallen world (4:4), good news is not always welcomed.

Paul and his co-workers end up 'being given up to death' (v. 11). 'Being given up' literally means to give or hand over to another, in the way that property is handed over so that another can manage it (Matthew 25:14). This verb is also frequently used of teachings being 'given over' to another to pass on accurately (for example, 1 Corinthians 11:23) and of arrests. When used of arrests, the idea is that someone is handed over to the power or use of another, as Jesus was handed over to the jurisdiction and authority of the governor (Luke 20:20). Paul himself had handed over Christians to be imprisoned (Acts 8:3). In 2 Corinthians 4:11, the prison system is personified as 'death' because death is the potential end result of serious accusations.

Life comes from death

And why are they accused? They are accused 'for Jesus' sake', not for their own evil-doing or obnoxious disrespect. Paul concludes with a marvellous paradox. They gave their lives over to Jesus. They were persecuted for their faith, but instead of death, Jesus' life was made visible. Jesus' life is revealed in their 'mortal flesh', symbolized by 'clay jars' (4:7). Because they are mortal, they have a life of difficulties when they promote the cause of Christ.

Jesus' love is so great because he gave his life for others (Mark 10:45). Similarly, Paul's team follow Jesus' example, giving their lives for the sake of others, in this case the Corinthians (v. 12). Persisting despite difficulties is one way they express their love. Paul had earlier stated a similar point (1:6) and he will conclude the letter with the same point (13:9). He even had the marks of his lashes on his body (Galatians 6:17; 2 Corinthians 11:23–25). Paul writes to a group of believers who are impressed by the 'super-apostles' who seek their own comfort to the detriment of others (11:20). Instead he wants them to appreciate leaders who are giving their all for others.

Blandina, the woman from Gaul who was tortured in the second century in an attempt to encourage her to repudiate her faith, was eventually hung on a stake and offered as prey to the wild beasts that were sent into the arena. No more despairing situation could seem to occur. However, the other Christians noticed that she seemed to be 'hanging in the shape of a cross, and by her continuous prayer gave great zeal to the combatants'. 'Their outward eyes saw in the form of their sister him who was crucified for them, to persuade those who believe on him that all who suffer for the glory of Christ have for ever fellowship with the living God.' None of the beasts would touch Blandina (Eusebius, *History* v.1.41–42). Christ's life was shown in Blandina by allowing her to persist in suffering, reminding others of Christ's gift of eternal life (John 3:16).

Not all Christians will have to die for their faith in Christ, as Paul and Blandina eventually did, but all Christians are called to give their lives over to advance Jesus' name and to await in what way 'life' will come into them to work among others.

PRAYER

*Thank you, Lord, for allowing yourself to be handed over to death
for our sins and for being raised for our justification.
Empower us too to give our lives for others for your sake
so we can see your life at work.*

Paraphrase of Romans 4:25

A PSALMIST MODELS FAITH

Paul develops the idea of 'life in you' (4:12) and ties it to its Old Testament basis.

Faith results in action

Paul highlights an Old Testament writer as a kindred spirit, a model for all of them. This psalmist was close to death: 'The snares of death encompassed me; the pangs of Sheol laid hold on me.' But in the midst of this distress and anguish, this poet called on the name of the Lord: 'O Lord, I pray, save my life!' (Psalm 116:3–4). Why did this Old Testament believer receive an answer from God? Because 'I believed, and so I spoke' (v. 13; Psalm 116:10). The Hebrew preposition *ki*, which the NRSV translates 'even when', can signify 'because, that, so that, when, for'. Both Paul and the Greek translation of the Hebrew (the Septuagint) chose the rendering 'so that'. The psalmist describes going through a two-stage process. A person believes (trusts, relies) in the Lord, and therefore goes on to speak to the Lord, or, in other words, to ask for the Lord's help in very difficult circumstances: 'I trusted so that I spoke.'

God is worthy of faith

If I were near death, the main characteristic about God that I would probably stress would be God's power. However, the psalmist highlights God's loving character: 'Gracious is the Lord, and righteous; our God is merciful' (Psalm 116:5). The Lord is gracious because the Lord 'heard' the psalmist's 'voice' and 'supplications' (Psalm 116:1). Similarly, the foundation for 2 Corinthians is the principle that God is the 'Father of mercies and the God of all consolation' (1:3). The psalmist presupposes that God is all-powerful. Paul states this fact (4:7).

Paul and his team trust because of a combination of God's mercy, power and reliability. In the midst of their difficulties (4:8–9), what kept them going? On what basis did they pray? They had confidence that in the same way as God the Father raised Jesus from death, so too would Paul, his team and the Corinthian believers be raised from death (v. 14).

What does this mean? On one level, Paul can simply be referring to the last times. All people will be resurrected at some future time; those who trust in Jesus' name will be caught up in the air with Jesus for everlasting life. (See also 1 Thessalonians 4:17.) Paul describes two parallel actions—'will raise' and 'will bring' (v. 14). 'Raise' suggests the act of being given life. 'Bring' suggests the act of presentation or standing together. Paul is confident not only that he and his co-workers will be resurrected to eternal life, but also that the Corinthians will be present too. Paul had expressed a similar idea already (1:14). In other words, Paul has confidence that their ministry among this group of rebellious Christians will be effective. This does not mean he is stating that he thinks every Corinthian will be saved, but it implies that he thinks, as a whole, they will turn out on the right side. And, amazingly, Paul did turn out to be correct. For example, after receiving 2 Corinthians they did give generously (Romans 15:26).

On a second level, Paul writes of their current situation. God's power was keeping their difficulties from developing into a worse result (4:8–9), illustrating God's ongoing 'resurrection' power. For Paul, being 'raised up' was sometimes quite literal: for example, in Lystra 'they stoned Paul and dragged him out of the city, supposing that he was dead'. But Paul 'got up' (Acts 14:19–20). Being 'perplexed, but not driven to despair' (4:8) is more a figurative 'death'. God has the power to resurrect both now and later, and the compassion to respond to our human situation.

The psalmist concludes with a pledge to declare thanks to God before others so that all might be reminded of God's mercy (Psalm 116:12–19). So, too, Paul reminds the Corinthians that God's mercy to him and his team has benefits for the Corinthians, with the long-term goal that many people will thank God (v. 15).

Like a person studying the facets of a diamond's reflecting light from different angles, Paul has revisited in this passage truths introduced in chapter 1: how their sufferings are for the sake of the Corinthians (4:12, 15; 1:6), how God rescues both Paul's team and the Corinthians (4:14; 1:10, 14) and how God's rescue results in thanksgiving (4:15; 1:11).

MEDITATION

Has God rescued you from any difficulties for which you should thank God in the midst of other people?

The INVISIBLE IS MOST HEAVY

What counts today? Marketing broadcasts the importance of what can be seen—the visual. Christianity also highlights the value of the material, because the material has all been created by a good God (1 Timothy 4:4). Nevertheless, Paul reinforces his attack against those who live merely for their own comfort and only the gain they can see.

Chapter 4 is well-rounded, beginning and ending with the same verb, 'we do not lose heart' (4:1, 16), which can also be translated 'we do not behave remissly or badly'. Paul and his team do not behave badly because their competence comes from God (3:5); they are being transformed into Christ's image in the new spiritual, life-giving, glorious, permanent, liberating covenant (3:6, 11, 17–18); they have received mercy from God (4:1); God shines in their hearts (4:6); Jesus' life will be made visible (4:10–11); God will raise them and grace will increase thanksgiving (4:14–15).

Outer and inner change

Paul has used several paradoxical images to describe the value of discerning what is really valuable—a treasure stored in a clay container (4:7) and a dead body being resurrected (4:10–11). Now he adds a third image—the outer physical versus inner spiritual nature. Studies have shown that the average eighty-year-old receives, processes and stores new information more slowly than the average thirty-year-old. Nevertheless, an older person has more experience, wisdom and ability to recall, recognize and perform things previously seen, heard and learned. The 'outer' physical nature (v. 16), that after the late twenties in most people begins to deteriorate in muscular tone, responses, memory and all-round health, is a symbol for the difficulties from opposition to genuine Christian ministry that Paul has cited in 4:8–9. Even as the body begins to deteriorate so that a person may look less 'glorious', in the same way Christians who have to undergo difficult circumstances may also look very unimpressive. Some people become so discouraged by their physical changes that they end up behaving badly, in ways not pleasing to God. However, even as age brings its competencies, so too does persistence. Genuine Christians need not be discouraged because their 'inner' nature, their truthful nature that reflects Christ's life and glory, is being renewed day by day (4:2, 10; 3:18).

'Renew' literally means to 'make new again'. In Colossians, Paul uses this rare word to describe how believers are becoming more and more like their creator, becoming impartial as God is impartial (Colossians 3:10). Therefore, the afflictions of 2 Corinthians 4:8–9 become 'momentary, insignificant' troubles in light of the inward change that looks forward to 'an extraordinary degree—to excess—fullness of glory' (v. 17). Paul writes here of a great deal of glory! He and his associates look forward to an unseen but eternal reward—to be in the likeness of Jesus—which keeps in perspective the outward glory of this age.

A spiritual pillar keeps us on track

To be in Jesus' likeness is an awe-inspiring process, but it is not visible to the literal-minded. When Jesus told his parable of the sower sowing seeds, one possible soil for the seeds was 'rocky ground'. 'This is the one who hears the word and immediately receives it with joy; yet such a person has no root, but endures only for a while, and when trouble or persecution arises on account of the word, that person immediately falls away' (Matthew 13:20–21). Paul, following Jesus, has noticed that troubles and persecutions can cause some people's desire to value the Christ-pleasing life to dry up.

So Paul warns his readers that they build their faith on rocky ground if they forget the 'eternal weight of glory beyond all measure' (v. 17) that awaits them in the future and the daily growth of their spiritual lives (v. 16). Instead, they should 'look' at 'what cannot be seen', which is eternal (v. 18), and build their faith on the Rock. Paul's paradox is that fixing our eye on a spiritual, not a stone pillar, of glorious weight, will help us complete our race straight into God's all-embracing arms.

PRAYER

You, O Lord, are a shield around me, my glory,
and the one who lifts up my head.

Psalm 3:3

LIFE WILL CONSUME MORTALITY

Paul's contrast between the outward and the inward person, what is seen and what is not seen, continues in a discussion of the earthly versus the heavenly tent. As Paul had been discussing the nature of his ministry in chapter 4 and will clearly return to the topic in 5:11, this paragraph also refers to the same topic.

Troubles are not glorious

Being 'naked' (v. 3) describes Paul's present mortal state—literally, being susceptible to cold and illnesses, and metaphorically, being susceptible to unfair accusations. If Paul had the glory of eternal life or a resurrected body, he would not have to endure what he now endures. He is indeed burdened by anxiety for the preservation of his work.

'Earthly tent', literally, is 'our earthly house of tent' that Paul contrasts to 'the building from God' (v. 1). 'Tent' or 'hut' occurs only here in the New Testament. It can also refer to the body as the tabernacle of the soul or to a dead body. Many ancient Greeks believed that the soul was good whereas the body or matter was evil. For example, in Poseidonian Stoicism, an ancient philosophy, when people were ruled by passions their souls would become encrusted with a mudlike substance. Therefore, at death, their souls would rise up only as far as the heavy air surrounding the earth. If people controlled their passions, their souls would rise up to the moon. Great moral philosophers such as Plato or Socrates would have their souls rise up as high as the fixed stars where they would hear the music of the spheres, the sound of everything working beautifully 'in its order'.

Matter is good

Even today, many people believe in a soul as a separate substance within the body. Therefore, some commentators have suggested that 'being naked' (vv. 2–4) refers to an interim state between death and the resurrection. Paul, then, would be fearing to be a spirit apart from the body. However, the 'soul' is used in the Bible not as a substance within the body but referring to a total living person. A soul is 'you'. For example, Paul says that Epaphroditus 'came close to death for the work of Christ, risking his life [not his soul] to make up for those services that [the Philippians] could not give [Paul]' (Philippians 2:30). Does Paul in 2 Corinthians 5 show that he has accepted or adopted the Greek idea that the body is evil, when he writes, 'While we are still in this tent, we groan under our burden' (v. 4)? He cannot have fully accepted the idea that the body is evil because, he says, we will be 'clothed' with a 'building from God' whereas, if matter is evil, no dwelling would be necessary at all. What Paul says in verse 2 agrees with his words in 1 Corinthians 15:44: a 'physical body' will be sown; a 'spiritual body' will be reaped.

Paul is using the idea of an 'earthly tent' to refer to a physical, mortal body in contrast to a spiritual body, the one received at the resurrection. Or, he could be using 'earthly tent' to refer more generally to temporal life, in contrast to eternal life in heaven or on the new earth.

'Pitching a tent' (v. 4) is used metaphorically by John to describe the incarnation of Jesus. The 'Word became flesh' is, literally, the 'Word pitched its tent' (John 1:14). 'Eternal tents' can refer to heaven (Luke 16:9), as does the 'true tent' or 'tabernacle', God's dwelling place (Hebrews 8:2; Revelation 21:3).

Considering that Paul, as a tentmaker, may very well have lived sometimes in his own tent as opposed to a permanent building, the contrast between 'earthly tent' and 'building' is quite striking. The tent is made by human hands and it is slowly falling apart. God's dwelling is not made by humans, and therefore it is eternal.

Paul says that we desire 'to put on over' ourselves our heavenly dwelling (vv. 2, 4). It is as if the heavenly dwelling were a permanent tent made of indestructible material. Paul here speaks either of a resurrected body or of eternal life that would remove him and his associates from all the great difficulties they experience in their ministry.

MEDITATION

Do you long not to have any difficulties or resistance to advancing God's kingdom? What hope does Paul give you?

At HOME *with* GOD

Verse 5 is phrased similarly to 1:21–22. Paul states a principle and then tells us who does it—God. Paul and his co-workers can always be affirmative (1:20) because God establishes and anoints and seals and guarantees (1:21–22). Believers can expect to be further clothed with life which devours mortality, because God prepares and guarantees (5:4–5).

God prepares and guarantees

God is described in two phrases in Greek: 'the one having prepared us for this very thing' and 'the one having given us the guarantee of the Spirit' (v. 5). 'Prepare' has the basic idea 'effect or gain by labour'. Thus, it can refer to the process by which something over time causes an effect, as in cultivating land. For example, in those who persevere, affliction can result in an 'eternal weight of glory' (4:17), or repentance can result in salvation (7:10). God is the labourer who is cultivating people so that they can be 'further clothed': in other words, they will be able to put on over themselves as an outer garment eternal life, an 'eternal weight of glory beyond all measure' (4:17; 5:4).

This glorious future is not a distant future which cannot be seen in any way. God not only cultivates the 'land', but also waters it. The 'guarantee' or down-payment, the pledge for a later full payment, is the presence of the Spirit, who can even now give the faces of believers a shining glow of God's presence.

Courage persists abroad

Therefore, believers are aware that they 'are away from the Lord' (v. 6). They have not yet received the full payment of the Spirit, nor yet has mortality ended (5:4–5). Nevertheless, 'we are always confident' (v. 6). To be 'confident' is to have 'courage'. When people are afraid, they need courage. Courage is not the same as being fearless. Fearlessness may simply be foolhardiness. Courage is doing something worthwhile even though that act may entail danger or disappointment. For instance, Jesus exhorted the paralyzed child, the haemorrhaging, ritually unclean woman and the terrified disciples to have 'courage' (Matthew 9:2, 22; 14:26–27). Jesus also exhorted perse-cuted disciples and even Paul himself, when death looked near, to have courage and hope (John 16:33; Acts 23:11). In the midst of afflictions received because Jesus' name is advanced (4:8–9), Paul and his co-workers are full of courage because God is the one who is at work preparing them for the future, already equipping them by the Spirit (v. 5).

The desire for eternal life that Paul and we have is a good one because God has made us for this purpose and has given the presence of the Holy Spirit as a deposit, guaranteeing (v. 5) that indeed our mortal state is temporary. Yet that desire cannot be fulfilled until we are in Christ's presence.

'While we are at home in the body we are away from the Lord' (v. 6) does not, then, refer to having or not having a body. We will always have a body. Rather, to be 'at home in the body' means to feel com-plete satisfaction and comfort in this life. To be 'at home' can refer not only to dwelling in a place, but also to living in a land, our own native land. To be 'away' means to leave on a journey, as well as to change our residence or move. If we feel completely content in this 'land' or life, then we are not looking forward to being in Christ's 'land' or presence, where we would have no difficulties (v. 8).

So what does it mean for us to walk by faith and not by sight (v. 7)? We must remember God's promises and down-payments and not begin (or continue) to serve merely this fleeting present world.

PRAYER

May I be filled with the knowledge of your will in all spiritual wisdom and understanding so that I may lead a life worthy of you, Lord, fully pleasing to you, bearing fruit in every good work, growing in your knowledge, being made strong with all the strength that comes from your glorious power.

Paraphrase of Paul's prayer in Colossians 1:9–10

JESUS IS OUR JUDGE

Paul now concludes and summarizes his paragraph. Whether we are in a mortal state or an eternal one, we can always aspire to be pleasing in the Lord's sight. To please God is Paul's ultimate goal and it should be the goal for every genuine Christian. No matter what our present situation, we can always aim to please God. If we are becoming more and more like Jesus (3:18), we will want to please Jesus.

Ambition is for pleasing

Ambition in itself is not wrong. 'Make it our aim' (v. 9) literally means to 'love honour'. The ethical question is who or what is the object of our ambition. In Romans, Paul says that his 'ambition' is to proclaim the good news where it has not yet been heard (Romans 15:20–21). Paul also exhorts the able Thessalonians to 'aspire' to work (1 Thessalonians 4:11). Ambition is wrong when the object is not worthy or when the means of reaching the goal is not God-pleasing. Here, the goal to which we should strive eagerly is to 'please' the Lord (v. 9).

What pleases God? God is pleased when we live in obedience by bearing fruit and growing in knowledge (1 Thessalonians 4:1–3; Colossians 1:10).

Judgment is inevitable

Why is it important to please God? Even though salvation or perishing are both processes (2:15), at some point each process will come to a sudden end. 'All of us must appear before the judgment seat of Christ' (v. 10). No one can avoid this judgment. Judgment will come either at our personal death or at Jesus' return: 'It is appointed for mortals to die once, and after that the judgment' (Hebrews 9:27). Paul preached to the Athenian philosophers that God 'has fixed a day on which he will have the world judged in righteousness' by Jesus, whom he has appointed (Acts 17:31). Jesus himself taught that God the Father had given all judgment to the Son and that eternal life in a qualitative sense would begin at the point a person believed Jesus' message (John 5:22–24). Jesus' return cannot be predicted because it will come at an unexpected hour (Matthew 24:44; 2 Peter 3:10).

Every day needs to be lived as if it were the last (Matthew 24:45—25:13).

The 'judgment seat' was a raised platform in the *agora* or market-place of many cities. Pilate sat on a judgment seat to judge Jesus (Matthew 27:19; John 19:13), and Festus sat on a judgment seat in Caesarea to judge Paul (Acts 25:6, 17). The judgment seat still stands at Corinth. A large, square platform, it stands about eight feet high with a stone staircase on the side. The proconsul Lucius Julius Gallio sat on this platform when he heard the complaints about Paul (Acts 18:12, 16–17). Paul pictures Jesus as sitting on such a platform, God's 'judgment seat' (Romans 14:10). The idea of judgment can be quite an intimidating thought, possibly because judges are sometimes pictured as adversaries. However, Jesus is the good judge who wants to advocate for each of us. The Lord does not want anyone 'to perish, but all to come to repentance' (2 Peter 3:9). God is impartial and just (Deuteronomy 10:17–18). Paul will later explain the lengths to which God will go to be reconciled with humans (5:18–21). But here Paul simply states the importance of living a God-pleasing life.

People will not be judged in a group. 'Each' will be judged for what each did during his or her limited mortal life (v. 10). Judgment will vary. To 'receive recompense' is basically a positive or neutral image. It can refer to receiving the money we have invested plus interest (Matthew 25:27). In this latter sense, life, land, time and possessions are all savings we receive at birth from God, entrusted to us to invest well. What did we do with God's savings? Will God think we deserve a reward?

MEDITATION

What have you done with your life to please God?
Do you expect a positive recompense from God? Why?

The FUTURE AFFECTS the PRESENT

Paul returns again to mention directly his main goal in this letter—to defend his and his team's leadership. Paul and his associates do fear the Lord. Therefore, they want to persuade people, but again, always in God's sight, or with a desire to please God ultimately.

Persuasion is needed

How many of us take seriously 2 Corinthians 5:10? 'All of us must appear before the judgment seat of Christ.' Paul and his associates took this future event very seriously. Persuasion or entreaty, in itself, is a neutral activity. What makes persuasion positive is the goal. For example, the chief priests and elders persuaded the crowds to ask for the release of Barabbas but the killing of Jesus (Matthew 27:20). Their goal was unjust. The same religious leaders also made up the lie that Jesus' body was stolen by the disciples and persuaded the governor that it was the truth (Matthew 28:13–14). Their persuasion was used to support a self-serving falsehood. In contrast, the goal of Paul's persuasion was to help others to be ready for future judgment.

Often Luke described Paul's speaking as a type of persuasion. Paul and Barnabas 'urged' the residents of Antioch of Pisidia to continue in God's grace (Acts 13:43). Weekly, when at Corinth, Paul would strive to 'convince' Jews and Greeks that Jesus was the Messiah (Acts 18:4–5). At Ephesus Paul 'argued persuasively' about God's kingdom, convincing many people that God was not made by human hands (Acts 19:8, 26). Even under house arrest in Rome, daily Paul urged his visitors to believe that the Old Testament prophesied Jesus' advent. Not all were persuaded (Acts 28:23–24). But negative response did not keep Paul from speaking.

Mutual pride is goal

Paul's main goal in 2 Corinthians might be picked up from verse 11: 'I hope that we are also well known to your consciences.' Paul hopes that the Corinthians might understand what he and his associates are all about, but from what he has heard from the associates who have given him news about the Corinthians, he does not think that they do understand his team's ministry goals and ways at all. Now that

Paul has explained how their motives are pure and their competence comes from God to be ministers of a living covenant in the midst of difficult circumstances, the Corinthians should be proud of Paul and his co-workers (5:11–21).

Boasting is not inherently wrong (v. 12). To boast or be proud of other Christians is a positive trait. Even as Jesus said that whoever confesses him before others, he will confess before his Father (Matthew 10:32), so too, when the Corinthians professed publicly their pride in Paul and his associates, they were confessing publicly their belief in all for which Paul stood.

The Corinthians should take pride in what is 'in the heart', not 'outward appearance' (literally 'the face', v. 12). 'The heart' is another word for the 'inner nature' (4:16), 'what cannot be seen' and the 'eternal' (4:18). Paul and his associates do not need an inanimate 'temporary' letter of recommendation because their letters are the Corinthians' faces engraved on their hearts (3:2–3). They do not preach the covenant that is fading away but rather the one that will be ever increasing in glory. This spiritual covenant changes the heart or essence of each person. Paul and his associates may not appear very impressive as they are 'afflicted', 'perplexed', 'persecuted' and 'struck down' (4:8–9), but the Corinthians need to appreciate that greater love had made them endure such discomfort.

Like the Corinthians, we need to ask ourselves, how often have we spoken up on behalf of someone who was not impressive but who did humbly serve God? Or, if we did speak up, did we resent the cost to our own public esteem because we spoke up for an unpopular person or cause?

PRAYER

Father, grant that I may be strengthened in my inner being with power through your Spirit, and that Christ may dwell in my heart through faith, as I am being rooted and grounded in love, with the power to comprehend the love of Christ that surpasses knowledge.

Paraphrase of Paul's prayer in Ephesians 3:16–19

LIVING *for* OTHERS

Paul, Timothy and others are not out simply to commend themselves. Instead they are completely driven by Christ's love.

God amazes and gives self-control

'Beside ourselves' (v. 13) literally means 'to stand out'. For example, if the Queen were to be walking by the Thames, police officers might instruct the crowd to 'stand out of' the way 'for' her. In the New Testament this verb refers to emotions, usually with positive, sometimes negative, connotations. When so many people came to see Jesus that he and his disciples could not even eat, his family thought Jesus had 'departed from' his own nature and tried to seize him (Mark 3:21–22).

The verb also refers to a type of amazement when seemingly impossible actions occur. For instance, people respond in amazement when Jesus heals the blind and mute demoniac (Matthew 12:22–23), resurrects a dead girl, and stops strong winds (Mark 5:42; 6:51). In the New Testament, this amazement usually comes from God's work in the world. Therefore, Paul and Timothy's amazement is not so much 'for' God (God as indirect object) but 'because of' God (God as cause or reason). God has been doing marvellous things in their lives—transforming them into Christ's glory (3:18), shining the glorious knowledge of Jesus in their hearts (4:6), raising them from near-death situations (4:14; 1:10), preparing for them an eternal weight of glory (4:17; 5:1).

In contrast, a 'right mind' is a 'sound mind'. The result of a 'sound' mind is self-control and moderation. For example, the demoniac 'Legion' used to be unrestrained and wild, but when the unclean spirit was removed, he was able to sit, clothed, in self-control (Mark 5:3, 15). To understand that our spiritual gift is worthwhile but that it does not make us superior over other Christians is to have a 'sound' or accurate perspective (Romans 12:3). When it comes to the Corinthians, Paul and Timothy are in full control of their emotions and actions (compare 2 Corinthians 1:17).

Love motivates

Verse 14 beautifully summarizes that love is the motivating force behind the action of Paul and his co-workers. Love is an action noun. Paul can either mean that their own love for Christ 'urges' their behaviour or that the love produced by Christ 'urges' them. 'Urge' literally means 'encircle', 'embrace', 'to hold or keep together, confine, secure'. 'Their own love for Christ' probably is what Paul intends, because he adds 'because we are convinced'. But their love is a result of Christ's loving action—one dying for all. Paul's and his co-workers' love for Christ or the love produced by Christ in them constrains or confines them so greatly that they are forced to act as they do. It encircles and embraces them, keeping them secure. Because Paul and the others had come to the conclusion that 'one has died for all; therefore all have died', they are filled with a great love for Christ that motivates all their actions.

Paul writes that 'one' (Christ) on behalf of 'all' died, not that one on behalf of 'some' died. Christ's magnanimous love expressed in his death is all the more generous because it is offered to all, both to those 'who boast in outward appearance' and also to those who boast in what is 'in the heart' (5:12). When Christ died, every human being died. No humans need to die to cleanse themselves from the evil they have done. They have died already, represented in Christ's death.

Why did Christ die on behalf of all? Christ died in order that 'the living no longer to themselves may live but' they may live 'to the one having died and having risen in behalf of them' (v. 15). The one died for all so that all may live for one. Paul has already explained that he and his associates do not abandon their faith in Jesus when they have difficult circumstances, because they then learn to rely on the life-giving power of Jesus (1:9; 4:11). Here he adds that they devote their life to pleasing God out of love. Since they have, in effect, 'died', they cannot live to please themselves, because then they would be striving to please a dead person. Some of the Corinthians may indeed have been living 'to themselves'. Paul will directly confront them in 6:1: 'We urge you also not to accept the grace of God in vain.'

MEDITATION

Paul describes three steps: (a) accepting Christ's death;
(b) dying or repenting of sin; and (c) 'living' for Christ.
Have you done all three stages?

A NEW PERSPECTIVE *in* CHRIST

Christ 'died for all' (5:15), therefore causing Christians to treat no one 'from a human point of view' or, literally, 'according to [the] flesh' (v. 16). To know Christ 'according to the flesh' might include seeing Christ 'through a veil', missing the glory that is captured in his humble life (chs. 3 and 4). Possibly, then, knowing anyone 'according to the flesh' in this context means to miss the reflecting glory that is hidden behind a life of difficulties. People in Christ might be 'a new creation', but they still may not look impressive.

God's knowledge

To know people in their inner self (5:12; 4:18) is a core characteristic of God. When Moses summarized God's essential nature, he described him as 'mighty and awesome', 'not partial', taking 'no bribe', executing 'justice for the orphan and the widow' and loving 'the strangers, providing them food and clothing' (Deuteronomy 10:17–18). To be impartial, literally, is to 'receive no face'. God does not evaluate people from their 'face' or outward appearance, which Paul will tell his readers is the problem with the super-apostles, who boast in their Jewish heritage (11:22). No wonder that, when God became incarnate in Jesus, Jesus too was not partial toward the rich or powerful. Even his enemies knew that Jesus showed 'deference to no one' for he did 'not regard people with partiality' (Matthew 22:16). Peter learned through a vision that Gentile believers were fully acceptable to God (Acts 10:11–16, 34), yet had difficulty under pressure in consistently acting on this truth (Galatians 2:6, 11–14). God's not favouring Jew over Gentile became one of Paul's major themes in his letters (Romans 2:11).

Christ died for all and all died in Christ (5:14–15): therefore we are all equal. We are all equally reborn babes with no economic, political, cultural, height or gender advantages (Galatians 3:27–28). Our attitude toward one another and toward Christ has changed (v. 16).

See the new country!

Paul is placing a wedge between a person's previous life outside of Christ and current life 'in Christ'. The difference between the two is as great as the difference between an old and a new creation (v. 17). Outside of Christ, humans persist in having a limited knowledge of each other and of Christ (v. 16). When humans are in Christ, their new creation is a state or condition, not a fleeting emotion ('has become', v. 17). The transition between the two creations is not a process but a one-time act ('the old has passed away', v. 17).

How can we reconcile this sudden passing away of the old with the slow process of becoming holy (2:15)? When 'anyone is in Christ', from God's perspective, that person's 'old' nature has immediately disappeared. The mind no longer is 'blinded' (4:4). Such people, as it were, have travelled from one country, the country of veiled minds, to another country, the country of unveiled faces (3:16, 18). They are a new creation, living in a new country, a new state which cannot be easily lost. But they still need to walk in this new country, becoming stronger, breathing better, seeing more clearly. That is the process of 'sanctification' or 'being saved' (2:15).

One example from the third century of someone whose perspective to Christ changed is Basilides, a soldier under Emperor Septimus Severus. Basilides led Potamiaena to be executed for her faith in Christ. Basilides treated her with compassion, keeping the insulting crowd away from her. After her death, Basilides was asked to take an oath as part of his official duties, but refused because he said he was now a Christian (Eusebius, *History* vi.5). Despite the fact that Potamiaena looked, from a human point of view, as worthy of all rejection, Basilides saw in her Christ's courageous, victorious and glorious self, worthy of emulation.

PRAYER

Thanks to you, God, who in Christ always leads us in triumphal procession, and through us spreads in every place the fragrance that comes from knowing you.

Paraphrase of Paul's benediction in 2 Corinthians 2:14

GOD *the* RECONCILER

All of this new creating comes from God (v. 18). 'Reconcile' literally referred to changing money and to exchanging one thing for another. In ancient Greece, 'to reconcile' could refer to exchanging prisoners and, metaphorically, to changing people from enmity to friendship, as when husbands and wives strive for reconciliation as opposed to separation and divorce (1 Corinthians 7:11). Humans are enemies of God because they continue to violate God's commands (v. 19). However, God has taken the initiative to change the nature of our relationship, changing it from one of enmity to one of friendship 'through Christ', who took the place of all humans, receiving their intended death (Romans 5:10).

Unreconciled we die

The Hebrews knew that the result of disobeying God's laws is death. Paul described this as payment: as 'the wages of sin is death' (Romans 6:23). For instance, when some of the Levites became envious of the Lord's appointment of Moses, Aaron and Aaron's descendants, God created an earthquake to swallow them up (Numbers 16:11, 31, 40). Or, when some of the more wealthy Corinthians began using the Lord's Supper to exclude the poorer Christians, the wealthy began to become ill and some even died (1 Corinthians 11:20–30).

The reconciled become reconcilers

God's action affects God's people, the new creation—Paul connects God's work with humans' work. In other words, God 'reconciled'; God 'has given' (v. 18). God 'was reconciling'; 'not counting'; 'entrusting' (v. 19). Each verse concludes with human action. In other words, what God did becomes the model for the new creation. After reconciling, God commissioned 'the ministry of reconciliation' (v. 18).

If 'reconciliation' referred to exchanging money, then God did not 'count' all our trespasses or sins (v. 19). If God had charged us for all our action that is displeasing to his perfect goodness, love and truth, then we would owe God so much that we would no longer own anything, even our own lives. Instead, God, as it were, paid all our debts, leaving us free from bankruptcy. We have a new start. And now, we are given the task to do the same for other people—to bring them from enmity with God and with one another to friendship with God and with one another. Paul's words echo Jesus' parable of the unmerciful servant: 'I forgave you all that debt because you pleaded with me. Should you not have had mercy on your fellow slave, as I had mercy on you?' (Matthew 18:32–33).

Reconciliation and giving are a process (v. 18). Reconciling, counting and entrusting are actions that began in the past but continue in the present (v. 19). Christ's sacrifice of atonement on the cross occurred only once and will not be repeated (Romans 3:25; Hebrews 9:28). God paid for our release. But this contract is made 'effective through faith' (Romans 3:25). It demands a response from the released prisoner (5:20).

One of the most poignant acts in life is the act of vicarious suffering. Even though his point of death was the climax of reconciliation, Jesus' whole life was a process of 'exchange' or reconciliation. Jesus, God of the universe, wealthy beyond measure, was born a human, in a poor transient household, laid in an animal's manger, because there was no place in the inn (Luke 2:7). His family could offer only two young pigeons for his purification, a sign of poverty (Luke 2:24). He who was Lord of all chose to be obedient to parents and submit to baptism (Luke 2:51; 3:21). Undergoing human temptations, Jesus fought the devil and the devil's spirits (Luke 4:2, 35). Instead of receiving adulation, he was persecuted (Luke 4:24, 29). Instead of living in comfort, Jesus, dedicated to others, lived a life of difficulties (Luke 9:58).

God in Christ came to offer eternal life and, instead of being welcomed, was reviled and killed (Luke 14:18–21; 20:14; 23:35). Rejected by his closest disciples, Jesus, who had harmed no one and instead healed thousands, was killed in place of a murderer and insurrectionist, Barabbas, who was released (Luke 23:19, 22). From the moment that the Messiah became human, the final process of reconciliation began.

MEDITATION

What form might the ministry of reconciliation take in your life?

AMBASSADORS

Because God reconciles, Paul and his associates summarize who they are and what they do: 'We are ambassadors for Christ, since God is making his appeal through us' (v. 20). In Greek the sentence begins 'for Christ', Paul emphasizing who sends them out as ambassadors and whom they must ultimately please—Christ. They are ambassadors for someone for whom they are full of love because that person freed them from death.

Maturity is appealing

'We are ambassadors' properly refers in Greek to age—'to be the elder or eldest'. In Israel, elders were treated with respect. Philo, the Alexandrian philosopher who lived during Jesus' lifetime, could assume, 'The sight of seniors or instructors or rulers or parents stirs the beholders to respect for them and decent behaviour and the desire to live a life of self-control' (*Embassy to Gaius* 1:5). When Philo and other elders were asked to entreat Emperor Gaius Caligula to stop the imperial command to place Gaius' statues in Jewish synagogues, they were acting as 'ambassadors'.

Paul and his co-workers represent God 'making his appeal' (v. 20). *Parakaleo* means 'to call to one's side', 'to summon one's friends to act as witnesses in a trial'. A defence lawyer, someone who pleads another's cause before a judge, was called a *parakletos*. Paul and his associates, speaking on God's behalf, were summoning the Corinthians to become loyal witnesses. God would be as the judge or the plaintiff who is summoning to court the defendant or the friends who should be loyal witnesses. Paul and his associates advocate on God's behalf. Their goal is friendship between judge and accused. The basis for this ministry of reconciliation is always love (5:14).

Paul then proceeds to make his appeal directly: 'We entreat you on behalf of Christ, be reconciled to God' (v. 20). 'Become friends instead of enemies with God.' This command is the second direct command to the Corinthians in this letter. Paul's first command was in 2:8: 'I urge you to reaffirm your love for [the person punished]'. Paul sees the Corinthians' behaviour as enmity with God because they have not welcomed God's messengers, whose lives reflect their message. 'Be reconciled to God' by listening to God's ambassadors. The Corinthians should take pride in Paul and his associates because they speak for what is 'in the heart' (5:12), out of love on behalf of Christ's love.

Atonement results in righteousness

'The one not having known sin—on behalf of us—sin became' (literally, v. 21). Paul repeats his earlier message (5:14–15, 19), but here he accentuates what we can never understand fully—the ramifications of the fact that the sinless God in the incarnate Jesus took upon himself the sins of all people past and future.

Paul alludes to the many sin offerings for atonement practised in his own time in the temple at Jerusalem and rehearsed for hundreds of years after God's instructions to Moses. The priests would lay their hands on the head of the animal, the animal would be killed 'in front of the tent of meeting' and the blood sprinkled as a sign of protection, but the flesh would be burned outside the camp (Exodus 29:10–14). The Day of Atonement included the additional practice of the high priest's confessing all the wrongdoing of the people while he laid both his hands on a live goat. Then the goat would carry upon itself 'all their sins' away into the wilderness (Leviticus 16:20–22).

In this section of his letter Paul draws at least two ramifications of Christ's death. People should live no longer for themselves, but for Christ 'who died and was raised for them' (5:15). People should 'become the righteousness of God' (v. 21).

Both clauses begin with the same Greek preposition, 'so that'. If Christ's death results paradoxically in a new way of living (5:15), now Christ's becoming 'sin' results in 'righteousness'. Christ's death affects the way people treat one another and also what people themselves become. 'Righteousness' is the characteristic of a judge. It includes both holiness and justice.

PRAYER

God, may my love overflow more and more with knowledge
and full insight to help me to determine what is best, so that in the
day of Christ I may be pure and blameless, having produced
the harvest of righteousness that comes through Jesus Christ
for your glory and praise.

Paraphrase of Paul's prayer in Philippians 1:9–11

WORKING TOGETHER *with* GRACE

Paul begins his charges to the Corinthians in chapter 6 with a call to action. Over and over again, he has set out the proofs for his claim that his ministry is a pure one and therefore worthy of the Corinthians' loyalty. He opened the letter with the claim that Christ's sufferings flowed over into his own and his co-workers' lives (1:5), then followed by detailing that these sufferings occurred in Asia and took him to the verge of death (1:8). His team's conduct, he declares, was exemplary and was clearly explained to the Corinthians in his previous writings (1:12–14). He and his colleagues were not like 'so many' trying to make a financial profit out of their ministry (2:17), and they did not come around with references and a CV like prospective employees (3:1). They did not use deception or distort God's word but were open both in people's and in God's sight (4:2). Hard-pressed as they suffer for Jesus, but not letting the persecution destroy their ministry because they know it is benefiting the Corinthians, they remain steady beneath the blows (4:7–12).

Grace must be welcomed

While Paul is constructing this argument, hoping to establish beyond a doubt the validity of his claim that their ministry is pure of profit motive and authentically under the calling of Christ, he is running another contrasting thread through these pages, challenging the impure motives of his competitors and calling for repentance. Paul, like a skilful verbal tentmaker, weaves together the two threads of thought (defensive and offensive) with which he has been working; and he has brought the Corinthians to a choice, providing an image of the selection Christ will make at the judgment seat (5:10).

Reconciliation of the Corinthians with Paul is in actuality reconciliation with Christ, for Paul and his team are Christ's ambassadors (5:20). The running argument concludes with Paul urging the Corinthians to be reconciled with God through the action of Christ. And now in 6:1 he implores the Corinthians not to let that gracious act of Christ's be offered to them in vain. Paul, we have heard over and over again, availed himself of Christ's gracious action on his own behalf (for example, 1:11; 3:6; 5:17), and he implores the Corinthians to do the same. God is generous and gives joy, pleasure and delight without any merit on the part of the receiver. But God's grace can be received 'in vain' or with no worthwhile goal if people do not 'work together' with other Christians and with God. Team ministry is a sub-theme of this letter, in contrast to a self-serving, hierarchical model of ministry (11:20).

As proof, Paul quotes word-for-word from Isaiah 49:8. The context in Isaiah 49 is not one of condemnation, but of hope and mercy. The Lord promises that the exiled Israelites will be brought back to Israel. Thus, too, Paul offers hope and mercy to the Corinthians. Isaiah describes God's decision. Paul now makes an application to the Corinthians, accentuating 'now'. A time for making a decision that affects salvation has arisen again, and that time is now.

Grace has no obstacles

Paul will ask the Corinthians to 'open wide' their hearts (6:13) to him and his co-workers—literally, 'enlarge' their hearts, to make room for Paul and his team and envelop them in the Corinthians' love and tangible, practical, affectionate actions. But Paul does not immediately voice his request, despite the fact that he has alerted them that a plea will be forthcoming. Instead, he provides reasons for the Corinthians seriously to consider granting the request he is about to make. Paul and his associates have wronged no one among them and therefore have not discredited the validity of their ministry. As proof, Paul will follow with a list, a catalogue of suffering (6:4–10).

Paul knows that the Corinthians feel ambiguously toward him. They want to be visited by Paul but are not fully affirmative of him, because enemies of Paul and Paul's gospel are among them, poisoning their minds against Paul. Yet, in the quiet moments of their hearts they remember Paul's loving, self-sacrificing acts among them. So he begins with a denial, that they put 'no obstacle in anyone's way', assuming his adversaries' challenge and beginning with its refutation (v. 3).

MEDITATION

*In what way(s) do you 'work together' for your own
and for others' salvation?*

GODLY SERVANTS ARE COMMENDED

What would we do if we had to defend ourselves before misguided people who were demanding that we had to do what their leaders had done, that is, to bring impressive recommendation letters? We cannot use the same misleading tactics but we must subtly do all we can to keep the people from abandoning the right road to salvation.

Held together by God

'Commend', literally, is 'set together, combine'. When we 'commend', we set or bring together people as friends, introducing someone to someone else. Paul uses this verb more than any other New Testament writer does, and more than half its uses are in 2 Corinthians (nine out of 16). The whole world is 'set' or 'held together' in Christ (Colossians 1:17) and by God's word (2 Peter 3:5). Paul is not against the concept of recommendations *per se* because he felt free to recommend Phoebe to the Romans (Romans 16:1–2). However, why would Paul and his team need letters of recommendation to people they had brought to the Lord and in whom they were investing their lives (3:1–2)? The Corinthians themselves should have commended them (5:12; 12:11)! Paul has already told them that they commended themselves by speaking and revealing the truth (4:2). Now he adds that they commend themselves by actions, too, as godly servants (v. 4) who obey God no matter the cost.

Held together for God

In verses 4–10 Paul compiles a lengthy list of his team's commendable godly actions. Later in the letter, Paul will more directly attack the self-commendation on ungodly bases of the super-apostles (10:12, 18; 12:11). Here Paul lists 18 attributes (vv. 4–7a). In Greek the preposition 'in' introduces every attribute, being repeated 18 times. This technique is called 'anaphora'. By the repetition of a word, a rhythm is established. It sets up an expectancy of each next addition to the pattern. Then each group of phrases becomes increasingly stressed. The first term, 'endurance', provides a broad overview of all that happened. Paul and his co-workers had been practising a 'great' amount of 'endurance' or 'perseverance' (v. 4). They were 'standing firm, holding out, bearing, remaining', just as Job kept persistently addressing God (James 5:11). Every entry that follows explains why perseverance was needed and how perseverance was enabled. The first group ('afflictions, hardships, calamities', v. 4) is more general, while the second group ('beatings, imprisonments, riots, labours, sleepless nights, hunger', v. 5) is more specific. 'Afflictions' is literally 'pressure', 'hardships' is 'force' and 'calamities' is 'narrowness of space'. Godly servants must persevere through narrow, forceful pressure.

The second group specifies the type of troubles through which they persevere. Examples of these troubles are recounted in Acts: stoned, beaten and imprisoned at Lystra, Philippi, Iconium, Corinth (Acts 14:5, 19; 16:23); buffeted by 'riots', anarchy and confusion at Antioch, Thessalonica, Beroea, Corinth and Ephesus (13:50; 14:13, 18; 17:5–6, 13; 18:17; 19:34).

The next group describes personal qualities Paul and his co-workers developed as godly servants: 'purity, knowledge, patience, kindness' (v. 6). 'Purity' describes the chastity of virgins (11:2), a trait given by God (James 3:17). The 'knowledge' to which Paul refers is personal knowledge of God (2:14; 4:6). 'Patience' is, literally, the holding of strong feelings over a long time. It can refer to 'endurance', which enables poor labourers to await patiently God's vindication (James 5:7–11), or 'compassion', a key attribute of God (Exodus 34:6). 'Kindness' is 'good for its purpose', the opposite of 'worthless' (Romans 3:12). It too is a trait of God, a synonym for compassion or mercy (Romans 11:22). Thus, as Paul and others serve God despite these difficulties, they are becoming more and more like the one they serve.

Paul concludes this first part of his list with four modified attributes (vv. 6b–7a). The Corinthians enjoyed flamboyant spiritual gifts (1 Corinthians 14:20–21); however, the Holy Spirit (REB) is manifested through difficulties, not by avoiding them. The Holy Spirit produces a 'genuine' or unhypocritical love, 'truthful' not deceptive words (compare 2:17).

PRAYER

Lord, make me increase and abound in love for other Christians and for all people, just as others abound in love for me.

Paraphrase of Paul's prayer in 1 Thessalonians 3:12

The RIGHT WEAPONS

Paul is still in the midst of describing where obedience to God takes a godly servant (6:4). But now, instead of repeating the preposition 'in' (6:4b–7a), he repeats 'with' or 'through' (*dia*, three times, vv. 7b–8a) and then 'as' (*hos*, vv. 8b–10), creating increasingly more complex and dramatic sets.

A weapon is righteous glory

Paul begins by referring to the 'weapons of righteousness' (v. 7). The right hand was traditionally the hand that grasped weapons for attack, such as the sword; and the left hand carried weapons of defence, such as the shield. Possibly, in 2 Corinthians, since Paul is fighting charges about their leadership, the weapon is their 'honour' and 'good repute' (v. 8), similar to the armour of righteousness (Ephesians 6:14).

Verse 8a is set up like the Greek letter called *chi* (a chiastic structure). Paul begins with honour, moves to dishonour, ends his first pattern, begins again with ill repute, and moves outward to end with good repute again. In effect this structure makes a listener or reader focus on the paradox of ministry. Unlike our normal mode of argumentation (parallelism), chiastic arguments carry a hearer to the extremities, the beginning and the end, and then back again to the centre.

'Honour' or 'glory' is a frequent word in this letter, even when Paul is highlighting difficulties. Christians aim to honour God (1:20; 4:6, 15). 'Glory' has been described as a shining presence on Moses' face, so great that the Israelites could not stare at him (3:7). The covenants both have this glory, but the new covenant even more of it (3:8–11). Therefore, as participants in the new covenant behold God's glory, they themselves increase in reflected glory (3:18). Since Paul has already told us that unbelievers do not see Christ's glory (4:4), we should not be surprised when Christ's followers are sometimes received in 'dishonour'. Paul contrasts 'dishonour' with 'honour', therefore setting up a contrast between the public's good and bad opinions of active Christians. What causes 'dishonour'? It is 'ill repute' or words of opposition, but 'honour' is caused by 'good repute' or words of praise. In 1 Corinthians 4:13 Paul explained that when 'slandered' or opposed, they responded in encouragement. Honour is their weapon (and their reward, 4:17), with which they must fight against the differing perceptions of those around them.

Life comes at the end of death

From verse 8b, Paul now uses the word 'as'. The first half of the pattern (8b–9a) builds up to 'see—we are alive' (v. 9); the second half ends with verse 10 and sets up verse 11, Paul's exhortation. 'As' is repeated seven times. The whole sentence in Greek begins in 6:1 and does not end until some 143 words later in verse 10. Paralleling a positive term with a negative one, Paul suddenly breaks the pattern in the phrase 'dying, and see—we are alive' (v. 9). The break in parallelism mirrors Paul's and now his readers' astonishment: 'We think we die—and—behold! We live.'

Who else was treated as an impostor? No less than Jesus was called an impostor by religious leaders of his time (Matthew 27:63). Some thought he had God's very goodness, others thought he was deceiving the crowd (John 7:12). But, like Jesus, Paul and his co-workers were in reality truthful. They were not ignorant ('unknown'), but rather thoroughly knowledgeable. 'Dishonour', 'ill repute', 'impostors', 'unknown' (or 'ignorant'), 'dying', all describe the weapons used to attack genuine Christians. But their defence in God's sight is that they possess 'honour', 'good repute', truth, thorough knowledge ('well known') and life (vv. 8–9; 2:16).

In the final grouping (vv. 9b–10), Paul continues taking successive pairs of opposite concepts that in God's servants can stand together, now intensified by a modifier ('not', 'always', 'many', 'everything'). If verses 8–9a present how they are perceived, verses 9b–10 present how they are treated by non-believers. They are 'punished' or scourged, made to be sorrowful and poor, 'having nothing'.

Paul's powerful proclamation is his own example of the living, life-giving God in action. Reflected is the preceding promise that carrying Jesus' death results in the revelation of Jesus' life (4:10–11). Jesus' life turns scourging from death, and sorrow and poverty to life, joy and generosity (v. 10).

MEDITATION

How can you have nothing but possess everything?
What do godly servants possess according to 6:4–10?

WIDE OPEN *to* TRUTH & LOVE

The rhythmic listing of how Paul and his team have commended themselves as godly servants has come to a surprising and dramatic end with an appeal. His appeal completes his earlier challenge: 'See, now is the acceptable time; see, now is the day of salvation!' (6:2). Here and now Paul indicates the action that he wants the Corinthians to perform—to welcome Paul and his team.

They are open to speak

Paul uses metaphorical language: 'our mouth is opened', 'our heart is wide open', 'you are not restricted', 'you are restricted', 'open wide' (vv. 11–13). The concept of 'frankness' occurred earlier in the letter as a description of Paul's actions and words (1:12; 4:2). The verb for 'open' is frequently used as we might use it, to describe the opening of doors (Matthew 7:7), a fish's mouth (Matthew 17:27) or treasure chests (Matthew 2:11). But when a mouth is opened, usually what follows is an extended speech, such as 'having opened his mouth...' Jesus taught (Matthew 5:2), Philip taught (Acts 8:35), Peter taught (Acts 10:34). Thus, because of its use elsewhere in the New Testament, 'our mouth is opened to you' alludes back to what Paul said earlier, that they write to the Corinthians so that they can be understood (1:13). They commend themselves by 'truthful speech' (6:7). 'We have spoken to you' at length in order that you understand the truth of the matter (v. 11).

They are open to love

And what does Paul want to communicate? He states the same thing, first positively, then negatively: 'our heart is wide open; you are not restricted among us' (vv. 11b–12a). Jesus described as 'wide open' phylacteries which were made big or broad so that all could see (Matthew 23:5). To be 'wide open' is to be spread over a wide space or 'broad'. A wide opened heart can be one which is sensitive to God's commandments (Psalm 119:32) or else to our own desires. Paul clearly uses the term in a positive sense, to express their love for the Corinthians. He will mention his love many times (for example, 7:3). In effect, Paul restates what he said earlier. Even as the Pharisees widened their phylacteries so that all could see, Paul, Timothy and others publicly express their affection for the Corinthians (3:2–3).

Now Paul challenges the Corinthians. Their own affections are what are restricted. 'Restrict' is the verb form of the noun used earlier for 'calamities' (6:4). People can be crowded together by one another, but also feelings can crowd out people. 'Affections' literally refers to the 'inward parts' of a human, especially the heart, lungs, liver and kidneys. Therefore, metaphorically, it is the seat of feelings and affections. We might call it 'gut-level feelings'. Titus has gut-level love for the Corinthians (7:15). From where do we humans receive 'gut-level love'? We receive that capacity from God ('*tender* mercy', Luke 1:78). Jesus, God incarnate, had gut-level concern for humans who needed a shepherd to protect them (Matthew 9:36), a healer to cure them (Matthew 14:14), a provider to feed them (Matthew 15:32), a parent to forgive them (Luke 15:20). The good Samaritan who responded with care to the half-dead robbed man had this gut-level love (Luke 10:30, 33), as did Jesus when he resurrected the only son of a widow (Luke 7:12–13). God's loving compassion results in loving action. This is what the Corinthians did not have. Their guts were tightened in resistance to those who cared for them.

Paul gives few commands in this letter because he did not have a good reception. But one of the few commands he does give occurs here: 'Open wide' (v. 13), literally, 'You also be widened!' To adults in a mature relationship, love is not something we can command. But the Corinthians are acting immaturely, thus Paul speaks to them as a spiritual father to children: 'Be opened to what we are saying! Welcome the truth! Welcome us!'

Love 'rejoices in the truth' (1 Corinthians 13:6). Often today people make love and truth conflict, but for Paul, because he loves he tells the truth, and the truth compels that he love. He can be subtle, but also direct.

PRAYER

God, help me to love all Christians and have faith in you, Lord, sharing my faith effectively while I perceive all the good that we can do for Christ.

Paraphrase of Paul's prayer in Philemon 5–6

The WEAPON *of* ATTACK

At this point, a passage occurs that has baffled New Testament scholars. So odd does it appear that Paul should suddenly swing into a discussion of being 'unequally yoked' (KJV) in 6:14—7:1, only to return to the identical phrasing about making 'room' in the Corinthians' 'hearts' in 7:2, that some have concluded that Paul did not intend the passage to be here at all. Some think a later unknown editor of 2 Corinthians simply rammed it in. Others conclude that the passage is indeed by Paul, but is a reworking of some other piece of tradition that Paul has had on his mind: while pausing, he remembers it and thinks, 'Why don't I put in that piece about not being unequally yoked before I forget it?'

Both weapons are needed

In fact, this passage is the second half of Paul's proof for his case for acceptance. The first reason Paul gave that the Corinthians should respond positively to his request to 'open wide' their hearts (6:2, 13) was that Paul and his associates had wronged no one among them and therefore had not discredited the validity of their ministry (6:3–13). The second reason Paul gives now is that the Corinthians need to remain pure (vv. 14–18).

Paul, having established his claims and pleaded for the Corinthians' understanding and acceptance, now addresses the rival claims to his. Paul himself is using 'weapons' of defence (6:3–13) and attack (6:14—7:1). The argument could be displayed in the following way:

6:1–2	Now is the day to act on God's grace
6:3–10	Paul's claims are proved by his suffering
6:11–13	Paul exhorts
6:14—7:1	Paul warns not to accept rival partnerships
7:2–4	Paul exhorts
7:5	Paul's claims are re-echoed
7:6–13	Titus confirms that the Corinthians' response to Paul's letter means they intend to obey Paul's requests.

Paul focuses the argument of the entire book on this central contrast between his and his rivals' claims. He attacks the bond between the Corinthians and his own accusers before he returns to restate his plea, reason number two having been now delivered. Verses 6:14—7:1 are not merely an aside by Paul or an insertion by an editor. They are a necessary part of Paul's argument. Paul is attacking all his rivals in one mighty slash: do not be aligned with pagans, non-Christian Jews, or 'super-apostle' apostates (and, of course, an application can be made to marriage).

Purity is relational

Paul has used a verb (to 'be mismatched') which occurs also in Leviticus. In the midst of other commands, God commands the Hebrews not to breed together different kinds of livestock, such as bull and donkey (Leviticus 19:19). This principle was also applied to believers. The Hebrews were not to intermarry with people who did not believe in the one living God (Deuteronomy 7:3–4).

What is true of sexual intimacy is also true of ecclesial intimacy. We have to beware lest we enter a liaison which might lead to diminishing our fellowship with God. However, Paul does not intend to require us not to associate with non-believers in the world (1 Corinthians 5:9–10). 'Mismatch' signifies sexual intimacy and 'fellowship' is economic intimacy (v. 14). The Corinthians had problems both with sexual immorality (12:21) and religious 'immorality'.

The correlation of loyalty to God with loyalty to spouse is fundamentally ingrained in the Holy Scriptures from the first words of the prophets, throughout the recorded ministry of Jesus, into the early Church. For God, the new Israel is a spouse, a bride in robes purified and glittering with the good deeds of the saints (Revelation 19:7–8); and to God, apostasy is adultery, plainly and simply. Rejecting Paul, God's ambassador, is not only a crime against the reign of God, Paul's commander-in-chief, it is a familial sin against a family member.

MEDITATION

Do you know someone with whom you should be reconciled?

GOD'S LIVING SANCTUARY

Paul is summoning the Corinthians to recall that they are not a marketplace where apostles of profit come to hawk their oratorical wares (2:17), but they, together with Paul and his co-workers, are the unified and holy temple of the living God.

God's temple is alive

In the history of Israel, four temples were built. The first, by Moses about the year 1500BC, was a movable temple. Its primary design was to provide a place where God dwells among humans (Exodus 25:8). Worship became synonymous with entering the temple because when we come into the presence of God, we worship.

The 'tent of meeting' (or 'tabernacle') had three basic sections: a court where the altar for burnt offerings stood; a holy place where the altar of incense stood; and the most holy place, the Holy of Holies, where the ten commandments, God's first written word, rested in the Ark of the Covenant beneath the mercy seat. The Spirit of God would descend like a cloud and envelop the tabernacle. The inner Holy of Holies, where God was most present, could be entered only once a year on the Day of Atonement, after an elaborate service of purification. God's presence made this most holy place so terrible that if a bell did not announce the entrance of the high priest, Aaron would be struck dead. God's presence was so holy that it was like a fire, purifying everything that entered it, instantly consuming anything impure.

When Christ died in our stead, his sacrificial death purified every human. Therefore the temple curtain to the Holy of Holies was ripped in two from top to bottom (Matthew 27:51). This signified that God's Spirit no longer dwelt in that place nor met God's people within the temple. God's Spirit rushed out into what was newly purified, and the people of God, the new Israel, became a new 'movable tent'. Greek has two words that are translated 'temple'. The first, *hieron*, signifies the whole temple, all the buildings, the grounds and the courts. But this is not the word Paul employs in 2 Corinthians 6:16. *Naos* ('sanctuary') was the holy place and the inner Holy of Holies. God has not made the Corinthians, together with Paul and his ministering team, merely the tent or the temple but the Holy of Holies! The implications are staggering. Wherever Christians go, God goes. And we have the privilege to represent God's most holy presence.

God's temple is a unity

This passage is not the first time Paul has reminded the Corinthians of this fact. For this reason Paul admonished them about their divisions and sexual immorality, since these sins destroy the entire structure, God's temple (1 Corinthians 3:17). 'Body' is singular but 'your' is plural (1 Corinthians 6:19). One Christian can affect the very sanctuary of God, affecting not simply a building or one individual but all Christians, all of the pillars, the living stones that comprise God's Church and that are laid upon the chief cornerstone, Christ. Therefore we, like the Corinthians, need to be very careful how we act. We must treat one another in the same way the Hebrews were taught to treat the Holy of Holies. If we destroy even the least of our brothers and sisters, lead any astray by our immoral acts, we have destroyed God's temple and God promises that we in turn will be destroyed.

To Paul, the believers at Corinth were like a building that belongs to God and on which Paul, Apollos and the other co-workers were labouring. As Christ's construction workers, Paul laid the foundation and Apollos built upon it. Adding in stones of false believers, pagan prostitutes and dissenters breaks the building down. Unyoking from Paul and from other true believers is splitting stones apart, a foolish act that threatens to topple the entire building down upon the Corinthians' heads, crushing and destroying their relationship with God. Rather, they should make in their own hearts room where love for Paul and for God can dwell. They should be using their time and energy in constructive ways, that is, ways that help to construct the temple of God. How can they do this? They can cement their relationship with Paul and with their fellow stones in the living temple by resolving their own disagreements, and being obedient to Paul and to their own promise to take up a temple offering to benefit their starving sisters and brothers, thus contributing to the collection Paul has been led to gather for Jerusalem.

PRAYER

Our Father in heaven, hallowed be your name. Your kingdom come. Your will be done, on earth as it is in heaven.

Matthew 6:9–10

ACTION BASED *on* PROMISES

In 6:2 Paul quotes word for word from Isaiah 49:8, but in verses 16–18 he quotes various Old Testament passages. Rabbis would string up various scriptures, as some people string up pearls, in order to enlighten one point of an argument.

Paul has just reminded the Corinthians of the marvellous truth that we mortals have become the sanctuary of the one living God (6:16a). Now he lists some of the Old Testament passages where God promises such a marvel.

God promises

'I will live in them' is a translation of a promise such as in Zechariah 2:10. 'I will live' is a common Old Testament word for people 'dwelling in' a land ('settle', Leviticus 26:32). Paul uses the same Greek word to describe the Holy Spirit dwelling among Christians (Romans 8:11). Thus, in the permanent way people settle down in a home and country, God settles down and lives among Christians, thereby making us God's sanctuary or 'home'.

The next Old Testament passage is Leviticus 26:12: '...and walk among them'. In Leviticus 26:11–12, God promises that if the Hebrews obey, God will set up a 'dwelling' ('tent') among them and 'walk' about among them; he will 'be' their God and they 'shall be' his people. Paul, therefore, includes in a passage dealing with God's tabernacle the necessity of obedience, a point he is about to reiterate in 7:1–2.

Paul next quotes Ezekiel 37:27: 'I will be their God, and they shall be my people' is a promise to the exiled Hebrews that they would return to Israel, and that, once there, God would establish an 'everlasting covenant' and set 'my sanctuary' (literally 'holy place') and 'dwelling place' among them. Thus, the nations will know that 'I the Lord sanctify Israel, when my sanctuary is among them forevermore'. This context refers to obedience to God and relates God's presence to the process of holiness (see Ezekiel 37:24, 26–28).

Paul reminds the believers of God's promise to be intimately present, and of the personal bonding and mutual commitment that results.

God warns

Then Paul makes explicit what was implicit in these Old Testament contexts (v. 17). If humans are to be close to a holy God, then their proximity to evil must be affected. God had promised the Hebrews in exile that the Lord would deliver them, and warned the priests, those 'who carry the vessels of the Lord', not to touch anything unclean and to be pure as they leave captivity (Isaiah 52:11). All believers are now God's very sanctuary, no longer needing priests as intermediaries.

'Separation' was an important Old Testament concept, since 'clean' animals had to be separated from unclean animals (Leviticus 20:25). God wanted the people to learn that they needed to be 'separated' away from evil because God is a 'separated' or 'holy' God (Leviticus 20:26). In this same way, at the final judgment, Jesus will separate people one from another (Matthew 25:32).

'I will welcome you' is a quote of Ezekiel 20:34 ('I will bring you') —again, a promise to the exiled Hebrews that they would be delivered. Of course, God would bring them out to the wilderness, as they were brought out before, for judgment, and the 'rebels' and 'those who transgress' would be purged out from among them (Ezekiel 20:35–38). Likewise, Paul will warn the Corinthians explicitly that he will punish transgressors (13:2).

Paul concludes his 'pearl stringing' by referring to God's promise to David that Solomon would build a 'house' for God (2 Samuel 7:13). God as 'father' adopted Solomon as heir (2 Samuel 7:14). But Solomon represents all future believers; thus Paul rephrases 'son' to 'sons and daughters' (v. 18). God promised David that sin would be punished but steadfast love would never be removed (2 Samuel 7:14–15); so too Paul implies that God will punish sin at Corinth but not remove God's steadfast love.

'Sons and daughters' are God's holy sanctuary, among whom God dwells, moves and is. God welcomes us and gives us rights of inheritance. Therefore, we must make an effort to be holy and to support holy, not rebellious, leaders.

MEDITATION

Which of God's promises do you find most challenging? Why?

GOD'S PRESENCE AFFECTS US

Paul's second appeal (6:14–18) and his string of Old Testament quotations build up to these direct exhortations. First, Paul commands the Corinthians to 'cleanse' themselves, using the first person plural ('we') to include himself in the command (v. 1). Then, Paul commands that they 'make room' for Paul and his team, using the second person plural ('you'), referring only to the Corinthians (v. 2).

A holy God deserves a holy people

Because God has promised to dwell among humans, we must therefore be pure. A holy God cannot dwell in an unholy vessel. Jesus has presented us as justified in God's sight, but God's covenant must be welcomed and made real. To 'cleanse ourselves' indicates an initial step on a new journey. 'Making holiness perfect' is a process, even as 'being saved' (2:15) is a process. Paul indicates what not to do and what to do, the negative and then the positive. Something must be removed, but then it must be filled anew.

To be 'cleansed' is not literal. Physical cleanliness is not next to godliness. Dirt on our body from manual labour can actually be glorifying to God (2 Thessalonians 3:7–9). 'Cleanse' in the New Testament often refers to ritual purity, or physical healing such as the healing of a leper with skin lesions (Matthew 8:2–3) or the welcoming of previously unacceptable food or people (Acts 10:15).

'Defilement' (molusmos) is a strong, although rare, biblical word. The related noun (molusma) is a 'spot' or 'taint'. When Joseph's coat was 'stained' with the goat's blood, it was 'defiled' (Genesis 37:31). When people ate 'unclean' food offered to other gods, their vessels were 'defiled' (Isaiah 65:4). Thus, 'defilement' is a spiritual state, like having blood on our hands from murder, which can never be removed by physical washing.

Paul describes two types of 'staining'—physical and spiritual, or sins of the flesh and sins of the spirit. Sexual immorality is an example of a physical sin (12:21). Selfishness, anger, jealousy and allegiance to the wrong leaders are examples of spiritual sins (12:11, 20). Both are equally displeasing to God.

The choice to be pure is an initial action. The process of becoming holy or fully like God is a long-term goal requiring many good actions. 'Making perfect' is to complete something, to finish it, to become fully mature. We are a new creation so that we can become righteous (5:17, 21). The 'fear of God' is involved because God through Christ will judge us (5:10). Working on holiness is a serious matter, and certainly for the Corinthians, whose sins were leading them further and further away from the right path.

A holy people want to be welcomed

Paul is ready now again (6:13; 7:2) to exhort the Corinthians: 'make room' (*choreo*) for us. What a sad day when Paul and Timothy, who introduced the Corinthians to Christ, have to beg them to make room for them! A 'room' or 'space' (*chora*) could be, literally, a country, a region, fields, the countryside or simply land. For example, the wise magi went back to their own 'country' (Matthew 2:12). Paul and his team want to be part of the Corinthians' 'country'. The implication here is that when Paul and his team are welcomed, then their sound teaching is welcomed. As Jesus said about his teaching on marriage, 'Let anyone accept this who can' (*choreo*, Matthew 19:12): let people 'welcome' or 'recognize the truth' of what he said. The Corinthians' allegiance to the super-apostles was becoming so strong that they no longer had 'room' to listen to the teachings and friendship of Paul and his team.

Paul summarizes in three verbs what he has been saying and defending all along, the reason why they and their teaching should be welcomed. They 'have done no one any wrong or injustice', they have 'corrupted' or ruined no one, they have not 'taken advantage' or greedily taken what is not theirs (v. 2). We shall see that these verbs will describe the super-apostles (11:20).

And Paul addresses these pleas to people he still calls 'beloved' (v. 1)!

PRAYER

Have mercy on me, O God, according to your steadfast love;
according to your abundant mercy blot out my transgressions.
Wash me thoroughly from my iniquity, and cleanse me from my sin.

Psalm 51:1–2

LOVE & BOASTING

Between these verses is a transition in Paul's argument. Verse 3 concludes the previous section (6:1—7:2) ('open your hearts to us') and sets up the next section (7:4—9:15) (Paul has confidence in the Corinthians).

Paul reaffirms their love

The difficulty with exhorting the Corinthians to change, and especially to abandon impressive people who are highly esteemed yet harmful, is that the Corinthians might become so insulted that they may leave Paul and his team altogether. Thus, Paul now wants to explain the reason for his previous exhortation and to shore up the Corinthians' self-confidence. If indeed the super-apostles have a domineering relationship with the Corinthians (11:20), then the Corinthians might not be thinking too highly of themselves, since they have allowed that to happen.

Therefore, Paul reaffirms his team's love for the Corinthians, affirming them. He is not ready to 'condemn' them (v. 3). The case is still being heard and the defendants still have the chance to change their lives. 'I said before' is in the perfect tense, signifying that what follows is something Paul has previously told them, yet the state of telling them continues through the current time. In other words, it is not past and done with. Paul will use the same verb and tense in 13:2 ('I warned') when he summarizes his argument in a forceful, direct way and exhorts the Corinthians to change. But here, Paul reaffirms his love, a love which is total, with inward feeling and outward action.

'You are in our hearts' (v. 3); 'you yourselves are our letter, written on our hearts' (3:2); 'our heart is wide open to you' (6:11). How many of us can express such love for people outside our families? Not just Paul, but his whole team ('our') is willing to do all for the Corinthians' betterment—'to die together and to live together' (v. 3). This is Christ-like love, to be willing to die for (and here 'with') someone else.

Paul first presents death, and then life. When Christ died, 'all died' (5:14). The Corinthians 'died' at one point in time, but they need to continue to die to their sins. Paul and his team are willing to walk with them as they endure the painful ongoing process of death. Then Paul and his team will not abandon them as newborn babes entering a new life. They will enjoy their friendships together.

Paul has hope for the Corinthians

Paul's encouragement of the Corinthians is only just beginning. He uses two synonyms to describe his positive expectations about the Corinthians—'boast' (*parresia*) and 'pride' (*kauchesis*) (v. 4). Paul used *parresia* earlier to describe their ministry style (3:12): it is one that is 'open and visible', speaking freely and without concealment or deceit. Here Paul states that he freely speaks about (and possibly 'to') the Corinthians, but not with premature condemnation (v. 3). Furthermore, he boasts not about himself but the Corinthians. There is such a thing as false boasting (11:12), which is not God-pleasing. But to boast on another's behalf is God-pleasing. Paul even hoped that the Corinthians and he would be able mutually to boast about each other (1:14).

And then Paul, filled with the Spirit who brings consolation from God (1:3), says that he is 'filled' and 'overjoyed' (v. 4). He is 'filled' with 'consolation'. 'Filled' is in the perfect tense, again, indicating that this is not a one-time event, but it happened in the past and creates a long-term state of 'filling'. 'Consolation' means advocacy, a major theme in chapter 1. Paul's advocacy for the Corinthians persists, even as his desire to 'die' with the Corinthians persists. As if this positive state were not enough, Paul reiterates in a heightened fashion that, literally, 'I am overflowing in joy'. Paul uses the verb 'to overflow' or 'to be over and above the number' to describe the greater glory of the new covenant (3:9) and the many spiritual gifts that the Corinthians have (8:7). But here he adds an intensifying prefix 'over': 'I am *over*-overflowing in joy' (v. 4). That's an awful lot of joy to have while going through difficulties! Why does he tell the Corinthians he is 'overjoyed'? He looks forward to the good news he received (7:6), reaffirms his positive expectations for the Corinthians, and, in microcosm, describes his leadership style, one where tremendous difficulties do occur, but nevertheless the joy present is 'super-overflowing'.

MEDITATION

Do you know someone whom you should encourage
by stating your pride in them?

LOOSENED *by* GOD

In verse 4, Paul concludes that he is 'overjoyed' in 'affliction'. Now he explains the extent of their affliction and why he is joyful.

Tightened strings

In Paul's recounting of his travels which form a thematic flow to this letter, he has now crossed from the seaport of Troas into the province of Macedonia. In 2:13 Paul explained that he had gone into Macedonia looking for Titus, but not until now does he tell us that he found Titus and learned what Titus had resolved with the Corinthians.

When they came into Macedonia, Paul and his team were in great distress. They were worried about Titus and worried about the Corinthians. Their bodies 'had no rest' (*anesis*, v. 5). *Anesis* can refer to loosened, as opposed to tightened, strings. Have you ever had so many troubles that you could not relax? You felt tense and stressed? That was their situation. They had 'disputes without and fears within' (v. 5). This letter shows their concern for the Corinthian spiritual condition, which indicated multi-level misunderstandings about a changed visit (1:15–17), a letter (2:3), an overzealous punishment (2:6–7), changing allegiance to false leaders (2:17; 6:13; 11:19–20), hesitation to give to other Christians (9:3) and numerous other sins (12:20–21).

Moreover, outsiders were causing trouble. 'Disputes' are 'battles', 'combat', 'fighting'. The word could refer to the combat of armies or to the verbal quarrels of individuals (2 Timothy 2:23). Paul and his co-workers were not fighting with each other. Paul could be alluding to the rioting of the crowd at Ephesus in Asia (Acts 19:23–41).

But Paul and his team also had 'fears within' (v. 5). How can they have 'fears within' when Paul had commanded the Philippians not to 'worry about anything' (literally, 'to be distracted', Philippians 4:6)? Paul counselled the Philippians that prayer to God is the answer to a distracted mind. That does not mean that prayer removes the knowledge that we have genuine things to fear. Paul and his team could fear losing their lives or being physically attacked or the ending of their ministry among the Corinthians. Courage is not about freedom from fear but about proceeding forward in prayer and action, despite fear.

Loosened strings

God acted to relieve Paul because God is 'the one *consoling* the downcast (v. 6, literally). God is always in the process of advocating for ('consoling') the 'downcast' or 'lowly' person. God is the court-appointed lawyer whose goal is to defend the poor person who cannot afford the expensive lawyer. All of us who have troubles in the midst of ministering should remember that God is always there to advocate for us.

That consolation was demonstrated by the appearance of Titus (v. 6). How relieved they were simply to see Titus!

God's 'consolation' was also demonstrated by the good news Titus brought (v. 7). Some scholars think that Paul could not have written in one letter about good news (ch. 7) and bad news (ch. 10). However, the good news here is not in regard to all of the spiritual issues with which the Corinthians had to deal. It had only to do with one matter (7:11). In George MacDonald's *The Lost Princess*, the wise woman asks Princess Rosamond to do her daily cleaning duties as a means of becoming more humble and good. After more than a day of wanton laziness, Rosamond wipes one streak of dust off a table in a fleeting moment of fear. The wise woman notices this one act and smiles 'like the sun peeping through a cloud on a rainy day in spring' (chs. 4—5).

So, too, Paul and Timothy are encouraged by this first step the Corinthians make, which shows that their relationship with them is not all ruptured. The Corinthians yearn after (lament) the loss, and jealously desire a good relationship (v. 7). A change of attitude precedes a change of action. When Paul saw the Corinthians' attitude, he was filled with even more joy because he had hope for a full restoration of their relationship with himself, his team and with God.

PRAYER

Blessed be you, the God and Father of our Lord Jesus Christ,
the Father of mercies and the God of all consolation,
who consoles us in all our affliction, so that we may be able
to console those who are in any affliction
with the consolation with which you, God, console us.

Paraphrase of Paul's prayer of praise in 2 Corinthians 1:3–4

GODLY & WORLDLY PAIN

Paul now returns to a topic he raised earlier—that letter of tears, the letter he wrote instead of a visit because he wanted to give the Corinthians a warning (2:1–7). He has developed since chapter 2 some additional reasons why he and his team should be welcomed: their competence comes from God to be ministers of a new spiritual covenant (3:1—5:21) and they have wronged no one, but rather the Corinthians need to be pure (6:1—7:3).

Paul's letter made the Corinthians feel pain. The verb and noun for 'pain' occurs seven times in these three verses ('made you sorry', 'grieved', 'grief'), indicating an important topic for Paul. 'Pain' can refer to bodily or mental pain. Paul discusses two types of pain—godly and worldly—and their length, goal and effect.

Pain has length and goal

Godly pain is temporary. 'Briefly' is, literally, 'for an hour' (v. 8). Apparently Paul's letter caused the Corinthians pain, but if Paul had visited, the pain would have been even greater (2:2–3). How many of us avoid pain at all costs and pursue pleasure with all zeal? Sometimes a temporary pain or conflict is worth it. In the past Paul had been regretting his letter, but now he no longer regrets it (having heard from Titus of its positive effect).

In godly pain, the goal is repentance, not pain and punishment. 'Repentance' begins with change of perception. One of Jesus' repeated calls to his audiences was, 'Repent, for the kingdom of heaven has come near' (Matthew 4:17). Having seen that God's reign is near, people should change. Jesus taught that he came 'to call not the righteous but sinners to repentance' (Luke 5:32). He said that when one sinner repented, the heavenly courts celebrated (Luke 15:6–7, 10). Therefore, the repentant person deserves forgiveness. If our friends repent even seven times in one day, we must forgive them each time (Luke 17:3–4). Therefore, Paul exhorts Christians to restore sinners gently (Galatians 6:1). This is what Paul is doing here in 2 Corinthians. As he expresses his deep love, he keeps focused on restoring the Corinthians to God's path.

Repentance is not punishment. 'You were not harmed' (*zemioo*,

v. 9) has to do with fines levied by courts or other financial losses. For example, when the sailors on the way to Italy were pounded by a north-east tempest, they had to throw the cargo and tackle overboard, suffering financial 'loss' (*zemia*) but not loss of life (Acts 27:21–22). The godly pain Paul caused the Corinthians was not a penalty. Its aim was to help the Corinthians avoid a penalty. Implied also here is Paul's conviction that he and his team did not take any financial advantage of the Corinthians (12:13, 18).

Pain has effect

While godly pain produces repentance which results in salvation (v. 10), worldly pain produces death. When Judas saw that his betrayal of Jesus resulted in Jesus' condemnation, Judas repented and returned the thirty pieces of silver to the chief priests and elders, declaring, 'I have sinned by betraying innocent blood.' He repented but, not being forgiven by the religious leaders or by himself, he ended up killing himself (Matthew 27:3–5). Zacchaeus, the wealthy tax collector in Jericho, changed his mind about defrauding others, showing his changed heart by a change in his behaviour, giving half of his possessions to the poor and paying back four times as much to anyone he defrauded. About Zacchaeus, Jesus said, 'Today salvation has come to this house', reminding his listeners that he 'came to seek out and to save the lost' (Luke 19:9–10).

One of the most remarkable uses of godly pain has been going on at the turn of this century in South Africa. The worldly pain mutually inflicted by the different people groups in South Africa is being handled in a godly manner. The Peace and Reconciliation Commission encourages victims and victimizers to express their feelings of pain, not in order to inflict penalties, but to stimulate acts of repentance in order to save a nation. This is a miracle of God at work among individuals affecting the national level, even as Paul in his time was an instrument of God at work at the local level.

MEDITATION

*Is there something of which you need to repent
or someone you need to encourage to repent?*

The SEVEN MANIFESTATIONS of GODLY GRIEF

If, in 7:8–10, Paul describes the length, goal and effect of godly repentance, in verse 11 he describes its outward manifestations.

Godly grief is reactive

Paul describes a seven-step process of repentance or 'pain' enacted in a godly way. First is 'earnestness', 'haste' or 'speed'. If we are genuinely repentant, we will act quickly. The Corinthians as a church tended to hurry to do things (8:7). Here, they hurried in a great way. This type of hurry should be true of leading and serving (Romans 12:8, 11).

Second is 'defence' ('eagerness to clear yourselves'). Procurator Porcius Festus explained to King Herod Agrippa and Bernice that Paul had the legal right to give his defence against the charge before his accusers (Acts 25:16). Peter, writing during Nero's time of persecution, also challenged his readers to be ready to make a defence of their faith to anyone who asked (1 Peter 3:15). Sometimes Christians think they should never defend their own rights, but God welcomes haste to clear up misunderstandings, because truth is important to God.

Third is 'indignation' (v. 11), literally, a physical pain or irritation. For example, when James and John had connived with their mother to ask for a special status, the other disciples were 'angry' (Matthew 20:24). When Jesus discovered that the disciples were not allowing people to bring little children to him, he was 'indignant' (Mark 10:14). Irritation can be caused by injustice, ignorance or jealousy. In godly repentance the basis is a desire for justice.

Fourth is 'alarm', 'panic flight' (v. 11). In the New Testament this is the most general term for 'fear'. 'Fear' can be reverence, treating God with respect and living a right life because God is our judge, or the fear we feel when we are attacked (7:1, 5; 5:10–11). In the context of chapter 7, fear appears to be a serious attitude in the process of repentance.

Godly grief is proactive

Fifth is 'longing' (v. 11). Titus himself described the Corinthians as having 'longing' and 'zeal' (7:7). We cannot turn our lives around if we do not move from the negative (defence, indignation, fear) to the positive, the yearning after or desiring what is absent or has been lost. Sometimes we yearn after possessions (Psalm 62:10), but godly repentance yearns after godly concerns. Paul has described how we yearn to be immortal (5:2). Christians also yearn to be with each other (9:14). The Corinthians were yearning for a restored relationship with Paul.

Sixth is 'zeal' (v. 11), a positive or negative trait, depending on whether it flows from God or the evil one. Positive 'zeal' promotes holiness. Negative 'zeal' is jealousy which undermines people's successes. For instance, the Sadducees were jealous of the apostles' growing influence in Jerusalem (Acts 5:17). But the Corinthians were jealous or protective of their relationship with Paul and with God. This type of positive jealousy could become a good motivation for dismissing ungodly leaders (11:2–4).

Seventh is 'punishment' (v. 11), the just decision of a judge (Luke 18:7–8). A judge may punish or vindicate. Punishment of our enemies belongs only to God (Romans 12:19–21). Jesus at his return will punish those who have rejected God's good news (2 Thessalonians 1:8). The final step of godly repentance is to seek complete justice. If a relationship is ruptured, justice should be the goal, not disguising truth, because God's love 'rejoices in the truth' (1 Corinthians 13:6).

What was the matter in which the Corinthians commended themselves as 'guiltless' (innocent, pure)? Paul had written to the Corinthians in a letter of 'many tears', warning and testing them (2:3–9; 7:8). Someone did wrong, while someone else was wronged (v. 12). Whatever happened we cannot be sure, but we can be sure that the Corinthians made haste to resolve this ruptured relationship. Still, however, they were not innocent about all matters. They were submitting themselves to heterodoxy (11:4). They still had problems (12:20–21).

PRAYER

As a deer longs for flowing streams,
so my soul longs for you, O God.

Psalm 42:1

REMEMBERING *the* VISIT

In this passage are revealed the interdependence, mutual respect and love between Paul, Timothy, Titus and the Corinthians.

A spirit at rest gives joy

Paul and Timothy are relieved that the Corinthians have manifested godly repentance (7:11, 13). However, even greater than their own 'comfort' or 'consolation', seeing Titus joyful and at rest gives Paul and Timothy joy. One group's maturity (the Corinthians') affects every concerned Christian because indeed we are family. Paul's spirit had no 'rest' when Titus had not met him at Troas (2:13), but now Titus' spirit had rest when the Corinthians responded in godly pain to Paul's letter (v. 13). What a diplomat Titus must have been, and yet his diplomacy flowed right out of his heart.

The Greek says that Titus' 'spirit' (*pneuma*, KJV), not 'mind' (*nous*), was set at rest. The human spirit is that aspect of a person that self-examines and self-observes, even as God's Spirit 'searches everything, even the depths of God' (1 Corinthians 2:10–11). The assurance that we are God's children is something that God's Spirit communicates to our own spirits; it is more than superficial cognitive knowledge (Romans 8:16). Thus, at the very depth of his being, Titus felt at rest after his visit with the Corinthians.

Paul had also been concerned about the Corinthians accepting the reliability of his word. Paul's word modelled God's word, and God can be fully relied upon. The faithfulness of Paul's plans (1:17), in his mind, was also related to the faithfulness of his expectations about the Corinthians (v. 14). Keeping a vow has several perspectives— what the Corinthians expected of Paul and what he expected of the Corinthians. Paul expected the Corinthians to repair this wronged relationship (7:12) and the Corinthians showed him to be correct. Paul draws out his lesson further: the faithfulness or reliability of his expectations for the Corinthians is analogous to the faithfulness of Paul and his team's teachings (v. 14). Paul's great love for the Corinthians does not eradicate his speaking truthfully.

Titus remembers his welcome

Titus' self-examining spirit was set at rest (v. 13). Moreover, his gut-level compassion kept remembering the Corinthians' 'obedience' (v. 15). They had 'obeyed' or 'listened' to Titus and to Paul. Their listening attitude was demonstrated by the way they 'welcomed' or 'received' Titus. Jesus had instructed his disciples to visit people in their homes with the good news. And he warned them that if they welcomed his disciples they welcomed the teacher who sent them (Matthew 10:12–14, 40). Thus, the way the Corinthians welcomed Titus indicated their attitude to all of Paul's team and eventually toward the very Jesus they proclaimed (11:4).

The Corinthians welcomed Titus 'with fear and trembling' (v. 15). 'Fear' is a proper human response to a mighty God (Luke 1:50). 'Trembling' ('quaking, quivering') intensifies 'fear'. The women disciples first responded in trembling, amazed fear when an angel told them that Jesus had risen from the dead (Mark 16:8). For Paul, 'fear and trembling' is a positive phrase, to describe his first visit to the Corinthians. Even though he was trained at the highest level (even Festus observed he had great learning, Acts 26:24), he chose not to use rhetorical arts to impress his listeners. Instead he describes his approach to the Corinthians as 'in weakness and in fear and in much trembling'. He preached 'Jesus Christ' 'crucified', reflected in a life of sufferings in imitation of Christ (1 Corinthians 2:1–3; 4:11–13). Christians should all manifest obedience to God and God's emissaries in 'fear and trembling' (Philippians 2:12). Thus 'fear and trembling' in the context of Paul's correspondence to the Corinthians reflected a wholesome fear of God, respect for God's workers, the beginnings of an understanding of the core of the gospel and a serious response to the current dilemma.

No wonder Paul could conclude that he has confidence in the Corinthians (v. 16).

MEDITATION

Is there someone you should affirm by welcoming him or her?

GOD'S GRACE ENRICHES *the* POOR

Paul discerns that, in Titus' confirmation (7:13–14), the struggle for the Corinthians' obedience has entered a new stage, and Paul has a reason for hope and confidence in them (7:16). Their response to his recent letter shows their zeal and affection for himself, Titus and the other co-workers. This action encourages him so that he can go on to make more difficult requests: their financial contribution (chs. 8—9) and later, their loyalty (chs. 10—13). Chapters 8 and 9 comprise what could be called in effect 'Paul's stewardship sermon'. He holds up the example of the poorer Macedonian churches before the materially comfortable Achaians, weaving example, proverb and plea together, alluding to past promises, present services and to God's great and generous gift of Jesus. His aim is to encourage the Corinthians and the other Christians in Achaia to add to the accumulated gift of all the Gentile churches to ease the famine-stricken Jerusalem church. At risk is nothing less than Paul's relationship with the churches and, by implication, the Corinthians' own salvation. Refusal would signify a rejection of Paul, Paul's gospel and partnership with the other churches in the body of Christ, and acceptance of rival false apostles. The stakes are clearly more than money, but parting with money, symbolic as it is of security, serves as a concrete indication of where the Corinthians' loyalty stands. We tend to vote with our purse, and Paul campaigns for that vote (not simply on his own behalf, for the money is not for his benefit), but on behalf of Christ's Church.

The Macedonians are models

Paul appeals to the Corinthians' sense of honour. He had used the Achaian example of willingness to give during the previous year to spur on the Macedonians (9:2). Now he turns and uses the Macedonians' example to the Achaians (v. 2). He initiates a healthy competition among the churches, encouraging each to strive to outdo the others in acts of kindness and generosity. Like a good teacher, he is creating a team identity with mutual support against a common enemy—want! In this way he enables each church to expand its vision to include its sister churches, working towards the same ends.

The irony of the matter is that the Macedonians were currently not doing well economically as a province. Paul describes them as in a time of 'poverty' (v. 2), the type of poverty a beggar might have—like Lazarus, covered with sores, who would have been happy to eat the crumbs that fell down from the rich owner's table (Luke 16:20–21). But this kind of poverty also includes the poor widow who gave proportionately more than any rich donor (Luke 21:3–4). And to think the Macedonian 'poverty' was 'extreme' (literally, 'reaching down into the depths')!

What caused this poverty? After Rome conquered Macedonia in 168BC, the Romans no longer allowed the Macedonians to farm their gold and silver mines for their own benefit or to cut their timber for ships. They also divided the province into four sections, banning all trading between the regions, and setting up armed guards along these newly created frontiers—'as mangled as an animal disjointed into parts' (Livy XLV: XVIII, XXX).

The poor relied on grace

Nevertheless, the Macedonians focused not on their need, but on God's grace, which extends out, giving joy, bubbling over into generosity, literally 'overflowing joy' (v. 2). And what was the result of this surplus of joy among an extremely poor people? They had a 'wealth of generosity'. 'Generosity' (*haplotes*) comes from the root 'single' or 'simple' (*haploos*), such as a metal without alloys. To be single-minded is to be simple-minded, open-hearted, hence liberal or generous. What you see is what you get. Similarly, Paul will exhort the Corinthians to keep their simple devotion to Christ (11:3). The Macedonians were literally poor, but in joy and open-heartedness they were wealthy, affecting their attitude toward giving.

PRAYER

O Lord God of hosts, hear my prayer... you are a sun and shield;
you bestow favour and honour. No good thing do you withhold
from those who walk uprightly. O Lord of hosts,
happy is everyone who trusts in you.

Based on Psalm 84:8, 11–12

The MACEDONIANS MODEL GIVING

What happens when God's grace is given to a church? Using the model of the churches of Macedonia, Paul describes the paradoxical results of the poor having a surplus of generosity. He describes how the Macedonians gave, why they gave and its effect on his team.

Capacity and choice affect giving

Paul describes how they gave in six ways, of which he says he is a personal witness. In Greek, Paul begins 'according to their means, and even beyond their means' (v. 3). He contrasts 'according to' with 'beyond'. 'Means' in Greek is *dunamis* (from which we get 'dynamite'). 'Means' or 'power' especially referred to bodily strength. In the New Testament it is often used of the ability to do supernatural wonders (12:12), but it can simply refer to the ability to do anything (for example, Matthew 25:15). Thus, Paul first describes the Macedonians as giving at the level of their economic capacity. And, second, he adds that they gave beyond their capacity. They began at the first level and then exceeded it. That is what God's grace does. Its power is 'extraordinary' (4:7)!

The third way they gave was 'voluntarily' (v. 3), of their own accord. Paul will repeat this point again in 9:7. Here in verse 3 it is modelled; in 9:7 it is exhorted. The Macedonians were not forced to give. Paul and his team may certainly have explained and exhorted, but they left the final decision to them.

Asking to give is commended by God

The fourth way they gave was 'begging us earnestly' (v. 4) or with much exhortation. 'Earnestly' is *paraklesis*, that trait of encouragement, consolation, advocacy that comes from God (1:3). Thus, since the churches had received God's grace (8:1), now they had God's power (v. 3) and God's encouragement (v. 4). *Paraklesis* was also used of 'invocation'. Thus, the Macedonians 'asked' ('beg'), really 'asking' ('invoked'). Why on earth would anyone beg to give? The answer is in verse 4: 'the privilege of sharing in this ministry to the saints'.

'Privilege' is 'grace'. The Macedonians, who were full of joy (8:2), saw giving as something which gives joy. God's grace (8:1) gave grace

(8:2) which gave more grace (v. 4). What the Macedonians modelled, Paul will explain later under the benefits of generosity (9:6–14). The Macedonians perceived giving as 'grace', not as depressing duty.

They also perceived giving as 'sharing' (*koinonia*, v. 4). Paul warned the Corinthians not to have 'fellowship' with darkness (6:14). But here light has fellowship with light. Paul had also discussed the fellowship his team and the Corinthians had because of sufferings and consolation (1:7). Here, that fellowship of consolation takes concrete shape. *Koinonia* in ancient times often had financial denotations, even as today we speak of financial partnership or joint ownership. When the Macedonians gave, they perceived themselves to be partners in a service or 'ministry'. They were not the owners of this service, but the 'joint' owners.

The fifth way they gave was 'not merely as we expected' (v. 5). They went beyond their own capacity to give (v. 3) and beyond their exhorters' expectations (v. 5) by giving in a sixth way. God's will was the means by which they gave first to the Lord, then to Paul's team. Their goal was not primarily to impress the Christians in Jerusalem, Macedonia or Achaia. They wanted to be commended by the Lord (a point Paul will later develop in 10:18). The Macedonians reactivated God's initial grace by giving themselves to God.

Thus, the Macedonians gave above their capacity, at their own choice, to an urgent call, with God's commendation. What was the end result on Paul's team? Paul and Timothy could use this example to encourage Titus (v. 6), who might have been feeling discouraged, wondering if he should return to Achaia. How many times, when we fall short of our spiritual potential, do we think about how we affect other Christians? The Macedonians' generosity spurred Paul's ministering team to keep serving. Service is more than zeal, beginning a good work; it is also perseverance, completing a good work. *Koinonia* among Christians has multi-level ramifications.

MEDITATION

After reviewing the ways the Macedonians gave, how can you spur yourself to give in a way you have not done yet?

EAGERNESS CAN BE LOVING

'Excel' is the action the Corinthians had in common with the Macedonians (v. 7). The Macedonians excelled or overflowed in joy and
generosity (8:2). The Corinthians overflowed in four virtues (v. 7).

Spiritual gifts

Faith, speech, knowledge and eagerness are Christian virtues. They
are also spiritual gifts. Paul had thanked God that the Corinthians
were so rich in the spiritual gifts of speech and knowledge (1 Corinthians 1:5–7). They were gifted in prophetic and language gifts (1
Corinthians 13:8–9; 14:2).

'Faith' is trust. All of us trust in something or someone. Every time
we sit down, we 'trust' that the chair will hold us up. What we need
to do is to find someone worth trusting and then keep trusting that
person (1 Corinthians 16:13), but only God is fully trustworthy. Paul
has been reminding the Corinthians to trust God's power, not impressive speeches (1 Corinthians 2:5). And 'faith' by itself is mean-
ingless. Christian faith rests on the resurrection of Christ and the
expectation that Christ's followers will be resurrected as well (1 Corinthians 15:14; 2 Corinthians 4:13–14). But 'faith' is also a spiritual
gift (1 Corinthians 12:9). Paul elaborates on 'faith' as the ability 'to
remove mountains' (1 Corinthians 13:2), alluding to Jesus' conversation with Peter about prayer (Mark 11:23–24).

Even as with faith, so too with 'speech': it is the content that
counts. Paul's words (or 'speech') are about Christ crucified, not about
impressive rhetoric or wonders (1 Corinthians 1:18–23). 'Speech' also
describes one group of spiritual gifts, the more verbal gifts that
traditionally befit the messenger of a ruler. The 'ministry of the word'
is done by apostles, prophets, evangelists, pastors and teachers
(Ephesians 4:11).

Paul mentions 'speech and knowledge' in both letters as constant
characteristics of the Corinthians. In 1 Corinthians he reminds them
that knowledge is less important than love. Knowledge by itself 'puffs
up, but love builds up' (1 Corinthians 8:1). Some Corinthians had
been flaunting their knowledge to the detriment of others (1 Corinthians 8:7). 'Knowledge' is also a spiritual gift which is related to

prophecy, even as wisdom is related to teaching: 'If I have prophetic powers, and understand all mysteries and all knowledge...' (1 Corinthians 13:2). Prophecy was speaking forth God's message for upbuilding, encouragement, teaching and revelation (1 Corinthians 14:3–12).

'Eagerness', or haste, energy, zeal, also typifies the Corinthians. The Corinthians had shown 'eagerness' or outward demonstration of godly repentance (7:11), but this gift was also a potential flaw. They could show zeal for Paul, but then be swept quickly away to follow the false apostles (11:4).

Developing love

The final virtue is 'love', but whose love is it? The initial source of the love is Paul's team, and it resides among the Corinthians. The main goal in writing 1 Corinthians was to exhort them to value love, or service to others for the gospel's sake, more than knowledge or right. Love gives life to all the spiritual gifts (1 Corinthians 13:1–4, 13). Did the Corinthians have it? Nowhere does Paul laud the Corinthians as being loving, but rather he wants them to demonstrate their love for him and for others (6:13; 7:2; 8:24). In 8:7 Paul does describe an overflowing love present at Corinth, but then qualifies it ('from us among you'), therefore showing it to be a potential love. In other words, the love is not yet brought alive by the Corinthians, but it is there, ready to be activated.

For what should their love and their overflowingly impressive gifts be used? The Corinthians should 'overflow' ('excel') in this 'grace' ('generous undertaking', v. 7). Of what use are spiritual gifts that do not reach out to others, such as to the needy Christians in Jerusalem? The 'genuineness' of the Corinthians' love needs to be demonstrated (v. 8).

PRAYER

Righteous Father, may the love with which
you have loved Jesus be in us.

Paraphrase of Jesus' prayer in John 17:25–26

POVERTY & PROSPERITY

Paul has presented the model of the Macedonian churches as an example of overflowing grace-filled giving (8:1–6), reminded the Corinthians of their own overflowing spiritual gifts (8:7–8) and now presents the model of grace lived out by Jesus himself (v. 9).

What do the Corinthians know?

The topic has been genuine love (8:8), and who is a greater example than God incarnate? Paul begins, 'for you (plural) know'—what Paul is about to elucidate is not new. To 'know' is to have knowledge grounded in personal experience, in this case the experience of 'grace' ('generous act'). 'Grace' (*charis*) or its related word 'joy' (*chara*) have occurred six times already in chapter 8. Paul will define grace with a christological statement that explains the person and work of Jesus in one well-rounded sentence, with profound practical ramifications for everyone.

Paul presents his statement about Christ by juxtaposing and inter-relating synonyms for wealth and poverty (in Greek they all begin with 'p'), highlighting its paradox and drawing the parallel of Christians to Christ: literally, he writes, 'For you, he became poor, prosperous being, so that you, by that poverty, prosperous might become'.

How can the rich be poor?

Christ 'became poor' (*ptocheuo*). The noun form (*ptocheia*) described the Macedonians' current economic condition (8:2). *Ptocheuo* is extreme poverty such as a beggar might have, the poor who cannot invite you back to dinner (Luke 14:13–14; 16:20). In what way did Jesus become poor?

First, he became poor by being born into a poor family (Luke 1:52–53). Jesus' family was not a desolate family without work or means of sustenance, but one that could afford not a lamb (Leviticus 12:8), but only two turtledoves or pigeons for its firstborn child's sacrifice (Luke 2:24). He was born in a manger 'because there was no place' for his family in the inn (Luke 2:7). As a carpenter, Joseph would have been part of the working, not the wealthy, class.

Second, Jesus became poor by becoming human. Jesus 'emptied

himself' of God's *shekinah* glory, taking on the outward form of God's own creation, a human. The contrast for God was analogous to a free-born ruler becoming a slave (Philippians 2:6–7).

Third, Jesus became poor by living a life of obedience. He obeyed God's commands, living in limitation in body and knowledge, persevering in his preaching, healing and teaching until he allowed himself to be crucified (Philippians 2:8).

Fourth, Jesus became poor by living for the poor. Shepherds were his first audience (Luke 2:15). He felt called to 'bring good news to the poor', release the 'captives', give 'sight to the blind', let the 'oppressed go free' (Luke 4:18). He healed, taught, fed and honoured the poor.

Fifth, Jesus became poor by being rejected by humans, first by the wealthy and the powerful and eventually by all. He had 'nowhere to lay his head' (Luke 9:58), no place or people who wholly accepted him for who he was, God incarnate. He was rejected because he elevated the status of devalued people: the poor, the semi-observant Jews, women, tax collectors, prostitutes, lepers, the demon-possessed, widows, strangers, the ill, the hungry, children. Jesus suffered and was persecuted (1:5).

Sixth, Jesus became poor by dying on behalf of human sin (5:14–15). At the moment of his death, when Jesus took on all human sin, God abandoned him because the Son had become 'sin' (5:21; Matthew 27:46).

However, Christ throughout his poverty was still 'rich'. He had all the physical provisions he needed (Luke 22:35). He was still God and Lord even though he was in human form (4:4–5). Despite his apparent defeat, he was triumphant (2:14), raised from the dead (4:14), the fulfilment of all of God's promises (1:19–20). 'Wealth' like the Macedonians' wealth (8:2) may look like poverty, but Jesus promises that if we put God's kingdom first, we will have enough for our necessities and enough to give away (Luke 12:29–33).

MEDITATION

What aspect of Christ's poverty moves you most to be generous?

A YEAR *of* GIVING

What year is this, what happened a year ago and why must the Corinthians give to the Christians in Jerusalem?

2 Corinthians was written in Macedonia in AD56–57. 1 Corinthians was written from Ephesus in Asia around AD56 (1 Corinthians 16:8, 19). Scholars deduce that about a year elapsed between the two letters, because of 2 Corinthians 8:10 and 9:2. Titus seems to have been the person who organized the Corinthians (8:6), while Timothy and Erastus may have prepared them (Acts 19:22).

Jerusalem saints in need

Paul had directed Corinth and also the churches of Galatia to save each week toward a special collection for Jerusalem. They were also to appoint people to accompany the gifts to Jerusalem (1 Corinthians 16:1–4). Why was Paul collecting money for the Christians in Jerusalem? When Paul and Barnabas had met with James, Peter and John earlier in Jerusalem, they had all agreed to 'remember the poor' (Galatians 2:9–10).

This was an especially difficult time in Judea. A prophet, Agabus, had predicted a severe famine which had especially affected Judea (Acts 11:28–29). This famine occurred in AD46–47, and was described by ancient historian Josephus, who said that Jerusalem 'was hard pressed by famine and many were perishing from want of money to purchase what they needed' (*Antiquities* xx. 2.5). Even Egypt, the refuge from hunger in Old Testament times, suffered from a famine around this time.

Making the situation more severe, Judea also suffered from both external and internal financial difficulties. The Roman procurators who reigned over Israel between AD44 and 66 stayed briefly and, instead of serving the nation, tried to take as much economic advantage as possible during their short stays. During Ventidus Cumanus' reign (AD48–52), about 20,000 Jews in Jerusalem lost their lives. In addition, although God had stated that God alone is owner of the land, after the kings began ruling, a few people took possession of large estates (Micah 2:2). When the collection was delivered in AD57, when Paul and his large team arrived in Jerusalem (Acts 20:4; 21:17), economic problems were spiralling.

The Jews had been instructed by God to care for the poor. The third-year tithe was to be designated for the Levites, resident aliens, orphans and widows (Deuteronomy 14:28–29). Indeed, Paul told procurator Felix that he had come to Jerusalem 'to bring alms to my nation' (Acts 24:17). Thus, Paul had good reason to be concerned for the poor, reiterating Jesus' charge: 'It is more blessed to give than to receive' (Acts 20:35). In addition to Paul's wish to support those who were poor for reasons outside their control (2 Thessalonians 3:10–12), he also wanted the Gentile Christians to express their appreciation materially for receiving spiritual blessings from the Jewish believers (Romans 15:27).

Giving has stages

In 2 Corinthians 8, Paul has not highlighted why the Corinthians should give specifically to the believers in Jerusalem, but he has been discussing why to give in general—the model of the Macedonian churches, the spiritual wealth of the Corinthians and the model of Christ (8:1–9). Now Paul reminds them of the interplay between intention and action. Positive response goes through these stages, each of which affects the next:

1. eagerness or willingness

2. will or desire

3. regular saving over time

4. completion of goal

First, their feelings were affected ('eagerness', v. 11) about the need to give. Second, they made a decision to give ('desire', v. 10). Third, they made a plan to give ('to do', v. 10). Paul had come up with this plan (saving every week on the first day of the week), but they had agreed. By saving, they could make sure they had the money they intended to give. Fourth, they would reach their goal ('finish... completing', v. 11). Thus, giving to the needy is an action which should be planned for and organized, as well as felt.

PRAYER

Give us each day our daily bread.

Luke 11:3

The PRINCIPLE of FAIR BALANCE

Once, at a church we attended, a young man who had been raised in the church, but had since drifted away, started attending. He had wanted to get married and, after counselling with a pastor, began again to participate. One Sunday, after the service, he told us he had found a reason for living. Delighted, we asked, 'And what is that reason?' He answered, 'Financial security, to make money.' Unfortunately, many people are like this man. Their security is in material possessions.

Fair balance is the same for all

In contrast, the Bible calls Christians to enter into a covenant of economic interdependence with other Christians, not to make some people poor and others rich but to make all equal with each other. Equality ('fair balance') with others (vv. 13–14) is the goal, not relief for one and pressure for another.

'Equality' has to do with proportions, ratios and impartiality. Paul exhorted masters to cause or bring about justice and equality for slaves (Colossians 4:1). Early Christians practised this teaching when they discovered that some widows were not being given food, while others were. They appointed devout believers from a neglected group (Hellenists) to oversee the distribution (Acts 6:1–5).

Equality is both the basis for action (v. 13, 'from equality') and its goal (v. 14). 'Equality' does not mean that all people had the same beginning characteristics. Some people had much, others had little (v. 15). Paul refers to Exodus, when God sent manna, a fine flaky substance, daily in the wilderness. Each family was supposed to gather only as much as it needed. After they measured each portion, those 'who gathered much had nothing over, and those who gathered little had no shortage'. Those who tried to hoard the heavenly bread found worms in it the next day (Exodus 16:18, 20). In other words, Paul implies by the context of Exodus 16 that lack of equality, building up storage barns while others are needy, is a type of greediness which shows lack of faith in God. Rather, the proportions should end up the same, because in reality the giver of all is the same, the one Lord of the harvest.

Receiving may be hard for some

God's master plan in giving is to create a family where each part is looking out for the other, relief flowing back and forth in love according to need. Such a relationship may have seemed superfluous to the currently successful *nouveau riche* Corinthians, but within twenty years of Paul's letter (AD77), an earthquake would reduce them from givers to recipients.

Some Christians are so proud that they will not accept help from anyone, thinking that there is some kind of special virtue in this attitude. All that this self-sufficiency does is to stunt the growth of the rest of the body of Christ by not letting it exercise its gifts of generosity and thereby grow spiritually. However, we should not keep more than our share of the world's goods. By doing so, we weaken the reciprocal nature of God's community. We need instead to be immediately passing goods on to brothers and sisters in need, being ready ourselves to receive from God's great cooperative bank of the saints when we stand in need. And we do not need to feel guilty for what we cannot give, if we are truly giving what we can.

None of us can outdo our Lord Jesus, however, who goes one step further. Jesus gave up riches to become poor so that by his poverty we might become rich (8:9). Jesus, who is not equal with us but is our master, went beyond equality with us to great sacrifice to ensure that we would be equal with each other. Likewise, the Macedonians gave not simply according to their means, but beyond their means (8:3). But all Paul asks for is equality, giving so that all people will get the same, even though their harvests may have been different. How could the Corinthians—how can we—reject so great a plea?

Therefore Paul's thought so far could be summarized as follows. How should we give? Plan ahead when possible; fulfil our obligations (8:10–11). How much should we give? We cannot give what we do not have (8:12). We should give proportionately, for the goal is equality with others, creating a reciprocal giving community (vv. 13–15).

MEDITATION

If indeed we should give more as we get more,
how can you enact the principal of proportionate giving?

TITUS' EAGERNESS *to* GO

The marvellous interconnection of God's sovereignty and human freedom are evident in these verses. God has been putting 'eagerness' for the Corinthians into several hearts, including Titus' heart, resulting in Titus going to Corinth 'of his own accord'. Titus has been the rich dark soil in which God's seed has thrived.

Grace boomerangs

'Grace' ('thanks') is a many-faceted word in this chapter. God's grace has been given to the Macedonian churches, resulting in their generosity (8:1). 'Grace' is God's bountiful, joyful love. God's grace was also manifest in the generous giving up of rights by Jesus for the sake of human enrichment (8:9). And now Paul returns God's blessing to humans by blessing or thanking God (v. 16)!

God has been giving Titus 'eagerness' (v. 16). 'Eagerness' (earnestness or zeal) is demonstrated by haste to do something. 'Eagerness' is one of the characteristics the Corinthians possess (8:7; 7:11), and Paul wants the Corinthians to direct this zeal toward others. 'Eagerness' was also a characteristic of the Macedonian churches (8:2, 8). Their zeal was directed toward the saints in Jerusalem. Titus' zeal for the Corinthians was similar to Paul and Timothy's zeal for them (7:4; 1:14). What a marvellous example to all of us to see a team of co-workers all so concerned for other Christians, in this case, the Corinthians.

Action should not enslave

Titus showed his 'eagerness' in two ways: he 'accepted' or welcomed their 'appeal' and he went out to Corinth (v. 17). Sometimes we Christians go to one of two extremes. We want to help people so much that we not only lead those we help as horses to water, but we also dunk their head in the water and grab their mouth to open and close it. (But the horse still must swallow!) Or we do nothing, tutting at the side, shaking our head in dismay at someone else's drifting away into sin. But Paul's team showed balance. First, they recognized that God is the ultimate source for concern for others. Then, Paul and Timothy communicated to Titus that they needed his aid.

Titus is a Gentile who helps by using his gifts of organization and encouragement. He had accompanied Paul and Barnabas from Antioch to Jerusalem, probably during the relief visit recorded in Acts 11:30 (Galatians 2:1–3). He has already met with the Corinthians about one matter which ended positively (7:6–7, 11). Later he will stay in Crete to 'put in order what remained to be done' and to 'appoint elders in every town' (Titus 1:5).

Paul's team needs Titus for another sticky situation, and Titus receives their summons as a host welcomes a guest (v. 17; compare Luke 16:4). What then happens? Titus becomes full of even more eagerness! And with that eagerness, 'of his own accord', he goes out from them. Titus received from God, listened to his co-workers and then acted.

Why is it so important for Titus to have acted freely, even as the Macedonian churches acted freely (8:3)? Giving people free choice is a key characteristic of genuine Christian leadership because it flows from a God who gives people free choice. God's good news brings freedom (John 8:36). In contrast, the super-apostles' leadership enslaved people (11:20). Free choice develops a strong, independent will that can freely choose to stand up for God in the midst of adversity. For instance, when Antiochus IV Epiphanes, in 169BC, required all Jews to eat pork, Eleazar, one of the leading teachers of the law in Israel, preferred 'death with honour to life with impiety', and 'voluntarily' submitted to torture instead (2 Maccabees 6:18–19). In the same way, countless Christians today all around the world continue voluntarily to act and speak to others about God's grace, despite the consequences. But allowing someone to self-choose does not mean that person should be kept ignorant of sincere Christians' appeals or independent of God's eagerness and grace.

PRAYER

God, give me your eagerness to reach out to someone this week.

An ACCOMPANIED GIFT

Sometimes in the church we think that if God has led us to do an action, we should do it spontaneously and immediately. To gather group support is worldly politics. These verses remind us of the importance at times of obtaining church support. Even as Titus finally went to Corinth of 'his own accord' (8:17), so too the church worked with Paul of its own accord.

Brothers and sisters

Having told the Corinthians that Titus is coming to organize the gift to the Christians in Jerusalem (8:17), Paul also introduces two or three other Christians who will come. They are each called 'brother'. When Jesus was dying, he formally instituted the Christian family as having priority over natural family ties, giving his mother, Mary, as mother to John, and John as son to Mary (John 19:26–27). Earlier he had taught the crowd that his true mother, brother and sister were those people who do the will of God (Mark 3:33–35). 'Brother' was a term that indicated equality. For example, Josephus, the historian, indicated that when Emperor Gaius called the god Jupiter his brother, he was giving himself an honour not appropriate for a human (*Antiquities* xix.1.1).

A Christian is elected

The first Christian brother's commendation comes from his work in proclaiming the good news, which is recognized by all the churches (v. 18). Normally when Paul refers to 'the gospel', he refers to the message of good news about Christ that he proclaims in word and deed (for example, 2:12; 11:4). However, some early Christians understood that in this passage Paul is praising the Gospel Luke recorded, because the Greek literally reads, 'the brother of whom the praise [is] in the gospel'. As early as the second and third centuries, Tertullian and Origen suggested that Luke 'wrote for Gentile converts the gospel praised by Paul'. Jerome and others repeat this tradition. Moreover, Eusebius explains that Paul was in the habit of referring to Luke's Gospel as his own (*History* iii.4; vi.25). Indeed, when Paul writes 1 Timothy (AD62–67), he quotes from the Gospel of Luke calling it 'scripture', on a par with the Old Testament (1 Timothy 5:18;

Luke 10:7). Paul also cites several words in 1 Corinthians 4:11–12 from the Beatitudes in the Gospel of Luke (Luke 6:21–29).

If Paul did indeed here refer to Luke's Gospel, then the Gospel must have been composed before AD56–57, the approximate date for 2 Corinthians. Luke has not visited Corinth, according to the New Testament, which would explain why his name is not mentioned here. Since around AD48 (that is, for about eight years) he had remained in Philippi, Macedonia. (The 'we' section ends in Philippi: Acts 16:17; 20:5–6.) We cannot be sure when Luke wrote his Gospel. Nevertheless, through the years, 2 Corinthians 8:18 has been associated with Luke.

This brother was Timothy and Paul's travelling companion (v. 19), a term also used of Gaius and Aristarchus (Acts 19:29). If indeed this 'brother' was Luke, he had certainly been the travelling companion of Paul and Timothy. Luke is described by Paul as the 'beloved physician' (Colossians 4:14), his 'co-worker' (Philemon 24), the only person who remained with Paul during his final Roman imprisonment (2 Timothy 4:11). Probably a Gentile (Colossians 4:11–14), he took leadership in maintaining the newly established church at Philippi, in which many women were active (Acts 16:12; 20:6). He was a loyal friend who persevered in difficult times. His treatment of Jesus' life shows evidence of a good education as well as sensitivity to the oppressed people of his time. Having highlighted Jesus' concern for the poor (Luke 4:18; 6:20), Luke would be a worthy delegate to make a collection for the poor in Jerusalem.

Most scholars think that the 'brother' of verse 18 is the same one as in verse 19. However, 'and not only' could be introducing another person, the 'travel companion' (v. 19). Whether Luke (v. 18) or someone else (v. 19), this person was voted by the churches to accompany the offering of 'grace' (v. 19).

MEDITATION

Would you consider keeping someone company
as (s)he makes an important visit?

TESTED BELIEVERS

The persons of integrity who are overseeing the gift to Jerusalem provide another reason for the Corinthians to give generously. This passage is a reminder today that we also need to choose carefully who will handle the financial giving of the church. In all this careful planning, Paul and his team are taking thought beforehand and including these persons of integrity, who are tested, enthusiastic, selected, praised people.

These brothers are recommended

Having stated that he himself and Timothy do not need letters of recommendation (3:1–2), Paul now recommends the gift overseers! Probably his reason to recommend is that the Corinthians do not know these believers, whereas Paul, Silas and Timothy were their spiritual parents. Unlike Phoebe (for whom Paul asks for help, Romans 16:2), these believers are not asking for help for themselves. Rather, in a time of banditry, especially among travellers, Paul wants the Corinthians to know that their contributions will be well guarded by reliable, godly, church-supported, enthusiastic people. Possibly also these people by their godly presence will spur the Corinthians to do their best (8:24).

Paul has told the Corinthians that he would be glad to send along with the gift whomever they approve (1 Corinthians 16:3). However, since they did donate, and the final list of people who travelled with the gift to Jerusalem included no one from the province of Achaia, they may be showing their confidence in the emissaries already chosen.

A Christian is tested

The second Christian whom Paul commends was someone who went through many difficult situations but remained 'eager' or full of ardour (v. 22). His eagerness, like Titus' (8:16–17), was directed toward the Corinthians because he had 'great confidence' in them (v. 22). Paul and Timothy were including among their delegates someone who was consistently positive. Being 'tested' is a necessary qualification for church leadership (1 Timothy 3:10). In contrast,

Paul had felt quite frustrated with Mark because he had deserted him in Pamphylia. However, Barnabas' trust in his potential was worthwhile (Acts 15:38–39) because Mark later became a crucial believer (for example, 2 Timothy 4:11). Possibly this second brother is mentioned in Acts 20:3–4 as one of those who accompanied the final offering: Sopater of Beroea, Aristarchus and Secundus of Thessalonica, Gaius of Derbe, Tychicus, Trophimus of Asia or (in Acts 19:29) Gaius of Macedonia. Here, Aristarchus and Gaius of Macedonia are called Paul's 'travel companions', the same term used in 2 Corinthians 8:19. Timothy and Silas (Silvanus) have already been mentioned by name so they are unlikely now to be called simply 'brother' (1:1, 19). If 2 Corinthians 9:3–4 indicates that the 'brothers' are not Macedonians, then the likely brother would be Gaius from Derbe or Tychicus or Trophimus from Asia. Paul describes Tychicus as a 'dear brother and a faithful minister' (Ephesians 6:21; Colossians 4:7–9). Trophimus was the Gentile who, without intending it, caused Paul to be imprisoned. Later he fell ill (Acts 21:29; 2 Timothy 4:20).

What is the goal of Paul's team in their giving? They want to glorify the Lord, express their 'goodwill' or 'eagerness' (8:11–12, 19), avoid being blamed for being overly generous (v. 20) and plan ahead what pleases the Lord and also people (v. 21). The woman who anointed Jesus at Bethany with costly ointment of nard was accused of being wasteful (Mark 14:3–4). Paul too feared that some would think they were too generous with the church in Jerusalem (v. 20). By summoning support from several churches and including several trustworthy and well-respected people, they hoped to avoid the criticism that the woman at Bethany unjustly received.

PRAYER

Lord, may I be generous, trustworthy and enthusiastic
as I handle money.

CHRIST'S GLORY IS INCARNATED

Paul began this chapter by telling the Corinthians what happens when God's grace is given (8:1). Now he concludes by repeating his earlier exhortations (8:7, 11, 24), highlighting what the Corinthians are to do (v. 24) and before whom they are to do it (v. 23).

What are they to do? The Corinthians are to prove or manifest their love by their generosity (v. 24). In other words, genuine love goes beyond feelings and promises.

Love proved before co-workers

To whom do they demonstrate their love? Paul summarizes his commendation of Titus and the two believers who are bringing the letter (v. 23). Paul describes Titus in two ways, one attribute pertaining to himself, the other to the Corinthians. 'Partners' were literally co-owners of a business, such as James, John and Simon who were partners in a fishing business (Luke 5:10). The Philippian church were financial partners with Paul's ministry (Philippians 1:5; 4:15–18). Paul did not allow the Corinthians to be his financial partners because of the misunderstanding it might cause (12:13). However, he did want them to be financial 'partners' with the church in Jerusalem (8:4, 24). Thus, Paul and Titus as 'partners' have a close working relationship, furthering the same goal.

Titus is also Paul's co-worker (colleague), but serving the Corinthians. In 1 Corinthians 16:15–16, Paul uses the term for a household of ministers, that of Stephana(s) (a Greek name which could refer to a man or a woman). Paul orders the Corinthians to 'be subject to such people and to everyone co-working and working' (my translation). These people are Paul's colleagues, ministering together with him, working side by side. Thus Paul can require that they be honoured as such, adjuring the Corinthians, 'Give recognition to such persons' (1 Corinthians 16:18). Worthy of note is that Paul does not use the gender-specific term *aner* ('male') to describe co-workers, but the generic pronoun, opening the term to all Christian persons. In Paul's pastoral team, co-working ministers were not only men like Titus and Timothy, but also women like Euodia and Syntyche who, as his 'co-workers', fought by his side in a spiritual military combat

(Philippians 4:2–3). Paul does not send Titus as a servant to the Corinthians, but neither is he their boss: he is a co-worker 'with' the Corinthians for their 'joy' (1:24; 6:1; 8:17).

Love proved before church

The Corinthians are also to demonstrate their love to the two 'brothers' who will be guarding the money (v. 23). Paul has already demonstrated how seriously he cares for Titus, his 'brother' (2:13). His care for Luke and the other worker would be no less.

Luke and this other man are 'messengers' (*apostolos*) of the churches. An *apostolos* was a 'messenger, ambassador, envoy'. Paul describes himself as 'an apostle of Christ Jesus' (1:1). An apostle of 'Jesus' was someone who had seen Jesus (1 Corinthians 9:1) and was sent out by Jesus (2 Corinthians 5:18–20). The apostles included the twelve disciples, Paul (Galatians 1:1; Acts 26:16), Barnabas (Acts 14:14), James (Galatians 1:19), Andronicus and Junia (Romans 16:7). All these people were witnesses to Jesus' resurrection (Acts 1:21–22).

Paul suggests a third recipient of the proof of their love—'the churches', literally, 'the face of the churches' (v. 24). Even as Paul had described a singular 'unveiled face' looking into a mirror (3:18), again he describes a singular face which witnesses the Corinthians acting out their love. Christians are not unconnected individuals, but part of one body, Christ's body. Therefore, when Christians are treated well, Christ's glory becomes incarnated in loving people and loving actions (v. 23).

PRAYER

How very good and pleasant it is
when kindred live together in unity!

Psalm 133:1

ZEAL *in* ACHAIA

Paul sounds as if he is re-introducing a topic which he has expounded already in chapter 8: the contribution for the Christians in Jerusalem. However, since the early Greek manuscripts included all these chapters, we can interpret these words as an explanatory apologetic. Paul has been very direct (8:24) and now he pauses and explains why he has done what he just did. He wants to tone down his previous exhortation because the Corinthians are super-sensitive.

Paul appreciates eagerness

'Flattery will get you nowhere,' we say, but where is the line between flattery and authentic, encouraging compliments? The difference lies in truth and love. In other words, harmful flattery is not truthful and it is self-serving. Paul's comments are true and they serve to advance God's purposes. Technically, for Paul to remind the Corinthians about their promised gift exceeds what is necessary (v. 1). A year earlier he had already reminded them (1 Corinthians 16:1–4). Paul repeats again that he knows they are eager to give (8:11–12; 9:2). 'Eagerness' (*prothumia*) comes from *pro* ('before') and *thumos*. The related verb *thuo* means 'to rush along, be in a heat, breathe violently'. Thus, for the Corinthians to be eager means that their feelings are at a high pitch. They are excited!

Paul has already warned them about making sure their feelings are directed not only to wanting a goal, but also to completing it (8:10–11). But now he will discuss the relationship between their feelings and receiving these emissaries who will precede Paul and the Macedonian delegates (9:3–5). Paul reminds them again that he has been boasting about them because he sees great potential in them (v. 2; 7:4, 14; 8:24). What makes this letter so complicated is that Paul is not sure the Corinthians will keep their word, and the Corinthians think Paul has not kept his word (1:17)!

Achaia has spirit

To whom is Paul writing? The introduction is addressed to both the Corinthians and the whole province of Achaia (1:1). The explanation for not visiting and the exhortation to be welcoming were addressed to Corinth (1:23; 6:11). But now Paul says Achaia was ready 'since last year' (v. 2), because the topic of financial giving is pertinent to the whole province. 'Achaia' was mentioned as early as Homer's Trojan war epic *The Iliad*. In 27BC, Augustus reorganized the empire, making Achaia a senatorial province under a proconsul who resided in Corinth. In AD15, Tiberius combined Achaia with Macedonia and Moesia, creating a vast imperial province governed by a legate based in Moesia. Claudius disbanded this arrangement in AD44, making Achaia and Macedonia again separate provinces. Thus, when Paul came to Achaia, he found Corinth once more the capital and government centre of the province, with Gallio as its proconsul (Acts 18:12).

The cities of Athens, Corinth and Cenchreae were all in Achaia, whereas Neapolis, Philippi, Amphipolis, Apollonia, Thessalonica and Beroea were in Macedonia (Acts 16:11—18:18). Modern-day Greece includes both provinces. The first people who became believers in the province of Achaia were the household of Stephana(s) (1 Corinthians 16:15–18).

Thus, Paul gives several reasons why the Achaians might think 2 Corinthians chapters 8 and 9 are excessive: Paul himself has been boasting about their year-long zeal, and their zeal has stirred up many people (v. 2). 'Zeal' (*zelos*) and 'stir up' (*erethizo*) are words which can have positive or negative connotations. *Erethizo* often means 'rouse to anger or to flight'. *Zelos* often means 'jealousy', but it can also refer to zeal or ardour (7:7, 11). Jealousy can be a godly trait when it refers to being singularly focused toward pleasing the one living God (11:2), but a demonic trait when it refers to wanting what is not ours (12:20; James 3:14). Paul uses these words in 2 Corinthians 9:2 in a positive way to indicate the ardour of the feelings of the Achaians and how their ardour has encouraged many, such as the Macedonians, to give. But the potential double meaning of these words is a reminder to us of the truth that every positive trait has its negative potential and every negative trait has its positive potential. Paul wants to encourage his readers to be spirited but to maintain that spirit to the conclusion.

MEDITATION

Consider what is the difference between zeal and jealousy
and how you can become zealous towards what is good.

WHY *the* BROTHERS ARE COMING

Paul as a wise ambassador has begun this section with positive comments about the Achaians (9:1–2). Now he explains why exactly he is sending Titus, (possibly) Luke, and one other Christian ahead before his own arrival. He has already explained why these Christians are qualified to go (8:16–23).

Be ready to give

The first two reasons are the same principle but from two perspectives, Paul's and the Achaians': the brothers will make sure the boasting by Paul's team about the Achaian giving will not be unjustified and that the Achaians are indeed ready to give (v. 3). Mutual boasting or pride is an important theme in this letter (1:14). Paul has been discussing ungodly types of boasting (for example, 5:12). To speak well of other believers who are serving God is a godly type of boasting. Paul has already mentioned his pride in the Corinthians specifically and Achaians generally several times (7:4, 14; 8:24; 9:2). 'In this case' (v. 3) indicates that Paul does not boast about the Corinthians in all matters.

Paul has already exhorted his readers to finish what they promised (8:10–11). In this internal summary he alludes to his previous comments ('as I said': literally, 'as I have been saying', v. 3). In the letters and in person, Paul has been repeating the same thing: 'be ready'. Literally, he writes, 'you had readied yourself' (v. 3). Paul describes an ongoing action, begun in the past, which the Corinthians had been doing for themselves. Now that action of saving up their gifts must come to completion.

Do not humiliate

The third and fourth reasons the brothers are coming have to do with avoiding humiliation of Paul and of the Corinthians. 'Humiliation' or 'put to shame, dishonour' (*kataischuno*) is an intensified version of 'shame' (*aischune*). 'Shame' is something one might do to others. In the New Testament, *kataischuno* often has the sense of someone being wrong because they do not have the truth. When Jesus was criticized for healing the bent-over woman on the sabbath, Jesus 'shamed' or showed his opponents to be wrong by mentioning their hypocrisy in caring for animals on the sabbath (Luke 13:17). Likewise, Christians should always have good conduct so that their accusers will be 'shamed' or shown publicly to be false (1 Peter 3:16). All believers in Christ will be vindicated in their faith (or not 'put to shame', 1 Peter 2:6). When the Corinthians rectified one of their errors, Titus was shown that Paul was accurate in his assessment of the Corinthians (7:14). Paul was 'not disgraced' or 'shamed'. Now, if the Achaians are ready with their gifts, Paul will again be shown to have had appropriate trust in them.

The fifth reason why Paul is sending these Christians ahead is to make sure the whole process of giving is a blessing (a 'voluntary gift'), not an 'extortion' (v. 5). Paul has used several different words to describe the financial gift: 'ministry' (*diakonia*), 'grace' (*charis*), 'generous gift' (*hadrotes*), 'proof (*endeixis*) of love' (8:4, 6, 7, 19, 20, 24). Now he calls it a 'blessing' (*eulogia*, v. 5). To 'eulogize', literally, is to give a good word or to celebrate with praises. 'Eulogy' describes the benediction given at mealtimes or the blessing of people (Luke 24:30, 50–51). What makes giving a blessing, not an extortion? Planning ahead. The brothers are to 'go on ahead' and 'arrange in advance' what the Achaians promised previously (v. 5). Gifts that are planned are a blessing to the giver and to the recipient as well.

PRAYER

O the depth of your riches and wisdom and knowledge, God! How unsearchable are your judgments and how inscrutable your ways! For who has known your mind, Lord? Or who has been your counsellor? Or who has given you a gift, to receive a gift in return? For from you and through you and to you are all things. To you be the glory for ever. Amen.

Paraphrase of Paul's prayer of praise in Romans 11:33–36

The PARADOX of GIVING

Today the arid hilly area around Corinth is full of fruit orchards. It is a centre for the export of currants, citrus fruits and olive oil. Strabo, the geographer, described the territory around ancient Corinth as 'rifted and rough', repeating the proverb, 'Corinth is both beetle-browed and full of hollows' (*Geography* 8:6.23). The soil is thin, with much limestone. But west of Corinth is the plain cut by the Nemean River, which Cicero described as 'the rich and fertile fields of Corinth' (*On the Agrarian Law* 1.5; 2.51). Living in a farming and commercial centre, the Corinthians well understood Paul's metaphor of harvesting.

Paul had concluded his apology for the messengers by explaining that if the Achaians planned ahead, their gift would be a 'blessing' (*eulogia*, 'voluntary gift', 9:5). Now he repeats *eulogia* ('bountifully', v. 6) to introduce another principle in the ministry of giving. If in 8:10–15 Paul describes the principle of 'fair balance' or equality, in 9:6–14 he describes the principle of generosity.

Generosity sows a harvest

Literally, verse 6 reads, 'the one sowing sparingly, sparingly also reaps, and the one sowing bountifully, bountifully also reaps'. The construction is almost a perfect parallelism, reflecting cause and effect in equal proportions. The way you act toward others rebounds to you. If the Achaians give a bountiful gift, they will be rewarded bountifully. A great gift to others, then, becomes eventually a great gift to oneself. If the Achaians give to the poor, they will not become impoverished. This principle of trade means that you will never have enough, unless you give it away. 'If you don't speculate, you won't accumulate'!

Every summer I plant a small vegetable garden behind our garage. I can never decide whether to plant the seeds right next to each other or to plant them at their final distance from the start. For instance, the broccoli seed packet instructs that I plant the seeds one inch apart and then, after the seedlings grow, transplant them to 15–24 inches apart. Nevertheless, one summer I decided to economize on the seeds and plant them 24 inches apart from the start. What happened? Some of the seeds did not grow and I ended up having broccoli plants every five yards! I sowed sparingly; sparingly I also reaped. When I sowed the seeds one inch apart, half of them died, half grew up too close to each other, but, after transplanting, I had well-spaced growing plants. I sowed bountifully; bountifully I also reaped.

The poor are generous

The same is true with giving. If we use our financial resources to help those in economic need, we will have economic and spiritual returns. Ironically, the poor rather than the rich tend to be more generous. In a 1989 survey of giving to charity in the United States, households who earned $50,000–$75,000 gave 1–2 per cent of their income, whereas households who earned less than $10,000 gave over 5 per cent of their income. Even 2000 years later, the poorer 'Macedonians', not the wealthier 'Corinthians', tend to be more generous. About the wealthy, some people say, 'you don't become rich by giving it away', but as Christians we believe 'you do become rich by giving it away', or, at least, rich enough for your needs.

What the Macedonians had learned is that when we trade with God, we are enriched. Proverbs 3:9–10 counsels, 'Honour the Lord with your substance and with the first fruits of all your produce; then your barns will be filled with plenty, and your vats will be bursting with wine'. Hoarding our money and property, as the rich fool in Luke 12 learned posthumously, is the very worst thing a believer can do. Proverbs 11:24–25 points out, 'Some give freely, yet grow all the richer; others withhold what is due and only suffer want. A generous person will be enriched, and one who gives water will get water.'

For this reason God told the Israelites in Malachi 3:10, 'Bring the full tithe into the storehouse, so that there may be food in my house, and thus put me to the test… see if I will not open the windows of heaven for you and pour down for you an overflowing blessing.' The Macedonians acted upon these truths, and from their deep poverty within testing troubles they overflowed with generosity in obedience to God and in partnership with Paul.

The Corinthians, who had a knowledge of business and the Old Testament, should all the more honour their promise to give (8:10–12).

MEDITATION

In what ways have you experienced a blessing for being generous?

How *to* Give

How should the Achaians give? Planned giving is an important way to make sure giving is voluntary. Paul has already told his readers that he does not want their donation to be 'an extortion', something they feel forced to do (9:5).

Giving is wholesome

No one can decide for another person whether and where to give. Paul spoke of the plural 'you' ('ye', KJV) to represent the province in 9:5, and now he speaks of the individual members of these churches (v. 7, 'each'). In the same way that Paul describes the individual members of one larger body to explain the interdependence of the spiritual gifts (1 Corinthians 12:12, 27), so in giving he points out that each member is responsible individually even though each is part of a larger community (the province of Achaia). To make up one's mind (*proaireo*) is not simply to decide or to choose, but to 'choose ahead' or 'choose deliberately'. His use of the perfect tense all the more emphasizes the past state of having chosen. *Proaireo* can refer to grasping, with the hand, produce from one's stores. Here metaphorically the 'store' is our own 'heart' (KJV). From the deep reservoirs of our inner being flows our choice to give. What is the opposite of this kind of wholesome, healthy giving? We might call it giving by being battered. 'Reluctantly' is giving that comes out from 'pain'. 'Compulsion' is 'force'. Giving may entail sacrifice, but heartfelt giving exercises a muscle, while forced giving wounds it. God, who created us, wants no mutilation, but rather heartfelt giving, the 'cheerful' or 'gracious' dispensing of produce (v. 7).

Why does God love a cheerful giver? A cheerful giver trusts in God (v. 8). The giver is cheerful because he or she is expecting good things to come (9:6). Some Christians might decide not to give because they are not cheerful about giving. While we should not let others force us to give, some of us need to act, to take a chance by putting our much-loved security into God's hands before we can fully trust God and experience the relief of cheerful feelings. If God does not love our way of giving, that fact does not mean we should cease giving entirely. We need to keep working on our attitudes. We can trust the God who searches our hearts to honour our intentions despite our sinful failings. Attitudes will follow actions. We act as the Christians we want ourselves to become, and we will become them.

God provides all

Verse 8 emphasizes that God is 'able'. Who or what is more trustworthy or powerful than God, the God who created and sustains the universe? What will God do? God will increase every grace. Our ability to give will increase. We need not be stingy about either the storehouses of our heart or our material cupboards because God has the power to provide 'every overflowing grace', which results in our own overflowing in four 'alls': 'so that in all (*pas*), always (*pantote*), every (*pas*) self-sufficiency having, you may overflow into every (*pas*) good work' (v. 8b, literally). Our 'self-sufficiency' or 'enough of everything' will affect place, time, quantity and need. We will overflow wherever we are and whenever we are, with whatever we have for whatever we need.

Autarkeia ('enough', v. 8) was a favourite virtue of the Stoics and Cynics. Walter Bauer's *Lexicon* notes that it was 'the state of one who supports himself without aid from others'. Paul has drawn a paradox here: the Corinthians' great self-sufficiency allows them to give more to others. Thus, God will continue to keep them self-sufficient so that they can give sufficiently to others. The interlocking relationship to God and one's neighbour is assumed. 'Enough' also implies not everything. God will cause to overflow what is 'necessary' for every good work, not necessarily everything we want. What we think we need for ourselves is often fuelled by external pressures. God wants us prepared for needs, not wants, of ourselves and of others.

So how were the Achaians to give? They were to plan ahead. Then they needed to be certain to fulfil the promises made in their plans. And finally they were to do this freely, trusting in God whose blessings fill the heart with joy.

PRAYER

To the King of the ages, immortal, invisible, the only God,
be honour and glory for ever and ever. Amen.

Paul's prayer of praise in 1 Timothy 1:17

SEED & HARVEST

What is the 'good work' (9:8) and why do it? Paul reminds his readers of the powerful apologetic for the righteous person in Psalm 112, because giving to the poor is a God-pleasing work.

The Old Testament models generosity

Psalm 112 begins, 'Happy are those who fear the Lord.' The psalmist describes righteous people's transitory happiness (vv. 2–3), effect on history (v. 6) and ability to withstand evil (vv. 7–8). They are a 'light for the upright' (v. 4), generous and just (v. 5). The 'poor' are those who work for their living, day-labourers, the 'poor' as opposed to the 'rich' (2 Corinthians 9:9), whereas the 'poverty' of the Macedonians is more aligned with that of destitute beggars (8:2). Thus, the psalmist imagines a land owner who generously pays workers. Paul implies that if the Achaians act generously they also can withstand evil (Psalm 112:8–10). Withstanding evil is a topic Paul will raise directly in the next chapter (2 Corinthians 10).

'Scatter abroad' or 'disperse' is a synonym for giving, alluding back to the imagery of sowing (9:6). The people who truly fear the Lord by dispersing their wealth to the poor maintain their own righteousness. Their righteousness will be remembered by God and by humans.

God is the source of all wealth

Paul has already told us that God is 'able' (9:8). Now he accentuates God's ability in a lengthy subject as 'the one supplying seed to the sower and bread for food' (literally, v. 10). 'Seed' and 'bread' represent the beginning and ending of harvesting. God has the power not only to cause seeds to grow (9:8), but also to give more seeds. God owns the garden centre and the supermarket! For that matter, God owns the very land and all the produce (Leviticus 25:23). The Achaians need not worry that they will have enough 'seed', for their current riches are a trifle in comparison to a generous God who is not stingy, but is continually in the process of 'supplying' seed.

Paul then describes two results of God's generosity: 'seed' and 'harvest' of 'righteousness' (v. 10). 'Seed' is material; 'righteousness' is a quality of character. God is concerned for both our material and spiritual well-being (Luke 12:28). God, the Lord of the harvest, will first give abundant supplies and then make those supplies multiply. Simultaneously, God 'increases' or 'strengthens' the 'harvest' or results of righteousness, going even beyond the psalmist whose righteousness is maintained (Psalm 112:9). God has been generous with the Achaians so that they can be generous with others. As they would see God take care of them, they would learn to rely more and more on God. And as God gave them more, they could give more.

Planting peanuts in our garden, I learned the farmer's creed: three peanuts are planted—one for God, one for the birds and one to grow. From one-third of the seed planted, many peanuts flourish. Living in thrifty New England, I was appalled to learn that I was supposed to pinch out a good number of the tiny peanut plants that I had sown so generously. Reluctant to do so, I found that none of them could grow into thriving plants while they all huddled together, competing for nourishment. In like manner, extra wealth becomes a blockage. While surplus wealth could be out enriching someone else, it becomes a burden on its keeper, dragging them down with worry for its safety, keeping the owner's eyes earthward and stunting spiritual growth. Our real fortunes are our Christian family and the God who is at its head. This God is all-powerful, the one furnishing all seed. All of us can rely on the ultimate source of all wealth.

What separates this from a theology of greediness is that, while God does return material benefits for material generosity, a lack of wealth such as the Macedonians had does not mean a lack of spirituality. As we see in the Achaians' case, presence of wealth is not a sign of spirituality. Not all wealth comes because people are generous, nor does spirituality only come from giving. Riches are not an end in themselves, for God is the great source of riches. They are provided to give an ability, and thus they create a responsibility—to give. God promises only to supply our needs, and God likes to do that through people, one to another, alternating as the giver and receiver. Abundance is worthwhile to God in this way: it has a potential to increase a giver's spiritual strength.

MEDITATION

In what ways has God supplied and multiplied your material and spiritual harvest? How can you be more generous?

RICHES RESULT *in* THANKSGIVING

In Greek, 9:10–14 is comprised of one lengthy sentence which flows from its subject, the one supplying seed to the sower and bread for food (9:10). Like an extravagant, intricate climax to a fireworks display, the ramifications of God's generosity go bursting out in all directions. Immediately, God as the source of all riches multiplies the material and spiritual aspects of the giver. How is this possible (v. 11)? And what are the ever-enlarging consequences for the church (vv. 11–12)?

Riches are for giving

Verse 11a might appear to say that because of one's generosity, one will become wealthier. Paul does earlier state that God will provide the giver with the material basis for giving (9:8) and Proverbs does indicate that if you place God as your priority in spending, you will have plenty for yourself (Proverbs 3:9–10). Rather, in 2 Corinthians 9:11, the aim or purpose of being enriched is 'for all generosity'.

'Generosity' (*haplotes*), another synonym for a gift, has already been used to describe the Macedonian giving (8:2). As Paul internally summarizes his arguments on giving in chapters 8—9, he will allude back several times to the model of the Macedonian churches (9:11–14; 8:2–4). *Haploos* had been used for the cloak without any fold versus the two-fold cloak. From this root developed the idea of singleness, simplicity, openness and open-heartedness. The Macedonians gave generously without any hidden objectives. So, too, God can empower the Achaians to give generously without hidden objectives.

Paul has discussed wealth or the abundance of external possessions in a paradoxical way in this letter. Paul's team and the Macedonian churches were each poor, and yet they were generous (6:10; 8:2). Jesus Christ was rich, but became poor in order to enrich the believers (8:9). What Paul asks of the Achaians is much less—simply that with their riches, they become generous (v. 11; 8:13–14). The Corinthians have already demonstrated that they treat what is given to them as if it had been earned (1 Corinthians 4:7–8), a danger about which Moses had warned the Hebrews (Deuteronomy 8:17–18).

Giving is for thankfulness

Generosity increases the giver's own righteousness (9:10), supplies others' needs (v. 12; 8:14) and, also, increases thanksgiving(s) to God (vv. 11–12). 'Thanksgiving' (*eucharistia*) literally is a 'good' (*eu*) 'grace' (*charis*), something which evokes good joy. One good grace is thanks. The Lord's Supper is called the 'eucharist' because Jesus 'thanked' God for the bread before he passed it around (Luke 22:19). Thanksgiving is not simply something someone does once, but it should be ever-multiplying. When believers pray for others and see God rescue them, a multitude of thanks will result (1:11; 4:15). And, as believers see God's grace work through their material gifts, many will be thankful to God (v. 12). Thanksgiving or appreciation is in effect a profession of belief in God ('confessing', 9:13). That is why Jesus asked where were the nine lepers who were healed but did not praise God. The tenth leper, who did praise God, was therefore both physically and spiritually healed: his 'faith' had saved him (Luke 17:17–19).

Paul uses both the singular and the plural for 'thanksgiving' (vv. 11–12). The singular 'thanksgiving' (v. 11) is another synonym for the gift. By the messengers bringing the gift to Jerusalem, it becomes like a thank offering to God. Among the Old Testament sacrifices was included the thank offering (Leviticus 7:11–18; 22:29–30). Part of the bread was given to the priest and the meat was eaten that same day after the formal sacrifice. The repentant King Manasseh offered sacrifices of thanksgiving on the altar during the process of restoring proper worship of the Lord (2 Chronicles 33:16). Offering thanksgiving sacrifices was a way to tell of the Lord's deeds (Psalm 107:22). Thus, when the Achaians gave to Judea, they were, in effect, thanking God for their present blessings (8:14) by sharing their material blessings with others. This 'eucharist' or thanksgiving from the givers, through the messengers, resulted in 'thanksgivings' (plural) by the receivers.

PRAYER

Praise the Lord! How good it is to sing praises to you, God;
for you are gracious, and a song of praise is fitting.

Paraphrase of Psalm 147:1

MANY REASONS *for* GIVING

Paul continues, explaining that the gift to the needy Christians in
Jerusalem overflows in thanksgivings because it also glorifies God
in several ways: by 'testing', 'obedience to the confession', by means
of 'the generosity' (v. 13) and by means of prayer (v. 14). In verses
10–13 Paul treats the gift from the giver's perspective, in verse 14
from the receiver's perspective, and then concludes with everyone's
view of God.

Giving is multi-faceted

Many words have already been used to describe the gift: giving (8:5),
'generous gift' (8:20), 'proof of your love' (8:24), 'bountiful gift'
(9:5–6), 'good work' (9:8), 'harvest' (9:10), 'thanksgiving' (9:11),
'ministry' or 'public service' (9:12). In verse 13, five more words are
used, only one of which is new: 'testing' (*dokime*, 8:2). The four
repeated words were previously used to describe the Macedonian
churches: 'ministry' (8:4, 19, 20; 9:1, 12), 'generosity' (8:2; 9:11),
'sharing' (8:4) and 'confession'.

Glorifying God is not simply done by the words we utter. As Jesus
explained, 'Not everyone who says to me, "Lord, Lord," will enter the
kingdom of heaven, but only the one who does the will of my Father
in heaven' (Matthew 7:21). The new glorious covenant (3:10–11),
because it is an internally transforming covenant (3:18), affects the
whole person. The unveiled heart (3:15) is reflected in unveiled or
'simple' direct action (v. 13). Good action (9:8) is proof (*dokime*) of
the transforming work of Christ's 'gospel' (v. 13). In effect, generosity is 'support for' confession of belief.

Giving is confession

A 'confession' is 'agreement' with and promotion of 'the gospel of
Christ' (v. 13). Normally it has to do with words, not actions. So, for
example, Paul can disparage those who 'profess to know God, but…
deny him by their actions' (Titus 1:16). Nevertheless, public verbal
profession of faith is crucial. Paul explains that belief in one's heart
that God raised Jesus from death justifies, but confession with the
lips that Jesus is Lord saves (Romans 10:9–10). Paul in 2 Corinthians

implies that if we indeed profess belief in the Messiah, then our confession is supported by our actions. Paul agrees with James: 'I by my works will show you my faith' (James 2:18). How can a donation be a confession? We give because we trust God. Giving is an act of faith. That is why God was given the first fruits in Proverbs 3:9–10. Giving is a sign of trust that God will make other fruits follow to supply our needs, and God rewards that faith.

Paul ends this chapter with his own confession, a brief doxology (v. 15). Paul repeatedly breaks out with words of thanksgiving to God (for example, 8:16; 2:14). Paul began the discussion on giving by describing the grace given to the Macedonian churches which resulted in abundant joy (*chara*, 'joy', is related to *charis*, 'grace', 8:1–2). When God gives grace (8:1), plenty of grace will be left over to return to God (v. 15). And who is the greatest example of generosity? Earlier Paul had described the generosity or grace of the Lord Jesus Christ (8:9). Human giving mirrors God's own generosity in giving the one great sacrificial gift of Jesus (v. 15). To the Corinthians, who already considered themselves rich in knowledge (8:7), Paul was demonstrating a new type of enrichment, a surpassing one (v. 14).

This is not the first time Jesus is described as a 'gift'. Jesus told the Samaritan woman that he was God's gift, a source of living water (John 4:10; Romans 5:15). *Dorea*, 'gift', can refer to a reward, wages for work done (Genesis 29:15; Exodus 21:2) or obtaining something for no cost (Numbers 11:5). In the first century, as in the Old Testament age, *dorea* could refer to the bounty of a legacy, privileges, the estate granted by a king. Further, Jesus is our inheritance, our estate, our legacy (v. 15). Being our inheritance, Jesus empowers us to generosity.

The doxology is brief (eight words) because the style reflects the content. Paul becomes almost speechless! 'Indescribable' (*anekdiegetos*) may very well be a word coined by Paul. To be 'describable' (*ekdiegeomai*) is to be narrated in detail (Acts 15:3). Paul adds the 'not' (*a*). When Paul dwells on God's 'gift', he is left without words.

MEDITATION

Review the different words for 'gift' that Paul uses in chapters 8—9. Which one(s) of them has been your most important motivation for giving? Which one would you like to explore more?

MEEKNESS & GENTLENESS

Paul ends chapter 9 with the exultant benediction: 'Thanks be to God for his indescribable gift!' He expresses praise in the third major section of his letter (6:1—9:15) because he remembers the joy of meeting Titus in Macedonia and of God's provisions for the believer. Chapters 8 and 9 are especially written to the entire province of Achaia because in Paul's review of his travels he stands at the entrance to Achaia, the province immediately south of Macedonia from where he is writing.

In 10:1, mentally he has entered into Corinth itself. Paul's mood dramatically changes as he confronts head-on the foes to whom he has alluded throughout—the opponents who have come to Corinth to undermine his whole ministry and the church that has welcomed these opponents. Paul stands now alone, without his co-workers, even as, once before, he entered Corinth alone (Acts 18:1–5). Paul describes how he and his co-workers do not act (in a worldly fashion, 10:1–18), and how they do work (11:1—12:18), and he summarizes his defence (12:19—13:11).

Paul begins by highlighting who makes the exhortation: 'I myself, Paul, appeal' (v. 1). This appeal comes not from any stranger but from the spiritual father who planted the seed of the Corinthians' new birth (12:14; 1 Corinthians 4:15). He appeals to the Corinthians; he does not command them. Paul, figuratively, stands between Christ's 'meekness' and 'gentleness' to make his appeal. 'Meekness' and 'gentleness' are two words that together emphasize one idea—humility.

Christ's meekness

'Meekness' (*prautes*), the noun, and its adjective, 'meek', occur only sixteen times in the New Testament, but wherever they occur they are significant. *Prautes* refers to both mildness and gentleness, with the adjective referring to 'mild, soft, gentle' things (such as a soft voice), persons, actions and feelings. Jesus describes himself as '*gentle* and humble in heart' (Matthew 11:29). Zechariah had prophesied that Jerusalem's king would come, gentle and riding on a donkey (Zechariah 9:9; Matthew 21:5). Mildness or 'gentleness' is one of the fruits of the Holy Spirit (Galatians 5:23). It is the way Christians should live

(Ephesians 4:2). It describes the way to restore someone 'detected in a transgression' or to correct an opponent (Galatians 6:1; 2 Timothy 2:25). Wherever it occurs, 'love' is never far away, as in 1 Corinthians 4:21 where 'love in a spirit of gentleness' is contrasted with a 'stick'.

Christ's gentleness

The second attribute of Christ, 'gentleness' (*epieikeia*), is reasonableness, fairness and equity. Contrasted at times with 'righteousness' (*dikaiosune*, 5:21), it is the opposite of the strict letter of the law. Paul uses *epieikeia* in contrast to violence and quarrelsomeness. 'Gentleness' or 'reasonableness' is a quality that an overseer should have (1 Timothy 3:3). Paul, in effect, says that his appeal is through the gentleness (*prautes*) that comes from love and the gentleness (*epieikeia*) that comes from reasonableness, all in Christ, who is gentle.

Christ's gentleness is not the outflow of a fearful spirit, but a loving spirit, God's great compassionate love. Paul has already told his readers about 'the Father of mercies and the God of all consolation' (1:3) and that their ministry comes through 'God's mercy' (4:1). He has reminded them of the grace of our Lord Jesus Christ, 'that though he was rich, yet for your sakes he became poor, so that by his poverty you might become rich' (8:9). The gifts are 'the proof' of 'love' that reaches out to others because of 'the surpassing grace' God had given them (8:24; 9:14).

Paul makes his appeal on the basis of God's compassion, Christ's gentleness—not on the basis of God's justice, because God's justice has already been met by Christ becoming 'sin' for humanity (5:21). The Corinthians have plenty of the world's critical spirit that chooses leaders who in turn criticize and subjugate. Paul appeals through the double columns of 'meekness' and 'gentleness' because he wants the Corinthians to learn about these aspects of God's nature. They did not comprehend God's compassion, gentleness and mildness, so they found Paul deficient because his aim was to be compassionate, gentle, mild—in other words, loving.

PRAYER

I thank you, Father, Lord of heaven and earth,
because you have hidden these things from the wise and
the intelligent and have revealed them to infants.

Jesus' joyful prayer, Luke 10:21

HUMBLE *but* BOLD

Who is Paul in the sight of the Corinthians? He is the one who is 'humble' when face to face with them, but 'bold' when away (v. 1)! Some people accused Paul, Timothy and Titus of living 'according to human standards', literally, 'according to the flesh walking' (v. 2). Paul had already discussed the Corinthians' complaint that his change of plans was 'fleshly' (literally, 1:17). Paul appears to them 'to be trying to frighten' with his letters. Some say, 'His letters are weighty and strong, but his bodily presence is weak, and his speech contemptible' (10:9–10).

Bold in Christ-likeness

In effect, the Corinthians were accusing Paul of being inconsistent. His personal presence contrasted with his absent style. When he was present among them, he looked to be lowly, meek and mild. But when he was absent he appeared to be 'bold' (v. 1). 'Boldness' is a theme that Paul has been discussing in this letter, explaining why he and his co-workers are indeed bold. They are 'bold' ('full of courage', 'confident'), despite their difficulties in this mortal life, because God has given them the Spirit as a down-payment for future glory (5:5–8). They have 'hope' for the Corinthians (7:16). 'Boldness' in the Bible contains a sense of hope despite difficulties, as when the midwife encouraged Rachel that, despite her difficult labour, she would have a second child (Genesis 35:17). Moses exhorted the Israelites to have hope in God's deliverance even though the Egyptians were advancing on them (Exodus 14:13). Not to be 'bold' connotes cowardliness. Thus, the Corinthians were implying that Paul was cowardly when present, but full of courage when absent. To them Paul was lowly, worldly, weak, ineffectual and unloving. His public esteem in a Gallup poll among the Corinthians at this time would have been very, very low!

Meek but not weak

Was Paul 'humble' or 'lowly' (v. 1)? *Tapeinos*, literally, means 'low', not rising far from the ground, as in low regions or low in stature. Who calls himself 'lowly'? Jesus is the one who is 'gentle' and 'humble' (*tapeinos*) in heart (Matthew 11:29), exactly as the prophesied Messiah was humbled (Isaiah 53:8). Paul describes Jesus as a model for believers because he 'humbled himself' (Philippians 2:1–11). Jesus describes the greatest person in God's reign as anyone who 'humbles himself' like a little child and welcomes such a little child in his name (Matthew 18:4–5). When Paul is accused of being too 'lowly', he proceeds to describe throughout his letter a 'lowly' leadership style, too lowly to accept a salary from the Corinthians (11:7) but lowly enough to mourn sin (12:21). Paul, again and again in this letter, takes the accusations of his critics and reinterprets their slander as compliments of appropriate and laudable behaviour for followers of the 'meek and gentle' Christ.

Nevertheless, Paul appeals, even begs (vv. 1–2) that the Corinthians do not make him turn his 'gentle' presence into a 'bold' one. Paul is certainly capable of 'daring to oppose' his adversaries. To 'dare' is to do or bear anything terrible or difficult. For example, Joseph of Arimathea went boldly to Pilate to ask for the body of a recently executed enemy of the state, Jesus (Mark 15:43). In contrast, what Moses lacked when he was standing before the burning bush was boldness (Acts 7:32). 'Boldness' has other connotations, negative ones, as in outrageous or shameless boldness—for example, when the Corinthians dared to bring other Christians to court (1 Corinthians 6:1) or when a certain Simon dared to accuse the high priest Onias of being a traitor (2 Maccabees 4:2). Did the Corinthians really want Paul to be bold? His boldness would be to reprimand them for doing evil (v. 2; 13:2–3, 10).

Paul repeats 'think' twice: 'I need (*logizomai*) not show boldness by daring to oppose those who think (*logizomai*)' (v. 2). *Logizomai* properly refers to numerical calculation, appropriate for Corinth as a business centre. Some people were doing 'calculations' about Paul's team and finding them of low value. But if Paul were to make any calculations, he would assess the entire enterprise of his opponents!

MEDITATION

Do words like 'meekness', 'gentleness' and 'humility' have positive or negative connotations for you? How can you understand them in a positive Christ-like way?

WAGING WAR *in the* FLESH

Some people accused Paul and his associates of 'acting according to human standards' (literally, 'walking according to the flesh', 10:2). Paul responds with a marvellous play on words: 'walking in the flesh not according to the flesh' (v. 3). He keeps their noun 'flesh' but introduces it with two contrasting prepositions, 'in' and 'according to'. Yes, they walk or live in the flesh. After all, Paul does not see matter as evil or unreal (see also 5:4). In addition, Paul and his co-workers have certainly had difficulties in their ministry: in other words, they live 'in the flesh'. 'Flesh' is in the first phrase a neutral word. But no, they do not fight or organize their life according to the flesh. The way they organize their ministry is not under the dominion or according to the rules of a world of sin.

Ministry may be warfare

Paul draws a sustained description of his ministry, using military terms that would appeal to the Corinthians, living as they did in the capital of a province overrun with military personnel. Paul states that 'we do not wage war' as the world does (v. 3), but then proceeds to describe how they do 'wage war' (battle or do military service). 'The weapons of our warfare', he explains, are powerful enough to destroy 'strongholds' or 'fortresses' (v. 4). These weapons are powerful because they are acceptable to and empowered by God. The 'fortresses' with which Paul has to deal are false arguments and reasonings—in other words, the false accusations against him and the false understandings of the Christian life. Another 'fortress' is the 'proud obstacle raised up against the knowledge of God' (v. 5). 'Proud obstacle', literally, is a 'height, elevation, stronghold'. As he wrote these words, Paul may have had in his mind the Acrocorinth, the fortified mountain that loomed 1,886 feet over ancient Corinth. Paul and his co-workers do wage a war, but it is a war against those people who have rejected the dominion of God. Consequently, when they are victorious, they too take 'captive' or 'carry prisoners' (v. 5), but their prisoners are thoughts that must become subject to obedience to Christ.

Warfare is not ministry

What principles can we draw from Paul's sustained metaphor? Paul and his co-workers do not fight a physical battle (v. 4). Later Paul will mention that he does not 'slap' people 'in the face' (11:20). Warfare and ministry are two things of unlike nature. Indeed, James uses warfare as a negative comparison to Christian living in his letter (James 4:1). But because the Corinthians may have had a positive view of the military, and the super-apostles themselves may have had a military-like demeanour, Paul compares Christian ministry with aspects of the military life: having 'weapons' (v. 4), offensive goals (vv. 4–5), enemies, victory, readiness to court-martial disobedient troops (v. 6).

Here Paul's enemies are not people, but false arguments, the opposing of true knowledge of God behind which people hide (vv. 4–5). Their prisoners, thus, are thoughts. 'Thoughts' (v. 5) are mental perceptions, concepts. If 'every' single mental concept is taken prisoner before the general (that is, Christ), rebellious thoughts may never become fully developed calculations, reasonings, systems of thought ('arguments', v. 4).

Paul alludes to what will become explicit at the end of the letter (13:2, 10): their 'disobedience' (or 'unwillingness to hear') will be punished, yet he wants the Corinthians themselves to participate in this 'court martial' (v. 6).

We too, therefore, should bring all our thoughts to Christ in prayer so that they can become Christ-pleasing, and we should strive, in steadfast, loving perseverance, to encourage others to abandon false arguments.

PRAYER

Holy Father, protect us in your name that you gave your Son, so that we may be one, as you are one. You have given us your word, and the world hates us because we do not belong to the world, just as Jesus did not belong to the world. Do not take us out of the world, but protect us from the evil one. Sanctify us in the truth; your word is truth. As you have sent Jesus into the world, so send us into the world.

Paraphrase of Jesus' prayer in John 17:11, 14–15, 17–18

WHY *the* LORD GIVES AUTHORITY

Paul is now using his heavy artillery. His more subtle arguments have been established, and these more overt arguments build upon them. As we readers evaluate the accusations made against Paul and his co-workers, we are filled with dismay that such an intimate relationship of spiritual parent and children should become so ruptured.

See the unseen

'Look' can be a command or a description (v. 7). 'What is before your eyes' can have positive or negative connotations. 'Look at what is before your eyes' (NRSV) means, 'Notice the obvious truth. I, Paul, am the genuine apostle of Christ.' 'You are looking only on the surface of things' (NIV) means, 'You are looking only at the superficial, worldly level.' My own preference is the NIV interpretation.

'Before your eyes', literally, is 'according to [the] face': 'the things, at a face level, you see' (v. 7). Even though the word 'face' in itself is not always negatively used by Paul in 2 Corinthians (1:11; 3:18; 4:6), to see things at a 'face level' is quite negative. To evaluate the success of one's life by 'what can be seen' is deceptive because 'what can be seen is temporary, but what cannot be seen is eternal' (4:18). People should not boast 'in outward appearance' (literally, 'in face'), but 'in the heart' (5:12). Paul's 'face to face' style had been the point of the Corinthians' complaint (10:1). And it will be the 'face' that Paul's opponents feel comfortable in striking (11:20)! Thus, after Paul's extended metaphor (10:3–6), in a brief sentence Paul reinforces his aside ('when your obedience is complete', 10:6) with a direct assault: 'You are only looking at the surface level!' (v. 7).

Now comes another complaint against Paul and his team. The first complaint was that they lived 'according to the flesh' (10:2; 1:17). The second complaint was that they were not 'of Christ' (v. 7). Possibly a third complaint was that Paul boasted about his authority (v. 8).

How twisted and malicious life can be, when those who are godly and loving are accused of being the opposite of what they are! But Paul will explain that such misconstrued challenges come ultimately from the Accuser, deceitful Satan (11:13–15). If today we are ever falsely accused, let us remember that so too were Paul and his co-workers. Nevertheless, Paul still deems to answer these complaints because Satan can stir up such hidden doubts.

Follow those who love

Even though Paul does not explicitly mention any external opponents until chapter 11, the previous difficulties he had with the Corinthians would create an environment conducive to agitation from outsiders who were opposed to his message. For example, many of the Corinthians did not regard leaders in a proper manner. Instead they pitted leaders against each other and factionalized behind them (for example, 1 Corinthians 1:10–16; 3:4–9; 4:6–7, 16–18; 11:18). Paul complained that the Corinthians imputed to their leaders the same kind of divisions that they were having with each other, for example, at the Lord's Supper. So they pitted factions following Paul against factions following Apollos against factions following Christ. Next they questioned Paul's and Barnabas' apostleship, their 'right' or 'authority' as apostles to receive hospitality, to be accompanied by spouses, to receive pay for their work (1 Corinthians 4:3–4; 9:1–6, 12, 18). Further, they were worried that Paul and Barnabas were going to depend upon them financially (1 Corinthians 9:6). Some were even questioning cardinal Christian doctrines: for example, Paul had to ask, 'How can some of you say that there is no resurrection of the dead?' (1 Corinthians 15:12). Thus, an environment of hostility and division is susceptible to outside agitation and heresy.

Authority, the power to do a thing, with its related rights, is a major topic in 1 Corinthians. But what is the purpose for having authority? Recently my son and husband demolished a wall in our garage. It took them one day and much physical force. It took over four weeks to build up the new walls, paint and decorate them. Paul insists on using his power to build up, not to pull down (v. 8; 13:10). In contrast, the Corinthians were more impressed by the flashy power that demolishes. Paul insists on the more loving edification because he follows Jesus' teachings on leadership. Followers of Christ should not imitate pagan tyranny, but rather Christ-like service (Mark 10:42–45).

MEDITATION

How can you use your power to build people up
rather than pull them down?

STRONG & WEAK

The complaints against Paul are mounting up until now, finally, we hear his opponents quoted. Of what exactly did they complain and what is Paul's initial response? His opponents contrasted the impressiveness of Paul's letters with his personal presence. Or, from a positive perspective, at least Paul's literary style was so awe-inspiring, they could not disparage it.

Strong is good

They were trying to present Paul as indecisive, inconsistent (1:17), hypocritical (v. 10). Paul's letters were frightening, causing alarm, terrifying (v. 9), but when he visited in person, Paul no longer frightened. His opponents complimented his letters, calling them 'weighty and strong' (v. 10). 'Weighty' (*barus*), literally, referred to being heavy in weight, having athletic strength and force or being heavily armed. It could refer to a powerful and dignified style. It could also be used negatively as burdensome, violent, indigestible, overbearing, infirm. In the New Testament it usually has negative connotations, such as the 'heavy', hard-to-bear burdens that the scribes and Pharisees made others carry (Matthew 23:4) or the 'violent' wolves who attacked a defenceless flock of sheep (Acts 20:29). Jesus also uses *barus* to describe the 'weightier' or more important aspects of the law—justice, mercy, faith (Matthew 23:23). 'Strong' also has to do with personal strength and power. A 'strong' literary style would be vigorous with strong syllables.

So what are they saying about Paul's letters? Are they describing the many prohibitions Paul has set down in an authoritative manner (v. 9)? Or are they describing Paul's effective and impressive writing style (v. 10)? Certainly 1 Corinthians has many difficult exhortations for the Corinthians, such as those on sexual purity (5:2), peacemaking (6:1), tolerance of different views on food (8:13), fleeing idolatry (10:14), not offending others (10:32), being united (11: 17–18), stressing prophecy over tongues (14:4), listening to one another (14:27, 31), not sinning (15:34). In addition, many biblical interpreters have complimented Paul's dynamic, profound and effective writing style. Augustine describes Paul as having 'a river of eloquence' (*On Christian Doctrine* iv. 7.20), while for Erasmus 'nothing could be lovelier or more fervent'. Paul was a well-educated man inspired by the fount of all creativity, God.

Weak is bad

However, Paul's opponents contrasted his letters to his 'bodily presence'. His physical presence was 'weak' and his words 'contemptible' (v. 10). 'Weak' usually refers to the physically ill. Thus, Paul's opponents found his bodily presence to be 'sickly', not overbearing or burdensome. In addition, they complained about his words, his 'contemptible' rhetorical style. When Herod and his soldiers mocked Jesus by putting an elegant robe on him, laughingly calling him 'king', they treated him with 'contempt' (Luke 23:11). Thus, Paul's opponents thought that Paul's speech was worthy of mockery, inferior, to be rejected.

On the other hand, Paul's opponents thought that they had a 'weighty and strong' bodily presence and enviable speech (v. 10; 11:20). But what did they miss? Like the scribes and Pharisees, they forgot the weightier matters of Christ's way. At the same time, Jesus' yoke is easy to carry and his burden is light (Matthew 11:30). God chose the low and 'despised' through whom to work and confound the worldly wise (1 Corinthians 1:28). Even though Paul was well-educated (he was probably taught rhetoric as well as Torah), he chose not to use 'lofty words or wisdom' or 'plausible words of wisdom', but rather to preach 'Jesus Christ, and him crucified' (1 Corinthians 2:1–4). Thus, Paul, unlike his opponents, is not concerned so much with overbearing bodily presence as with word and action. What Paul wants the Corinthians to 'understand' or 'calculate' (10:11, 2) is that all his team's words are consistent with their actions.

PRAYER

O Lord, I have heard of your renown, and I stand in awe, O Lord,
of your work. In our time revive it; in our own time make it
known; in wrath may you remember mercy.

Habakkuk's prayer, 3:2

75

MEASURING *by* GOD'S CANON

In chapters 10—13 Paul entreats the Corinthians to change so that
he will not have to discipline those people who suspect his team of
acting in a worldly fashion. Paul explains that his team's warfare is not
like worldly warfare (10:1-6) and that the accusations made against
him are untrue (10:7-11). He then argues that any boasting he does
is not an untrue boasting in someone else's work (vv. 12-18).

Some measure themselves

Paul has alluded to 'such people' (10:11) and 'those' (10:2) earlier
and now he begins his more extended description of what these
opponents are like and how their values contrast with his values.
Paul has used indefinite pronouns such as these to refer indirectly to
those who oppose him: 'if anyone has caused pain' (2:5); 'some'
need 'letters of recommendation' (3:1); 'if anyone is in Christ' (5:17);
'we intend that no one should blame us' (8:20); 'those who think we
are acting according to human standards' (10:2); 'if anyone is confident that he belongs to Christ' (10:7, NIV). These indefinite pronouns will increase in use: 'let no one think that I am a fool' (11:16);
'when someone makes slaves of you' (11:20); 'no one may think
better of me' (12:6). When 'such boasters' are called 'false apostles,
deceitful workers' (11:13), then what is implicit has finally become
explicit.

God measures

Paul now uses a consistent imagery from the world of commerce and
government—measurement. When anything is measured, it needs
some standard by which to judge. Originally, *canon* (vv. 13, 15-16,
'field', 'sphere of action') came from the Semitic word signifying
'reed' or 'straight like reeds'. A *canon*, literally, was a straight rod or
bar that kept something straight. It could refer to staves that preserved the shape of a shield, a weaver's rod to which alternate threads
of the warp were attached, a line used by masons or carpenters, a
ruler, curtain-rod and bedposts. In art, it was a standard or model; in
grammar, a general rule; in history, a table of dates; in geography, a
boundary. Before placing tiles on a floor, today, homeowners make a

chalk line at which the first line of tiles is placed. Consecutive tiles are then placed to the right or left of that first set of tiles. Thus, that chalk line would be a *canon*. In the same way, the Bible is a *canon* or standard by which believers evaluate their own lives.

Even as one tile by itself cannot be a measure by which to determine the correct position of another tile, Paul says that people cannot measure themselves by looking at one another. They must use 'the measure of the standard (*canon*) with which the God of measure measured out' (literally, v. 13). God's standard for measure is what matters. Therefore, to seek to be approved or included by those humans who commend themselves is of no use at all. Paul, of course, alludes to such self-commendation in chapter 3. In chapter 10 he uses the extended metaphor of measuring space as a springboard to discuss some people who were trying to receive credit for work done by others (vv. 15–16). In contrast, three times Paul repeats that his team does not boast 'beyond limits' (vv. 13, 15–16).

One of the unseemly undersides of some churches is the practice of winning Christians to their congregation away from another church or taking for their own credit what was done by someone else. Once I attended an interchurch service where parishioners boasted about the greatness of their particular pastor by saying how many other church buildings they had to pass in order to reach their specific church: 'I passed 15 churches to get here!' 'That is nothing! I passed 40 churches on my way.' They measured their pastor in comparison to other pastors, rather than seeing all the churches as colleagues in the same battle. How that must grieve the Lord when Christ's body is set at odds with itself!

What is the antidote to such ungodly behaviour? To follow Paul who has hope that as people's 'faith increases', then every minister's 'sphere of action... may be greatly enlarged' (v. 15). Lack of faith is the problem. If we all trust God more, instead of stealing those already growing in Christ, we can all together reach out to spread the good news among those who are not yet growing in Christian community (vv. 13, 16).

PRAYER

Teacher, I believe; help my unbelief!

Mark 9:17, 24

BOASTING & COMMENDATION

Paul has been discussing the wrong type of boasting—taking credit for work done by others (10:16). Now he tells us of the proper sphere of boasting in the Lord (v. 17). If people seek to satisfy God's standard of measure in their work (10:13), then indeed they can be sure they will be declared 'approved' by the Lord (v. 18).

Boast in the Lord

'Boasting' is an important theme for Paul in his correspondence to the Corinthians. Seventy per cent of the uses of the verb occur in 1 and 2 Corinthians (54 per cent in 2 Corinthians, 20 out of 37 New Testament references). The concept to which Paul alludes is contained in Deuteronomy. Moses warns the Hebrews that when they settle in their new land and eat their fill and build fine houses, and their herds and flocks multiply, and silver and gold multiply, and all they have is multiplied, they must not exalt themselves, forgetting all the Lord their God did for them in leading them out of Egypt, out of slavery, and through the desert while giving them water and food: 'Do not say to yourself, "My power and the might of my own hand have gotten me this wealth." But remember the Lord your God, for it is he who gives you power to get wealth' (Deuteronomy 8:11–18a).

For a few years I ministered as an instructor in 'English as a Second Language' among Hispanic inmates at a maximum security prison. In one way, that ministry was easier than ministry among those not incarcerated—most inmates readily agreed they were sinners. Many readily agreed they needed God's help. But the moment they heard they were to be paroled, their ears closed. Now they thought they could handle matters themselves by their own power and might.

The central truth of Deuteronomy 8 is alluded to in a prayer by Hannah (1 Samuel 2:1–10) and repeated by the Lord to Jeremiah for the Jews who would soon be in exile: 'Do not let the wise boast in their wisdom, do not let the mighty boast in their might, do not let the wealthy boast in their wealth; but let those who boast boast in this, that they understand and know me, that I am the Lord; I act with steadfast love, justice, and righteousness in the earth, for in these things I delight, says the Lord' (Jeremiah 9:23–24).

Wisdom, strength and wealth provide three different types of human success—the mental, physical and material. From Deuteronomy we learn that all such success comes ultimately from God. From Jeremiah we learn that no type of success can compare with knowing God. 1 Corinthians, like Hannah's prayer in 1 Samuel, highlights that God chooses those who are not humanly successful, those lacking wisdom, strength and wealth, to remind us that God is the source of everything good (1 Corinthians 1:27–31).

Boast in others

But if Paul exhorts his listeners to boast in the Lord (v. 17), why then should he want the Corinthians to boast about Paul and his co-workers and why has he been boasting about the Corinthians to others (5:12; 7:4, 14; 9:2)? In Greek, the word for boasting has negative connotations such as 'speak loud, boast, vaunt oneself'. We all should celebrate and praise, but who or what? For believers to praise one another is God-pleasing: 'If one member is honoured, all rejoice together' (1 Corinthians 12:26b). For people to praise the source of their blessings is God-pleasing: 'Save us, O God of our salvation... that we may... glory in your praise' (1 Chronicles 16:35). But to praise ourselves or someone else for what is not our own or theirs (10:13, 16; 11:12) is a type of blasphemy. In idolatry, God is not given credit for what comes from God (Romans 1:20–23).

2 Corinthians 10:18 is a practical verse by which to guide daily actions and long-range plans. Does my action please God? When I bow before the Lord at judgment, will God say, 'I am well pleased with you. Stand up and be crowned'? Will the Lord commend us? We, on the other hand, find ourselves tending to submit to the pressures of humans who commend others, using these as a standard. Paul is certainly not against following the model of devout believers (1 Corinthians 4:16–17), but the follower must always remember that other humans are models only insofar as they follow God's standards.

MEDITATION

*Think of examples of how you could boast in positive
rather than negative ways.*

PURE BETROTHED LOVE

Although Paul has described something of the manner in which he and his co-workers work in chapter 10 (waging war for their ruler-God and measuring by God's standard), his strategy has been to explain how they do not work (waging war as the world does, inconsistency between words in presence and in absence, and measuring oneself by human standards). The 'foolishness' Paul introduces in chapter 11 is his need to defend his ministry more directly. The Corinthians would not 'bear' with Paul's defence (v. 1), but they would 'bear' with false teachers' boasting (11:4, 19–20).

Paul is matchmaker

For a dearly beloved family member to defend his foundational principles is indeed foolishness. Nevertheless, the Corinthians have forced Paul to do so. Accordingly, he uses the analogy of a father and daughter. As a father would arrange a marriage and give away the daughter to the groom, similarly Paul, as the person who introduced the Corinthians to Jesus the Messiah, is a spiritual parent. 'I feel a divine jealousy for you' (v. 2) aptly describes not only his earnest concern for the Corinthians but also his zeal for everything he did in life. When he did not believe in the Messiah, he zealously persecuted Christians. When he did believe in the Messiah, he zealously served Christians. Paul, as any loving father, has concern for the well-being of his daughter, God's people. Paul 'promised... in marriage' the Corinthians as a pure virgin to 'one husband', Christ. Many ancient engagements required a year of preparation in which both the bride and groom would save their funds for the forthcoming marriage. Revelation 19:7–9 uses similar imagery when teaching about a forthcoming marriage supper of the Lamb.

The serpent encourages infidelity

Paul explicitly confronts the Corinthians at this time. Consistent with his imagery, he compares the Corinthians with Eve who was 'deceived' by the serpent's 'cunning' (v. 3; Genesis 3:1). The 'cunning' serpent's conversation with Eve is an archetypal example of being misled by deception (as opposed to committing sin by knowledge).

Paul is afraid that the Corinthians 'might be led astray' (literally) from their 'sincere and pure devotion to Christ'. Paul uses the subjunctive form of the verb ('might be led astray') to indicate that the Corinthians have not yet completely disobeyed God as Eve eventually did. They stand like Eve, admiring the tree of the knowledge of good and evil (Genesis 3:6). Knowledge has always been a temptation to the Corinthians. Paul was also to use the analogy of Eve to the Ephesians, who also desired to be great 'teachers of the law' (1 Timothy 1:7). They were also being misled by false knowledge from false teachers. At Corinth, the whole church was affected. At Ephesus, ignorant women were especially susceptible (1 Timothy 2:12–14).

The sexual purity that God requires of the bride and groom would be analogous to the spiritual purity of believers. Paul had earlier described the behaviour of himself and his co-workers toward the Corinthians as one of 'holiness and sincerity' (1:12) because their motives were pure. The churches of Macedonia also were sincere and open-hearted ('generous', 8:2). But were the Corinthians similarly 'sincere' and pure'? Was their repentance complete?

PRAYER

Your law, Lord, is perfect, reviving the soul; your decrees, Lord, are sure, making wise the simple; your precepts, Lord, are right, rejoicing the heart; your commandment, Lord, is clear, enlightening the eyes; your fear, Lord, is pure, enduring forever; your ordinances, Lord, are true and righteous altogether. More to be desired are they than gold, even much fine gold; sweeter also than honey, and drippings of the honeycomb. Moreover by them am I, your servant, warned; in keeping them I have great reward. But how can I detect my errors? Clear me from hidden faults, O Lord, my rock and my redeemer.

Paraphrase of David's Psalm 19:7–12, 14

PAUL'S OPPONENTS

Would a sincere and pure fiancée become devoted to another man? Paul believes that the Corinthians, although they might not 'bear with' Paul's defence, certainly seem to 'bear with' people who proclaim 'another Jesus than the one [Paul and his co-workers] proclaimed', receiving 'a different spirit from the one [the Corinthians] received', and accepting 'a different gospel from the one [they] accepted' (11:1, 4). To whom does Paul refer? He refers to the false teachers he calls the 'super-apostles', (v. 5), the 'beyond-measure-apostles'. They masquerade as apostles of Christ, but in reality, they are servants of Satan (11:13–15).

Who are these people who think Paul, Timothy and his other co-workers live by 'human standards' (10:2)? Next to the number of letters contained in 2 Corinthians, interpreters disagree most about the type of opponents Paul combated in Corinth and their relationship to opponents in other places. These opponents claimed they were better apostles than Paul.

Evidence from 2 Corinthians

Paul does not explicitly state the heretical teachings of the 'super-apostles'. We can gather that they emphasized their Jewish background (11:18, 22), but did not emphasize sharing Christ's sufferings (11:23–33; 13:4). Claiming to be followers of Christ, in reality they were deceitful (11:4, 13–15, 23). They were characterized by their haughty consideration of themselves as being better apostles than Paul was. They had impressive appearances and wielded authority in an autocratic style (11:20). They spoke skilfully and probably boasted of special revelations from God. They took money from believers (11:12), ensuring a more comfortable lifestyle than that of Paul and his co-workers.

Summoning up such explicit identification suggests that other vaguer references in the epistle also apply to the false apostles. They probably are the peddlers of God's word, retailing the gospel like merchants, provisioning the saints with spiritual food like tavern keepers (2:17). These are the ones who bear letters of recommendation (3:1), who falsify God's word, using trickery and cunning (4:2).

Priding themselves in appearances (5:12, 16; 10:12), they boast in another's labour (10:15–16; 11:12). Probably they were some kind of legalists (10:5; 3:3, 7, 17).

Evidence from other letters

We can compare these opponents in 2 Corinthians with those in Acts, Philippians 3:2–11, Galatians and Romans 16:17–20. Acts seems to indicate a persistent Jewish movement within the Christian Church to set Paul's and Peter's understandings of the gospel against each other (compare Galatians 2:12). In Acts 11:1–3 a group from Jerusalem, called the circumcision party, criticized Peter for eating and fraternizing with Gentiles. They were silenced when they heard of Peter's experience in Joppa (Acts 11:4–18). Again, we see the same concerns voiced in the region of Judea and within Jerusalem (Acts 15:1–5). Further, the Jerusalem council's decision to free believers from most of the legal regulations applied only to Gentiles (Acts 15:23). When Paul returned to Jerusalem before his imprisonment, James and the elders told him that thousands of Jews who had become Christians were still zealous for the law and wanted their children circumcised (Acts 21:20–26).

Clearly there was a movement of Jewish Christians actively antagonistic to Paul's message and methods. Whether they followed Paul from city to city (as hostile Jews from Antioch and Iconium did in Acts 14:19) is speculative. There are many similarities between Paul's opponents at Corinth, Philippi, Galatia and those referred to in Romans. All were Jewish Christians who accentuated their Hebrew heritage: they had confidence in their earthly status, they did not emphasize the need to share Christ's sufferings, and Paul considered them to be evil and deceitful.

In Corinth these believers accentuated dissensions, preaching and living out another gospel, tampering with God's word. Were these the smooth-talking flatterers who caused divisions, deceiving with contrary teaching and serving their own appetites in Romans 16:17–18? If so, they were potently effective, for even Barnabas under pressure weakened and joined Peter, according to Galatians 2:13. Theirs was a renewed bondage (Galatians 2:4; 5:1).

MEDITATION

Paul fought pagans and Judaizing believers to protect the Corinthians. Do similar false teachers threaten the Church today?

UNTRAINED *in* SPEECH

Paul is 'in no way' inferior to the 'super-apostles' (11:5). He does not actually say he is 'untrained in speech' (v. 6). Rather, he has chosen not to use persuasive words (1 Corinthians 2:1–5).

Not all training builds up

Literally, Paul says 'but if even untrained in speech' (v. 6). He uses the conditional 'if', stating it as if it were fact. The conditional phrase relates to the main phrase. Even if Paul were untrained in oratory, he was still trained in knowledge. From this one clause we cannot tell if Paul had been 'trained in speech' or not. 'Untrained' (*idiotes*) referred to people without professional knowledge or skill. It could also simply refer to a private individual as opposed to one holding public office. An *idiotes* was the common or average person. At its worst it degenerated to mean 'ignoramus'. Paul uses *idiotes* for the common person ('outsider') visiting the church, who does not understand speaking in tongues and therefore cannot learn from the service (1 Corinthians 14:16, 23). The religious leaders marvelled that fishermen like Peter and John could be so bold, at ease speaking publicly, even though they were 'not trained' (Acts 4:13).

The ancient Jews had three levels of education—elementary, *mishnah* and *talmud*. The elementary (approximately 5–12 years of age) focused on basic reading, writing, maths, Hebrew and study of the Old Testament. The *mishnah* stage focused on oral repetition of scripture and interpretation. The *talmud* stage (age 15 and above), or higher education, focused on interpretation and study of the teachings. Peter and John would not have had the *talmud* level of education, but all Jewish males were required to have the elementary level. Paul had all three levels of education. Some rabbis even taught their advanced students Greco-Roman rhetoric. Paul's writing style shows remarkable use of the Greek language, but he has not agreed with his critics' accusations that he cannot do personally what he does in writing (10:11). Rather, Paul has clearly told the Corinthians that he will not win them over to the gospel by charming them with his speech (1 Corinthians 2:1–5). He will not present the gospel in the form of a professional orator or sophist, unlike the super-apostles who built their message on this type of oratory.

Oratory puffs up

Oratory was one of the most popular forms of entertainment, rivalling the theatre. In contrast to philosophic rhetoric, which sought to discover truth, sophistry used artificial rhythms, exotic words, novel figures of speech, and quotable sentences, accompanied by music, to attract wealthy students. Dionysius of Halicarnassus tells us that these rhetoricians/sophists, whose focus was not philosophy but the art of persuasion, appeared in his generation (30–8BC). As he saw it, 'another Rhetoric stole in and took' the place of the old philosophic Rhetoric:

> *Intolerably shameless and histrionic, ill-bred and without a vestige either of philosophy or of any other aspect of liberal education. Deceiving the mob and exploiting its ignorance, it not only came to enjoy greater wealth, luxury and splendour than the other, but actually made itself the key to civic honours and high office. (*The Ancient Orators *1)*

Philo describes 'sophists' as experts in 'decoying, charming, and bewitching' their hearers using a 'most meagre admixture of truth' with 'large portions of false, probable, plausible, conjectural matter' (*On Dreams*, I.XXXVIII.220). City after city was being won over by these orators and the whole world was honouring them for their 'hair-splitting' and 'clever inventiveness' (*On Husbandry*, XXXII.143).

Paul, instead of being deceptive, bewitching or incomprehensible in his oratory, openly and publicly communicated his own wealth of knowledge of God to the Corinthians (v. 6; 4:6; 10:5).

PRAYER

Lord, help me to explain what I know about you to others,
by elevating you, not simply charming my listener; being
informative, not simply entertaining; clear, not incomprehensible;
true, not deceptive; open, not secretive; illuminating,
not exploiting ignorance; commended by you,
not simply seeking my own wealth or status.

SALARY *as* MINISTRY

The reader now understands that the Corinthian charge that Paul is 'lowly' ('humble', 10:1) means that Paul is too 'lowly' to charge the Corinthians for his ministry (v. 7). However, Paul used money as a means to advance people's spiritual growth.

Why Paul did not accept support

In a passionate defence, in 1 Corinthians 9:1–18, Paul pointed out that he and Barnabas, like Peter, the Lord's brothers, and the other apostles, had the right to be paid for their teaching. Paul saw nothing inherently wrong in being paid for preaching. He took up his trade of tentmaking whenever he wanted to impress a point on a congregation. For example, he did not accept any money from the Corinthians because they appeared to be afraid that Paul and Barnabas were out to take advantage of them (1 Corinthians 9:6; 2 Corinthians 12:13–18). Furthermore, the false apostles had confused the Corinthians, convincing them that one of the criteria of true apostleship was receiving money. Ironically, then, when the false apostles were taking financial advantage of the church, they were by their standards proving their apostleship (2:17; 11:12).

The Corinthians both feared being taken advantage of financially and desired to pay in order to prove the recipient's worth. Since their view of money was so completely warped, Paul did not want to allow them to support him financially. Such a move would have confirmed the false apostles' claims and undermined what Paul was trying to teach the Corinthians. As Acts 18:5 suggests, Paul stopped working as a tentmaker in Corinth only when Timothy and Silas arrived from Macedonia.

Interestingly, Paul did not allow the Thessalonians to support him financially either, but for different reasons. For their edification, he, Timothy and Silas worked among them in order to show that a person does well to work with his hands. So in 1 Thessalonians 5:14 he writes, 'And we urge you, beloved, to admonish the idlers' and 'aspire to live quietly, to mind your own affairs, and to work with your hands... so that you may... be dependent on no one' (1 Thessalonians 4:11–12). Thus, in 2 Thessalonians he can command them to 'keep away from believers who are living in idleness' because 'we were not idle when we were with you, and we did not eat anyone's bread without paying for it; but with toil and labour we worked night and day, so that we might not burden any of you. This was not because we do not have that right, but in order to give you an example to imitate' (2 Thessalonians 3:6–10).

Why Paul did accept support

Therefore, to be allowed to contribute financially to Paul and his ministry was a privilege. As far as the Bible tells us, the Philippians were the only church consistently allowed by Paul to help him financially (Philippians 4:15). What does that tell us about the Philippians? They had a healthy view of money. They did not hesitate to work. When they contributed to a person's ministry, they did not feel enslaved by that giving, nor did they feel that when they paid a church worker, they were being exploited. And, conversely, they did not believe that financial remuneration proved a person's worth or authenticity, as happens sometimes when people are valued by how much salary they get.

The Philippians had suffered as Paul had and they had grown to a position of equality with him, partnered with him in a way no other congregation was. As 2 Corinthians 8:1–2 indicates, the churches of Macedonia had suffered a severe affliction at least five years earlier and were now in extreme poverty. Nevertheless, not only did the Philippians give, but they were very generous, while the Corinthians in contrast had financial abundance (8:14) and were hesitant. Of course, not everyone at Philippi was necessarily poor. Lydia of Thyatira, who had insisted on housing Paul and Silas when they were in Philippi about ten years earlier (Acts 16:15, 40), was probably well-to-do as a dealer in purple cloth. Probably Lydia was a generous contributor toward Paul's support, but as a group the Philippians were poor, even if individuals among them were wealthy. But whether poor or rich, the Philippians were generous. They had a proper attitude toward money, an attitude Paul longed for the Corinthians to emulate.

MEDITATION

What do you need to improve to have a proper attitude toward financially supporting others?

PAUL ATTACKS *the* SUPER-APOSTLES

Apparently Paul's opponents received money and led a more comfortable life than he and his co-workers led, for after Paul has refuted the charges that he has been a financial burden on the Corinthians (11:7–11), he concludes that he wants to remove the basis of the claim of those who contend that they work on the same terms on which he and Timothy work (v. 12). The Jewish philosopher Philo has well described a teacher who puts on airs and financially exploits the student, a description that fits the super-apostles:

> *Often on the other hand some teacher of the lower subjects, who has chanced to have a gifted pupil, boasts of his own teaching power, and supposes that his pupil's high attainments are due to him alone. So he stands on tiptoe, puffs himself out, perks up his neck and raises high his eyebrows, and in fact is filled with vanity, and demands huge fees from those who wish to attend his courses; but when he sees that their thirst for education is combined with poverty, he turns his back on them as though there were some treasures of wisdom which he alone has discovered.* (Preliminary Studies *XXIII*: 127–28)

Such false teachers were the super-apostles, full of vanity, disparaging loyalty, humility and other virtues, manipulating the Corinthians for financial gain.

Trees are felled

Paul in 11:13–15 is finally completely direct. The subtlety he has been using is finally transformed into forthrightness. Here is Paul's goal: to cut away the very foundation of his opponents' base of operations. The phrase 'deny an opportunity' (v. 12), although giving the general sense of Paul's original Greek words, does not communicate the intensity of those words. He states that he will continue refusing to accept financial support from the Corinthians (11:8–9), literally, 'in order that I might cut off (*ekkopto*) the base of operations (*aphorme*) of those wanting a base of operations' (v. 12). To 'deny' or 'cut off' is a strong verb. The root *kopto* means to 'cut', 'strike', 'smite'. The prefix *ek* intensifies the verb, resulting in 'to cut out of' or 'to cut from within'. For example, if *kopto* means to 'chop off' trees, *ekkopto* means to 'lay waste' the whole forest. Jesus uses *ekkopto* when referring to false prophets. False prophets, like these false apostles, come in sheep's clothing, but inwardly they are ravenous wolves. How will people recognize them? By their 'fruits', the qualities of their lives, the results of their speech and actions. Fruit-bearing trees that do not bear fruits are better 'cut down' (*ekkopto*), thrown into a fire for heat (Matthew 7:15–19). Paul, too, wants to cut down completely not the super-apostles *per se* but their 'base of operations'.

Wars are fought

'An opportunity' (*aphorme*) is the starting point of a war, its base of operations. It is a banker's resources or capital. Earlier Paul had been trying to give the Corinthians the reason or resources for them to boast about Paul and his team (5:12). Used in a negative sense, personified 'sin' seizes as its 'base of operations' the commandment against coveting to produce covetousness (Romans 7:8); or younger widows, unhappy with their decision not to marry, give Satan a 'base of operations' (1 Timothy 5:14); and freedom should not become a 'base of operations' for self-indulgence (Galatians 5:13). Thus, Paul wants to attack the very basic philosophy of his opponents.

Paul's opponents wanted to be seen as the equals of him and his team. They particularly gloried in 'the dignity of being Apostolic missionaries', but, as Alfred Plummer explains, 'They saw plainly that in this particular they were at a disadvantage as compared with St Paul.... they were a burden to the Corinthians' and Paul was not. Apostles did have the right to financial support (1 Corinthians 9:4–12), but the real reason that these super-apostles asked for financial support was because they were in reality 'false apostles' and 'deceitful workers' (v. 13).

PRAYER

Hear a just cause, O Lord; attend to my cry; give ear to my prayer from lips free of deceit. From you let my vindication come; let your eyes see the right.

Psalm 17:1–2

The FALSE ANGEL of LIGHT

When I was in seminary in the early 1970s, hardly anyone in the United States believed any longer in the existence of Satan as a personal spiritual presence. Some theologians assumed that the belief in Satan was part of a premodern, primitive society. However, when the movie and book *The Exorcist* came out in 1971, many ordinary people showed eagerness to relearn about supernatural evil.

Who is Satan?

'Satan' is a transliteration of the Hebrew, an 'adversary, opponent, accuser, enemy'. Revelation 12:9 summarizes many of his names: 'The great dragon was thrown down, that ancient serpent, who is called the Devil and Satan, the deceiver of the whole world'. Each name highlights a different aspect of Satan's character. 'Satan' is the one who opposes humans and God in purpose and action. 'Dragon' and 'serpent' allude to Genesis 3:1, being described as the most 'crafty' of all animals. Abilities which could have been used for good were instead used for evil. 'Devil' is the false accuser, even as 'adversary' (1 Peter 5:8) is the opponent in a legal suit.

'Tempter' is the one who always tests, in order to encourage evil. 'Beliar' (6:15) signifies 'lord of the wilderness' (*Beliar*) or 'worthlessness' (*Belial*), with whom Christians cannot become partners. 'Beelzebul' is 'lord of dung or filth', alluding to idolatry (Matthew 10:25). The 'god' or 'prince of this world' (4:4; John 12:31) highlights Satan's temporal power. Satan is a 'god' that detracts worship away from the one living God (Matthew 4:3–10).

'Deceiver' and liar (John 8:44) are aspects of Satan's character which Paul highlights in 2 Corinthians. Satan has the power to keep unbelievers from seeing Christ's glory (4:4).

What is transformation?

In verses 13–15 Paul brings out Satan's ability to deceive, transforming himself into an attractive outward form but having ugly evil inside. Transformation in itself is not evil. At the resurrection, Jesus will transform believers' lowly bodies into glorious ones (Philippians 3:21). What makes Satan's transformation wrong is its lie. Satan is not an angel of light. Satan's servants are neither servants of righteousness nor apostles of Christ (11:13–15). As Jesus explained, Satan 'was a murderer from the beginning... When he lies, he speaks according to his own nature, for he is a liar and the father of lies' (John 8:44). When Satan deceived Eve and Adam into eating the forbidden fruit, he promised they would not die (Genesis 3:4). Since they did die, Satan is a murderer, and still continues to entice people to physical and mental illness and death (Luke 13:16) in the guise of giving them what looks attractive. Sometimes the outward form reflects what is real (Philippians 2:7) and sometimes it does not. Paul has already warned the Corinthians to look at the eternal, the 'unseen', not the temporary, the 'seen' (4:18). Here is one reason: only if people are focusing on God's eternal qualities will they not be misled by the illusion of the transitory.

And how are these super-apostles misleading people? Their beliefs stress their 'outward' credentials (5:12), their Jewishness (11:22). Further, they are deriding Christians like Paul who remind the listeners of the 'crucified Messiah' (1 Corinthians 2:2)—God's anointed one, to whom victory came, but by way of suffering in the crucifixion. To deride suffering and humility for Christ's sake is to promote Satan's purposes. When Peter rebuked Jesus for planning to suffer in Jerusalem, Jesus challenged Peter, 'Get behind me, Satan! You are a stumbling block to me; for you are setting your mind not on divine things but on human things' (Matthew 16:23).

The philosopher Simone Weil writes that one of the most difficult aspects of writing fiction is portraying good and evil for what they are truly: 'Nothing is so beautiful and wonderful, nothing is so continually fresh and surprising, so full of sweet and perpetual ecstasy, as the good. No desert is so dreary, monotonous, and boring as evil. This is the truth about authentic good and evil' ('Morality and Literature'). One deception of Satan is that victory and success lie with the Evil One. However, not only do followers of Christ have authority over Satan (Luke 10:17–19), but also Satan will be judged along with everyone else (v. 15; 5:10).

PRAYER

God, who shines in the darkness, help me to see your eternal qualities shine through the world and let me not be deceived by Satan's transformations.

PAUL'S IRONIC BOASTING

When Søren Kierkegaard writes to the religious but insincere church of Denmark of his time, he uses primarily indirect communication. To him, direct communication 'presupposes that the receiver's ability to receive is undisturbed':

> For there is an immense difference, a dialectical difference between these two cases: the case of a man who is ignorant and is to have a piece of knowledge imparted to him, so that he is like an empty vessel which is to be filled or a blank sheet of paper upon which something is to be written; and the case of a man who is under an illusion and must first be delivered from that.
>
> (The Point of View for My Work as an Author)

Paul has been writing to people 'under an illusion', and in chapter 11 he intensifies the dramatic irony of his words to try to break through the Corinthians' illusion—their admiration for false apostles. The meaning Paul intends to communicate conflicts purposely with the language and tone he uses. He wants to bring out the incongruities that occur between the reality and the appearances of the behaviour of the Corinthians. He also uses verbal irony many times. 'Irony' comes from the Greek *eironeia*, ignorance purposely affected to provoke or confound an antagonist. 'Super-apostle' is irony. Paul intends to communicate the opposite—'inferior-apostle' (11:5). In verse 18 Paul alludes back to his opponents who were falsely boasting (11:12). Paul's 'boasting' and 'foolish' words are irony .

The wise fool and the foolish wise

The Corinthians consider themselves wise (v. 19; 1 Corinthians 4:10); however, in Paul's estimation, they are misled. Paul asks the Corinthians to receive him as a 'fool' so that (as a fool and before fools) he, too, may have an opportunity to boast. What Paul is really saying is that only fools boast and that the Corinthians only listen to fools who boast a lot (11:1, 19). Therefore, Paul claims that he must pretend to be foolish and boastful to be heard by them (v. 16). But Paul will not boast 'according to the flesh' (1:17; 10:2–3; 11:18). In fact, he does not really boast at all. The Corinthians are foolish to desire false leaders and to believe that Paul is the unwise person.

Paul boasts by not boasting

Paul sets up a comparison between two types of boasting—boasting 'the way the world does' and ironic boasting (boasting that shows that God must be at work in one's life). Many Bible students misinterpret Paul's boasting as pride in all the difficulties he suffered. However, Paul intends the very opposite. No one at Corinth, and especially not the super-apostles, would be impressed by suffering.

Paul's perspective has been clarified to me even more by studying Jeremiah 9:23–24, which is quoted by Paul in 1 Corinthians 1:31 and 2 Corinthians 10:17. If God has told the wise, strong and rich that only boasting in their knowledge of the Lord is worthwhile, then Paul, in contrast, has described to the Corinthians the foolish, weak and poor. Paul had told the Corinthians that God chose the foolish, weak, lowly and despised so that no one might boast in God's presence (1 Corinthians 1:27–31). Paul also has used each of these concepts in 2 Corinthians: 'Let no one think that I am a fool, but if you do, then accept me as a fool' (v. 16); 'If I must boast, I will boast of the things that show my weakness' (11:30). Paul's speech is 'contemptible' (10:10): 'I who am humble when face to face with you' (10:1). Paul implies that if he and his co-workers indeed show themselves to be weak, foolish, lowly and contemptible, then they have the qualifications to be chosen and used by God, and indeed that is what happened. God worked through their outwardly unimpressive lives to bring genuine Christ-like success (4:7).

Paul's real goal is not to impress the Corinthians but to teach them about authentic Christian leadership (Luke 9:23). 'Boasting' of our own accomplishments is impossible if it is God who sustains us in difficulties.

PRAYER

There is no Holy One like you, Lord; there is no Rock like you, God. Let not arrogance come from my mouth; for you, Lord, are a God of knowledge, and by you actions are weighed.

Paraphrase of Hannah's prayer in 1 Samuel 2:2–3

ABUSIVE LEADERS

Paul allows the Corinthians to keep identifying themselves as 'wise', but he attacks that self-perception indirectly as he describes exactly what is entailed in the wisdom of the Corinthians: wisdom to allow enslavement, exploitation, theft, rejection and physical abuse. The Corinthian 'wise' are patient even with their own enslavement!

These leaders 'murder'

Paul uses images of slavery, eating, hunting and lifting to describe the type of leadership the Corinthians unwisely seek. To 'make a slave of' (*katadouloo*) contains the verb 'enslave' (*douloo*) plus the prefix *kata*, 'down'. *Kata* intensifies the verb to signify 'reduce to slavery' or 'oppressively subjugate'. Paul uses the same verb to describe the false believers, the circumcision party, who tried to restrict the freedom Paul and others had in Christ Jesus 'so that they might enslave us' (Galatians 2:4). When the Egyptians forced the Hebrews to build cities, 'ruthless in all the tasks that they imposed on them', they oppressively enslaved them (Exodus 1:11–14).

To 'prey upon' (*katesthio*) also has the prefix *kata*, intensifying the verb 'to eat' (*esthio*), 'to eat up, devour, consume'. From its earliest appearance in the Bible, *katesthio* had been used both literally and metaphorically. For example, when the famine was severe in Israel, Jacob and his family ate up all the grain they had brought from Egypt (Genesis 43:2). Sometimes *katesthio* was used to describe the way animals would 'eat up'. Joseph's brothers claimed that a wild animal 'devoured' Joseph's body, leaving only his bloodstained, torn robe (Genesis 37:20, 33). Thus, metaphorically, *katesthio* frequently signifies a destructive act toward another, such as scribes who 'devour' or 'steal' widows' possessions (Mark 12:40).

To 'take' (*lambano*) means to 'take advantage of, grasp, seize'. One possible use of *lambano* is to fish or hunt, where the fisherman catches the fish unawares so as to seize or take advantage of it (Luke 5:5).

To 'put on airs' (*epairo*), literally, is to 'lift up and set on', 'raise' and, metaphorically, to 'exalt, magnify'. Often it is used simply of 'lifting up' the eyes, head, voice or hands. However, Paul uses *epairo* in a negative sense in 2 Corinthians. In 10:5 it was part of his imagery of warfare. In ancient Israel and Greece, fortresses such as the Acrocorinth were built or 'raised up' on the tops of mountains. People who are self-righteous, but not righteous in reality, 'lift' themselves up: 'There are those who are pure in their own eyes yet are not cleansed of their filthiness. There are those—how lofty are their eyes, how high their eyelids lift! There are those whose teeth are swords, whose teeth are knives, to devour the poor from off the earth, the needy from among mortals' (Proverbs 30:12–14). Enslaving, consuming, fishing and war all result in the object losing its life. These are all metaphors of death and destruction.

These leaders abuse

Finally, Paul concludes with a literal description: to 'slap' or strike the face (v. 20). The religious leaders who condemned Jesus for blasphemy spat on him and hit him (Mark 14:64–65). The high priest Ananias ordered Paul to be struck on the mouth when Paul claimed to live his life with a clear conscience (Acts 23:1–2). Like the high priest Ananias, the super-apostles thought they had the right to strike people. Their leadership style removed Christian freedom in Christ, misappropriated money, took away what was not their own, made life into a battle, treating people as condemned prisoners. The super-apostles, though impressive in their rhetoric, were arrogant, autocratic bullies who spiritually, economically and physically abused the Corinthians. They were like non-Christian Gentile rulers who 'lord it over' and tyrannize their people (Mark 10:42). If these actions are 'strength', then Paul and his team in comparison were 'weak' (v. 21). Paul states, therefore, ironically, that they are 'too weak' to treat the Corinthians as would slave traders, exploiters, robbers and bullies. In reality Paul's team was following Jesus' exhortation that the 'first among you must be slave of all. For the Son of Man came not to be served but to serve, and to give his life a ransom for many' (Mark 10:44–45).

MEDITATION

To what kind of leader are you attracted? Look for leaders who free
you to become more Christ-like.

CHRIST'S FOOL

For the whole of chapter 11, Paul is writing 'foolishly', having to defend himself before the challenges of the 'super-apostles' (11:1, 5; 12:11). Paul should have been commended by those he lovingly nurtured.

A fool speaks to fools

In 1 Corinthians 9:22–23, Paul explained that he is willing to 'become all things to all people, that I might by all means save some. I do it all for the sake of the gospel.' He was willing to become a slave, a Jew, a Gentile, weak, in order to win slave, Jew, Gentile and weak— even though in reality he was 'free with respect to all' (1 Corinthians 9:19–22). But would he be willing to become a fool in order to win fools? Yes and no.

The New Testament has several different Greek words translated 'fool'. About half of the New Testament references to 'stupid' (*moros* and *moria*) occur in 1 Corinthians and those to 'without sense' (*aphrosune* and *aphron*) occur in 2 Corinthians. *Aphron* is, literally, without reason or purpose. Religious leaders who do not perceive the truth (Luke 11:40), greedy rich who build larger barns rather than share their harvest with the poor (Luke 12:20), doubters who cannot understand the resurrected body (1 Corinthians 15:36), drunkards who do not use their time to understand and do God's will (Ephesians 5:17–18), false critics (1 Peter 2:15), are all 'fools'. Thus, foolishness, at its heart, is the inclination to think and act as someone who does not believe that God exists and therefore does not seek after God (Psalm 14:1–2). Paul is not this kind of fool because he speaks the truth (12:6). He is no longer blinded by the 'god of this world' (4:4).

However, since some Corinthians already consider Paul a 'fool' and listen only to fools, and since Paul is willing to become 'all things to all people', he is going to defend himself, and in defending himself, become as foolish as those who criticize him (11:16, 19).

Fools flaunt ancestry

Paul begins where the super-apostles end and quickly dismisses the claims they flaunt about their Jewishness: 'Hebrews are they? I also.

Israelites are they? I also. Descendants of Abraham are they? I also.' (v. 22, my translation). Paul emphasizes their claims by placing the direct objects first: Hebrews, Israelites, descendants of Abraham. These three phrases are all synonyms with only subtle differences in meaning, highlighting one common point.

In New Testament times, a 'Hebrew' was someone who spoke Hebrew (Acts 6:1). The Hebrew language of the first century was Syro-Chaldee, a mixture of the Aramaean of Daniel and Ezra with the ancient Hebrew. Many Jews had become so influenced by the larger Hellenistic culture that they were no longer fluent in Hebrew. Thus, when the angry mob in Jerusalem heard Paul address them in Hebrew, they became respectful (Acts 22:2).

'Israelite' may highlight religious training, as Jesus said of Nathanael: 'Here is truly an Israelite in whom there is no deceit!' (John 1:46–48). 'Israelite' goes back to 'Israel' or Jacob (Genesis 32:28) who represents the twelve tribes. Paul writes that to the Israelites 'belong the adoption, the glory, the covenants, the giving of the law, the worship, and the promises... the patriarchs, and... the Messiah' (Romans 9:4–5). Thus, to address a crowd as 'Israelites' was a way to awaken pride in God's appointment of a people (Acts 13:16–17; 21:28).

To be a 'descendant of Abraham' highlights the individual connected over time with others of a common race or ancestry. Mary sings in praise that her child is a fulfilment of a promise made to descendants of Abraham (Luke 1:55). Being a descendant of Abraham was cause for pride (John 8:33). In Romans 11:1, Paul also calls himself 'an Israelite, a descendant of Abraham', when he defines Abraham's real descendants by faith, not race (Romans 9:7–8). The super-apostles were highlighting their racial qualifications, and, by implication, we can infer that they were persuading Gentiles that becoming Jewish was a necessary prerequisite to Christianity. But Paul's brief, elliptical 'I also' shows how little significance he places on the super-apostles' claims of Jewishness: he can easily match them (v. 22).

PRAYER

Lord, help me become all things to all people, that I might by all means save some for the sake of your gospel.

Paraphrase of 1 Corinthians 9:22–23

The LIFE *of a* GENUINE MINISTER

Paul has now set aside the weapons of attack (11:1–20) and grasped again the weapons of defence (11:21—12:13; 6:7). Paul wants the Corinthians to see exactly how he and the 'super-apostles' compare as genuine leaders. However, Paul describes difficulties they endure, not ones they inflict on others (11:20).

Service costs

Paul's questions (11:22) take on an increasing cadence that moves the reader quickly to verse 23: 'Ministers of Christ are they?' Finally, here Paul breaks the parallelism because as 'ministers of Christ' Paul and the super-apostles are not parallel. Paul uses irony when he announces that he talks 'like a madman'. He does not think he is mentally immature or unbalanced, but he writes in this defensive way (that he would prefer to avoid) in order to help a 'mentally immature' Corinthian church to comprehend the truth. Paul, in effect, appears to be 'mad' to the Corinthians' mental immaturity!

'I am a better one' is literally 'I even more'. Paul omits the verb 'am' and the second half of the sentence, '…a minister of Christ than they are'. By omitting the end of his sentence, Paul plunges into a description of his life before the reader knows exactly what Paul intends to communicate by this list of trials. Paul requires his readers to complete, and therefore pause and reflect on, the missing words: 'I [am] even more [a servant of Christ than they are]'. Paul will extensively illustrate what it means to be a 'minister (or servant) of Christ'.

How is Paul a 'better' 'servant of Christ'? In 'far greater labours, far more imprisonments, with countless floggings and often near death' (v. 23). 'Countless' and 'better' have the same prefix as 'super-apostles' (11:5). The super-apostles had 'super' comfort while Paul had 'super' difficulties. The irony rests in these happenings being cause for 'boasting'. Certainly such difficulties would not impress the 'superlative' apostles. Yet Paul's goal is not to impress them; rather, it is to teach them what authentic leadership is all about. No one can boast about difficulties if God is the one who sustains a human in those difficulties.

Ministry is hard work

Paul uses a marked and hurried rhythm as he describes his many troubles. This rhythm is created by omitting conjunctions, which impresses the details vividly on the reader, and by repeating 'with' (literally 'in') eight times (vv. 23, 27) and 'danger' eight times (vv. 26–27). Images of prisons and death create a bleak picture indeed. Forty lashes were considered tantamount to a death sentence. For this reason, Jewish law prescribed that one less lash should be administered (v. 24). Paul has had to experience every kind of danger from nature, from people, from non-believers and from so-called believers.

Bandits were a common danger in ancient times. Thus, travellers would often join with large groups for protection (Acts 20:4; Luke 10:30). 'Wilderness' (*eremia*) could refer to literal or emotional solitude. Thus, the philosopher Epictetus described 'forlorn' (*eremia*) as 'the condition of one who is without help. For someone is not forlorn merely because he is alone, any more than a person in the midst of a crowd is necessarily not forlorn' (*Discourses* iii.xiii.i). And indeed Paul looked to be 'without help'. The phrase 'toil and hardship' summarizes and emphasizes what Paul has had to endure for the Lord's sake (v. 27).

Finally, Paul's list ends abruptly in verse 28: 'Besides other things ['apart from what I leave unmentioned'], I am under daily pressure because of my anxiety for all the churches.' Can it be possible after all these experiences that Paul has left something 'unmentioned'? Previously he has described physical discomfort from persecution and from travelling about in order to proclaim Christ. Now he adds mental anguish as well because of his responsibility and passionate concern for the spiritual well-being of believers. The image of 'pressure' well describes this new hardship. Even as a physical pressure can cause long-term discomfort, similarly concern for the well-being of others has caused Paul long-term mental discomfort.

Paul's 'boasting' is no boasting at all. He has listed the difficulties he has been enduring to show the kind of life that proves the genuineness of a servant of Christ. Only for the sake of Christ would anyone endure such difficulties.

MEDITATION

What has discipleship of Christ cost you?

WHEN WEAKNESS IS WORTHWHILE

Paul had taught the Corinthians that 'God chose what is weak in the world to shame the strong' (1 Corinthians 1:27). He explained that he purposely presented himself in a speaking style that the world of rhetoric might look down upon: 'I came to you in weakness and in fear and in much trembling' (1 Corinthians 2:3). Nevertheless, the Corinthians did not understand. Their eyes were blinded to the treasure within this 'clay jar', agreeing with the complaint that Paul's 'bodily presence is weak' (2 Corinthians 10:10). But because God is all-powerful, Paul can redefine 'weakness', the very word of slander, as a virtue, even as he earlier redefined 'boasting'.

Weakness can mean a lot

In verse 29 Paul first uses 'weak' in a positive way to describe himself. A 'weak' person might be someone tempted to 'stumble' or sin. Such people would cause Paul to be anxious (11:28). The second 'weak' (v. 29) refers to being 'indignant', having empathy with the person made to sin and outrage at the person who caused the temptation (Luke 17:2–3). Paul identifies with the tempted person and is indignantly angry against those who caused this fall, or, as he wrote: 'To the weak I became weak, so that I might win the weak' (1 Corinthians 9:22).

Paul uses 'weakness' in verse 30 as an internal summary word to describe a servant of Christ: 'If I must boast, I will boast of the things that show my weakness.' 'Weakness' is sometimes defined as moral defects, sins or personal deficiencies.

'Weakness' literally refers to lack of physical strength. In the Gospels it often refers to diseases (for example, Luke 5:15). In the New Testament the verb, noun and adjective are used metaphorically to refer to 'weakness' 45 times. Paul uses them 39 times (thirty times in 1 and 2 Corinthians, fifteen of those times in 2 Corinthians 10—13).

Although people do need to repent of their wrongdoings (for example, Luke 18:9–14) and acknowledge their limitations so that God can empower them (Exodus 4:10–12), Paul does not use 'weakness' in this passage to refer to sins or psychological limitations.

Weaknesses reflect servant leadership

The immediate context is always the most important determiner of meaning. Paul employs 'weakness' in 2 Corinthians 11—12 to refer to the physical and mental discomfort he has had to endure because of his desire to preach the good news of Christ. 'Weakness' is an internal summary word to describe a genuine servant of Christ (11:23). It refers to physical discomfort due to persecution, physical discomfort due to travelling about and encountering natural disasters and robbery, physical discomfort from hard work and living without all physical necessities, and mental anguish from continual responsibility for the churches (11:23–29). Paul's escape from Damascus is another example of danger he had to incur because he preached Christ (11:32–33). People who live the way 'the world does' (10:3) might see such discomfort as 'sickness'. Unlike the arrogance and desire for comfort of the 'super-apostles', Paul lived a difficult but unflamboyant life of self-sacrifice. To reinterpret 'weakness' as individual traits might excuse an interpreter in living more comfortably, whereas Paul's use of 'weakness' requires the willingness to take risks and the possibility of a change of lifestyle. Verse 30 can be rephrased, 'If I must boast [that is, find something that is a sign of a true servant of Christ], for the sake of Christ, I will boast of a life of affliction which is looked down upon by others.'

The cost of being a genuine follower of God in a time of unbelief was not only taught by Jesus (Luke 14:26–33) but also lived out in even Old Testament times. The prophet Jeremiah is an example of a person whose faith was costly. Especially poignant was when King Zedekiah allowed Jeremiah's enemies to drop him into a cistern, lowering him into mud, without food and water (Jeremiah 38:5–13). Like Jeremiah, Paul too had to give up comfort to follow God's calling.

PRAYER

Now my soul is troubled. And what should I say—
'Father, save me from this hour'? No, it is for this reason that
I have come to this hour. Father, glorify your name.

Jesus' prayer in John 12:27–28

THROUGH *a* WINDOW *in the* WALL

Readers of 2 Corinthians have asked why Paul placed this extended narrative where he did and what precedent he set by escaping.

Damascus narrates weakness

The passionate, moving list of difficulties in 11:23–27 builds up to verses 28–29, followed by Paul's internal summary in verse 30. Now Paul continues his examples of 'weakness' (vv. 31–33), which are, as John Calvin explains, 'those things which might, in the view of the world, bring him contempt, rather than glory'. Augustine writes, 'I cannot sufficiently express how beautiful and delightful it is when after this outburst he rests himself, and gives the hearer rest, by interposing a slight narrative' (*On Christian Doctrine* iv.vii,12ff). The earlier illustrations are grouped by type, not time—rivers and robbers, Jew and Gentile, urban and rural, sea and false believers (11:26). Acts records only a few of these events—flogging and imprisonment in Philippi (Acts 16:23; 2 Corinthians 11:23), stoning at Lystra (Acts 14:19; 2 Corinthians 11:25), danger from Jews and Gentiles at Damascus, Antioch of Pisidia, Thessalonica and Corinth (Acts 9:23; 13:50; 17:5, 13; 18:12; 2 Corinthians 11:26).

In verse 32 Paul lists probably the earliest major difficulty he experienced in his ministry, during the first three years of his conversion. On Paul's way to the synagogues at Damascus with permission to bring Christians bound back to Jerusalem, Jesus confronted Paul and communicated, through Ananias, Christ's call 'to bring my name before Gentiles and kings and before the people of Israel; I myself will show him how much he must suffer for the sake of my name' (Acts 9:15–16). At Damascus 'Saul became increasingly more powerful and confounded the Jews', but then when the Jews plotted to kill Paul, Paul managed to escape (Acts 9:22–25; 2 Corinthians 11:32–33). What glory in the midst of such difficulties!

Paul begins this narrative by reiterating that he tells the truth (v. 31). Truth-telling has been an important theme for Paul, in contrast to the deceit of the super-apostles (11:4, 13). Earlier, he had been accused of lying to the Corinthians about his forthcoming visit (1:17), and, as here, he called on God as his witness (1:23). He describes his team as persons sent from God, not 'peddlers of God's word' (2:17). They commend themselves by the 'open statement of the truth' (4:2), 'truthful speech' (6:7), truthful claims (10:13, 15; 11:10). Paul's divine witness is described in a lengthy subject: 'The God and Father of the Lord Jesus, the One being blessed forever' (v. 31, my translation). The participle 'being blessed' or 'being praised' indicates that God is worthy of continual praise. Whenever they referred to God in passing, often pious Jews would do just that, praise God: 'the Holy One, blessed is he' (for example, *Mishnah, Aboth* 3:2).

The 'governor' was the ruler of a tribe or nation, a delegated overseer. Paul's conflict with the 'governor' occurred between AD37 and 39 when King Aretas ruled over Damascus, probably the oldest continuously inhabited city of the world. Even today a hole can be found in a wall in Damascus which is claimed to be the one Paul used. He was not the first Jew to escape through a city window. Rahab let down Joshua's spies through Jericho's walls, 'for her house was on the outer side of the city wall and she resided within the wall itself' (Joshua 2:15). When I visited ancient Tortosa in Spain, I saw clothes hung outside a window by people who still live in the ancient city walls. Such walls could be as much as eleven to thirty feet thick.

Unjust judges should be avoided

Was Paul a coward or did he evade justice? The unbelieving Jews who sought out Paul were not seeking to bring Paul to court for a crime against the state. They were 'plotting' or contracting to kill Paul (Acts 9:23). In the same way as officials warned Paul not to speak to the crowd at Ephesus (Acts 19:31), or the tribune removed him from Jerusalem so that he would not be killed (Acts 23:16–35), or believers protected Paul in Beroea (Acts 17:10), so believers in Damascus protected him from criminal activity (9:25). These particular criminals had simply found a governmental official to assist them. This governor was not God's servant 'to execute wrath on the wrongdoer' (Romans 13:4). Rather, he was a pawn for wrongdoers.

MEDITATION

Do you know of any believers who have been attacked unjustly?
What can you do to help?

A VISION FOURTEEN YEARS AGO

Paul speaks of himself in the third person ('I know a person in Christ') because, although the Corinthians might very well be impressed by his visions and revelations, such flashy events are not what they should look for when trying to find the genuine servant of Christ. Paul 'boasts' only of actions which show his 'weaknesses' (12:5). No doubt the super-apostles boasted of special revelations from God. By using the third person for himself, Paul also describes his experience in a more impartial and objective way. But clearly in 12:7 he acknowledges that he is that person ('me').

Better not boast

Paul restates again his theme of boasting (v. 1) which he introduced in 11:18–21, only because that is the only way he can reach the foolish Corinthians. But he repeats that 'nothing is to be gained by it' (v. 1). Commending ourselves before those who should be commending us is not the 'best' action to take, but sometimes it is necessary.

Paul goes on to visions, but they are not events that he can brag about as self-achievements and the difficulty that follows is not something people would desire (12:7). Paul describes an event that took place fourteen years previously (v. 2). If 2 Corinthians was written around AD56–57, this vision occurred around AD40–42, about seven years after his conversion in AD33–35. After preaching for three years in Arabia and Damascus, Paul had then returned to Tarsus, Cilicia and Syria, so he is describing an event that took place probably in Tarsus, the place of his birth.

The Lord communicates

A 'vision' (optasia) is 'something seen' (v. 1). In the New Testament all other uses of optasia refer to events 'in the body'. Zechariah, for example, saw an angel at the right side of the incense altar in the temple, and dialogued with the angel (Luke 1:11–22). Mary Magdalene and the other women who visited the empty tomb after Jesus was resurrected saw and spoke with angels (Luke 24:4–10, 23). When Paul was converted, he saw a light, heard a voice and received a message. In the Bible, visions (horama) can come to people awake or asleep, individually or communally. In the book of Acts, visions occur to spur people to do very difficult actions, contrary to what they have learned or what seems safe. For example, the Lord spoke to Ananias in a vision to pray for a man who had been persecuting Christians like himself (Acts 9:10–14). An angel of God in the afternoon commanded the Gentile Cornelius to send for a Jew (Acts 10:3–6). In a noon trance God commanded Peter to kill and eat unclean animals (Acts 10:10–19). In Troas Paul was called into Macedonia in a night vision, where he would minister among women (16:9–13).

Paul also mentions 'revelations' (v. 2). In the Bible the concept refers to the disclosing of something not fully known (Romans 16:25–26), like the second return of Jesus in judgment (1 Corinthians 1:7; 2 Corinthians 5:10). Paul has always claimed that his knowledge of the resurrected Jesus was by special revelation (Galatians 1:12; Ephesians 3:3; 1 Corinthians 9:1). Paul had more 'visions' and 'revelations' (plural), although here he describes only one event.

Paul specifies that these visions and revelations come from the Lord at God's initiative (v. 1). This is an important distinction to make. Humans can create their own visions or ecstatic experiences. Sometimes drug-induced experiences, by forcing people to dwell on hidden emotional feelings, can push them into chronic mental illness. The ancients were also well acquainted with hallucinogenic drugs. But Paul's experience was not self-induced or mentally unwholesome. He was carried into God's presence by God's genuine spiritual beckoning.

PRAYER

One thing I ask of you, Lord; that will I seek after:
to live in your house all the days of my life, to behold your beauty,
and to inquire in your presence.

Paraphrase of Psalm 27:4

PAUL IS TAKEN AWAY *into* PARADISE

In the Greek, Paul ends verse 2 with his climatic phrase 'having been caught up, such a person, as far as third heaven'. He begins, 'I know a person' but before he tells the reader what happened to that person, he dismisses in parenthesis when and how it happened. In verses 3–4, Paul repeats the introduction and elaborates more on what happened.

Caught up to the third heaven

We can learn from these verses that the 'third heaven' is a synonym for 'Paradise' where Paul heard words, but he does not spend time dwelling on the mechanics of his experience. All he trusts is God, who knows those mechanics. He uses the verb *harpazo* ('caught up, seized and carried off, taken by force, taken away', vv. 2, 4) in the passive voice to highlight that this experience was not self-induced. *Harpazo* was sometimes used of robbery (Matthew 12:29), attack (John 10:12), forcible arrest (Acts 23:10) or being overpowered (John 6:15). But it can also have positive connotations. When evangelist Philip finished baptizing the treasurer of Ethiopia, the 'Spirit of the Lord caught Philip' and the eunich saw him no more (Acts 8:39). Who 'snatches' us affects the positive or negative nature of the trip. Similarly, followers of Jesus 'will be caught up in the clouds' to meet the Lord (1 Thessalonians 4:17). Being snatched by God is a safe place to be.

What do the 'third heaven' and 'Paradise' mean? 'Third heaven' occurs only here in the Bible. In the centuries that follow, apocryphal writers have referred to a multitude of heavens: seven (3 Enoch), ten (2 Enoch) and five (3 Baruch). The Testament of Levi describes the third 'uppermost heaven' as the place where dwells 'the Great Glory in the Holy of Holies superior to all holiness' (ch. 3). However, Paul, in contrast, writes of only three heavens, which for others would seem only a stepping-stone to a more spiritual state.

Probably the simplest interpretation of 'third heaven' is best. In Genesis God made a firmament or dome and called it 'heaven' (Genesis 1:8, KJV). Thus, the first heaven would simply be the atmosphere above us with its clouds. The second heaven would be outside earth's gravity, in the sphere of the sun and moon (Genesis 1:14–18). These first two 'heavens' are God's physical creations. The third heaven is a spiritual place, the place of God's presence (Deuteronomy 26:15). God, as spirit, cannot be limited to one physical place (John 4:24; Acts 17:28). Yet 'heaven' is a euphemism for God's holy presence, which is why we pray to 'our Father which art in heaven' (Matthew 6:9, KJV). Possibly Paul described his experience as in the 'third' heaven because he will later describe the 'three' appeals he will make to God (12:8), or perhaps he simply wanted the readers to know he was in God's presence, not simply up in the physical clouds.

Caught up into paradise

'Paradise' means an enclosed park, a pleasure-ground, a garden or orchard. In Eden was a garden (Genesis 2:8), the 'garden of the Lord' (Genesis 13:10; Isaiah 51:3; Ezekiel 28:13). Jesus uses 'Paradise' as a synonym for 'heaven' when promising the repentant criminal that he would come into God's presence (Luke 23:43). When John is carried in the Spirit, he sees the tree of life in God's future paradise (Revelation 2:7; 21:10—22:5). In it are no sun or moon, as there are in the second heaven. Thus, Paul experienced a foreshadowing of the magnificent city of gardens we call the new Jerusalem.

Unlike the later apocryphal writings which go into quite extensive detail about what God says (for example, 2 Enoch 22), Paul heard words 'unspeakable', which 'no mortal is permitted to repeat' (v. 4). The modifying clause explains that these spoken words were indeed understandable, but Paul was told not to repeat them. He received different commands than John, who was ordered to share his vision as a warning to others (Revelation 1:1). Paul will shortly share other words that God revealed to him (12:8). Why, then, did Paul experience this rapture? John Calvin suggests, 'This took place for the sake of Paul himself, for one who had such arduous difficulties awaiting him, enough to break a thousand hearts, required to be strengthened by special means, that he might not give way, but might persevere undaunted.'

MEDITATION

When do you most feel you are in God's presence?

No Better *than the* Truth

Sometimes the newly rich are those who most vaunt themselves. They have not learned that with money and possessions comes responsibility, and they have forgotten how much of what they have was given to them. Such were the Corinthians. In less than twenty years of its refounding, Corinth became the wealthy capital of the province of Achaia and the administrative seat of the Roman government's proconsul for southern and central Greece. Without an aristocracy, Corinth's new money and power became the rule of the day. This spirit of boasting also infected the church. Thus, we have already seen how the topic of 'boasting' has been a major theme in 2 Corinthians, one to which Paul builds up in 12:8. He must engage his critics in comparisons at some level (12:1). Thus, Paul has at least a dual goal: to defend his team's leadership style and to redefine the meaning and place of boasting.

To boast or not to boast

The super-apostles were apparently boasting of or flaunting accomplishments which were not theirs (10:13–16). Paul, in contrast, reiterates that 'I will be speaking truth' (v. 6); 'I do not lie' (11:31). He apparently wants the Corinthians to become aware of his extraordinary revelations (12:1, 7), of which he briefly described only one (12:2–4) so that the super-apostles could not claim to be more impressive than the genuine apostle, Paul. However, in keeping with his thesis, he excludes revelations from his personal arena of 'boasting'. Paul himself 'boasts' of or describes only difficult situations where God's power must be at work to sustain him (v. 5). Physical discomfort from persecution and travelling, and mental discomfort for Christ's sake (11:23–33), highlight the Lord's mercy and power (Jeremiah 9:24; 2 Corinthians 1:3; 10:17).

The wise love truth

Even though Paul has stated that he will act as a fool who boasts (11:16–17) so that he will be understood by the foolish Corinthians (11:19), here he reiterates how he is in no way like a fool. He speaks the truth (v. 6). His 'foolishness' is in having to commend himself—

something the Corinthians should have done on his behalf (5:12). Paul refrains from vaunting or boasting about his accomplishments. When people flaunt their own accomplishments, then those who listen may end up less likely to evaluate a person by the evidence before their eyes—'what is seen... or heard' (v. 6).

To 'think', literally, is to 'credit' or to 'charge to someone's account'. Will Paul's listening accountants give Paul's credit–debit sheet the correct amount of credit? 'Better' (huper, v. 6) is the same prefix as in 'super-apostles' (huperlian, 11:5), 'exceptional character' (huperbole, v. 7) and 'elated' (huperairo). Paul, even with his 'super' (or 'exceptional') revelations, and probably because of his genuine 'super' revelations, can afford to be modest. He does not want anyone to credit him with having done anything 'better' than what he actually did (unlike the 'super' or so-called 'better' apostles).

For Paul and all the biblical writers, historical evidence is crucial to faith. Paul's team speaks 'as persons sent from God' (2:17), living 'the open statement of the truth' (4:2), having 'truthful speech' (6:7). As John explains, 'We declare to you what was from the beginning, what we have heard, what we have seen with our eyes, what we have looked at and touched with our hands' (1 John 1:1). Paul earlier told the Corinthians that Christ 'appeared to Cephas, then to the twelve. Then he appeared to more than five hundred brothers and sisters at one time' (1 Corinthians 15:5–6). Timothy reminded the Corinthians of Paul's 'ways in Christ' (1 Corinthians 4:17). The Philippians should 'keep on doing the things that you have learned and received and heard and seen in me' (Philippians 4:9). These are only a sampling of the many New Testament passages which reiterate what Paul now stresses to the Corinthians. The evidence of sight and sound are crucial for determining truth and Paul wants the Corinthians to recognize that he, not the deceptive super-apostles (11:13), is giving them the truth about God. Paul's actions speak for themselves, in the same way as did the actions of his Lord: 'The works that the Father has given me to complete, the very works that I am doing, testify on my behalf that the Father has sent me' (John 5:36).

PRAYER

God, help me to speak the truth and see the truth.

The TORMENTING THORN

After having reminded the Corinthians of the exceptional character of the revelations, Paul emphasizes why he was given 'a thorn': 'to keep me from being too elated'.

Over may not be above

'Too elated' (*huperairo*, to 'lift or raise up over', v. 7) is one of Paul's *huper* words. One way Paul expresses his passion in 2 Corinthians is by the frequent use of the preposition *huper* by itself or in composition. Often it simply means 'on behalf of' (for example, in 12:5). However, its root idea of 'over' can also mean 'above' or 'beyond' as in 'I am a better one' (11:23). This use of *huper* brings out the astonishingly positive experiences of genuine Christians in the midst of astonishing difficulties. Paul and his team were 'so utterly, unbearably' crushed, but God rescued them (1:8–10). An 'extraordinary power belongs to God', but it is kept in 'clay jars' (4:7). A glory 'beyond all measure' awaits those who persevere through a 'slight momentary affliction' (4:17). Paul was 'overjoyed' in all their 'affliction' (7:4). Similarly, Paul had to withstand a thorn so that he should not become too elated by his 'extraordinary' revelations (v. 7). Truth often contains paradox.

These revelations that Paul had were so 'exceptional', so beyond the norm, that he may have been tempted to lift himself up or give himself airs. Paul had identified this as the problem of the 'lawless one': 'He opposes and exalts himself (*huperairo*) above every so-called god or object of worship, so that he takes his seat in the temple of God, declaring himself to be God' (2 Thessalonians 2:4). This was the problem of the 'beyond—exceedingly' (*huperlian*) apostles (11:5; 12:11). Like Satan, they were 'overstepping' (*huperekteino*) their limits (10:14), taking credit for what they did not do.

In the *Star Wars* series, this is the problem of the gifted young man with a danger to use his gifts for evil, who becomes Darth Vader. Should he never have been trained? God's solution would have been to allow the youth's difficulties to become a means of humility.

A stake can be struck

Because Paul uses metaphorical language, commentators differ over its literal meaning. A 'thorn' is anything pointed, such as a splinter or stake, with which an enemy might impale one's eyes (Numbers 33:55) or thorns which block one's way (Hosea 2:6). Paul's 'thorn' pierces the flesh. It is also 'a messenger' from Satan who 'may torment' (*kolaphizo*). *Kolaphizo*, literally, is to 'strike with the fist'. When Jesus was accused of blasphemy, some of the religious leaders 'struck him' (Matthew 26:67). Paul too, is 'beaten' (1 Corinthians 4:11).

These metaphors—a thorn piercing, a messenger hitting—suggest external, localized, periodic problems. Therefore, most commentators understand the 'thorn' as some kind of physical suffering. Some suggest physical persecution for the faith (for example, in 12:10). The verb 'torment' was elsewhere used of unjust persecution. Certainly Satan, the 'adversary', tries to use such persecution to advance his cause. However, why then would Paul ask to have removed what he says 'we are destined for' (1 Thessalonians 3:3)?

Another possibility is Paul refers to a specific physical ailment that he may have. Since the 'thorn' '*may* torment' (v. 7), not 'will torment' or 'always torments', and it is a striking with the fist—a piercing, not an all-consuming illness—the language suggests an intermittent, not a continual, problem. While Paul was able to stare at people (for example, Acts 13:9), he appears to have had an eye problem: 'You know that it was because of a physical infirmity that I first announced the gospel to you; though my condition put you to the test… you would have torn out your eyes and given them to me' (Galatians 4:13–15). 'See what large letters I make when I am writing in my own hand!' (Galatians 6:11). Ophthalmia is one such intermittent eye problem. Doctor Stephen Price, a physician, suggests that these physical symptoms fit more specifically the inflammatory Reiter's condition (which also affects the joints) or intermittent glaucoma, that causes the eye pressure to rise at times.

Whatever the precise meaning, the tormenting 'thorn' appears to be physical suffering which was part of the Satanic dominion. God periodically allowed it in order that Paul should not exalt himself.

MEDITATION

*How have you experienced the extraordinary nature
of God's presence?*

A PRAYER IS HEARD

Paul's passionate discussion of 'weakness', boasting and power reaches a climax in verse 9, when God says to Paul, 'My grace is sufficient for you, for power is made perfect in weakness', and Paul concludes, 'So, I will boast all the more gladly of my weaknesses, so that the power of Christ may dwell in me.' Paul has taken negative words used to criticize him and reinterpreted them in a positive way so that he can even say he 'gladly' boasts in weaknesses.

Prayer can be urgent

Because of the torment from the 'thorn', Paul 'by prayer and supplication' let his request 'be made known to God' (Philippians 4:6). Paul has previously used more common New Testament words for 'prayer': *deesis* ('prayer for needs', 1:11; 9:14), *eucharisteo*, ('pray in thanks', 1:11; 4:15; 9:11–12). 'Appeal' (*parakaleo*), which is a word the ancients often used to describe communication with the gods, refers to 'prayer' only here. In the context of 2 Corinthians, *parakaleo* is an apt word for Paul to use because he wants to highlight the urgent nature of his prayer and remind readers of the opening paragraph where he describes God as the source of all appeal ('consolation', 1:3–4).

Paul summons God to his aid three times, because he does not know God's response and he expects a response from God, the just judge. His prayer is quite specific—that the 'thorn' might be removed. If the 'thorn' indeed is Paul's eye problem, which was interfering with his ministry (it put the Galatians 'to the test', Galatians 4:14), and since, through Paul, God had healed many people, why could Paul not be healed? Especially if this infirmity might cause some people to 'scorn or despise' Paul (4:14), removing it would appear to help him minister.

Paul's prayer is answered

This time, what Paul heard was not secret (12:4). God 'said' (v. 9), so Paul no longer needed to ask. The quality of God's strength is figuratively presented as a person taking up residence ('may dwell'), alluding to Christ's incarnation (John 1:14) and the descent of God's *shekinah* glory (Exodus 25:8; 40:34–35). Moses could not enter the tabernacle when God's glory was present, but Paul could be filled by God's glory while alive.

God's grace is sufficient for Paul because God imparts strength and power to the person who looks weak or powerless. Paul's 'weaknesses' are the 'insults', 'hardships', 'persecutions' and 'calamities' ('constraints') he undergoes during his ministry. When Paul willingly lives this life of difficulties for the greater cause of advancing God's reign, Christ's power comes down to Paul as the *shekinah* glory descended upon the mercy seat in the Tabernacle, and 'takes up its abode' (v. 9). Paul ends his discussion with the paradox, 'At the time that I am not strong, then I am strong' (v. 10, my translation). Power cannot come unless preceded by 'weakness' (humility of life). Power is what the Corinthians want. They want a burdensome and powerful presence to match a powerful writer (10:10). They forget this paradox: difficulties encountered in advancing God's reign are opportunities for God to empower and for genuine leaders to demonstrate sincere intentions. Paul has restated and personally appropriated Jesus' teachings (Luke 6:22–23; 9:23). Accepting all difficulties, in itself, is not God's intention. Rather, troubles should be welcomed only 'for the sake of Christ'.

How, then, can we discern the false from the genuine Christian leader? The false Christian despises a life of danger, physical discomfort from persecutions, insults, calamities, frequent nearness to death, infirmities and mental anguish for the sake of Christ. When Paul was chosen along the road to Damascus, Jesus told Ananias that Paul would 'bring my name before Gentiles and kings and before the people of Israel; I myself will show him how much he must suffer for the sake of my name' (Acts 9:15–16). Paul discovered that some people thought his difficulties were a sign of his lack of power, but he learned that his difficulties were an opportunity for God to work through him.

PRAYER

Though the fig tree does not blossom, and no fruit is on the vines;
though the produce of the olive fails and the fields yield no food;
though the flock is cut off from the fold and there is no herd
in the stalls, yet I will rejoice in the Lord; I will exult
in the God of my salvation.

Habakkuk 3:17

SIGNS *of an* APOSTLE

The glove has finally been pulled off the iron fist. The 'foolishness' in which Paul has indulged has come to an end. After a letter that has moved concentrically from less to more direct communication, Paul concludes this section with a direct elaboration of the problems he and the Corinthians have with each other.

Paul was compelled to be foolish

The Corinthians compelled Paul to be 'foolish', in other words, to defend himself, although they themselves should have defended him. Since the Corinthians themselves were foolish (without reason), gladly putting up with fools (11:19), Paul had to become a fool in order to reach them.

Apparently the super-apostles brought impressive letters of commendation to Corinth, which the Corinthians thought should be emulated by Paul and his team. But for Paul to bring such a letter to Corinth would be like parents bringing a letter of commendation to their own child. The bond of parent and child is greater and deeper than any letter. Paul's team commends itself by the Corinthians themselves, the team's love expressed in responsive lives enduring many difficulties on their behalf (3:1; 6:4), a love which rejoices in truth (4:2) and in the Lord (10:18), not false self promotion (10:12).

Paul demonstrated miracles

In verse 11 Paul directly states the main topic of the letter: 'I am not at all inferior to these super-apostles.' Even if Paul were 'nothing', he would still not be 'inferior' to the 'super-apostles' because the 'super-apostles' were oppressive heretics (11:13–15, 20)! Nevertheless, Paul summarizes two reasons he is not inferior to the 'super-apostles': he has exhibited the 'supernatural' types of gifts such as healing and exorcism that encourage people to repent (v. 12); and his team refused to take financial advantage of the Corinthians (12:13–18).

Possibly the Corinthians only needed to have been reminded of verse 12 to have disparaged the super-apostles. In the same way as Philip did more impressive miracles than Simon (Acts 8:6, 13), and Moses than the Egyptian sorcerers (Acts 7:36), Paul could have done more impressive miracles than the super-apostles, overpowering the Corinthians with his power. However, the Bible presents a mixed message when it comes to 'signs and wonders and mighty works'.

These three terms highlight one major point: supernatural acts show that God is at work. A 'sign' is a 'mark' by which something is known. The shepherds were told to look for the 'sign' of the Saviour: 'a child wrapped in bands of cloth and lying in a manger' (Luke 2:12). When Paul personally signed his letters, he marked his 'sign' of authenticity (2 Thessalonians 3:17). Jesus' 'signs' as the true Messiah (John 20:30) included turning water into wine (John 2:11), healing the sick (John 4:54, 6:2), multiplying bread and fish (John 6:14) and resurrecting Lazarus (John 12:17–18). Thus, Paul as a messenger (apostle) from God persevered in being God's vehicle to show the Corinthians marks or signals that he indeed preached God's authentic message.

However, Paul had warned the Corinthians that signs by themselves would not bring them to a saving, persevering faith (1 Corinthians 1:22–23). The demanding of signs can become simply the testing of God (Matthew 16:1) and in that way evil (Matthew 12:39).

'Wonder' in the New Testament always occurs together with 'sign' as an intensifier. A 'wonder' could be some terrifying change in the sun or moon (Acts 2:19–20). Like 'signs', wonders can be performed by false messiahs and prophets to lead people astray (Matthew 24:24; 2 Thessalonians 2:9–10).

'Mighty works' signifies 'power' or 'strength'. Luke writes that God did 'extraordinary miracles through Paul, so that when the handkerchiefs or aprons that had touched his skin were brought to the sick, their diseases left them, and the evil spirits came out of them' (Acts 19:11–12). Thus, God gave Paul the power to heal and to remove demons.

By focusing on these miraculous deeds, Paul could have dazzled the Corinthians! But Paul tucks these overwhelming actions into one sentence, because he does not want the Corinthians to get sidetracked into loving power rather than loving the Messiah who could have commanded legions of angels but instead allowed himself to be crucified to save others (13:4; Matthew 26:53).

MEDITATION

What wonders have you experienced that show
God is at work in your life?

PAUL'S FINANCIAL INDEPENDENCE

After stating the simplest defence for apostleship (12:12), Paul now returns to what he considers to be one of Corinth's core problems—finances. With a church that is presently in a state of financial 'abundance' (8:14), we would imagine that finances would be no problem at all. But life is stranger than reason.

Corinthians misunderstand money

The Corinthians were enjoying their life of comfort. Only a hundred years earlier, Julius Caesar had decreed the refounding of Corinth. Their parents and grandparents may have been among those people who emigrated to Corinth to build a new life for themselves. 'Already you have all you want! Already you have become rich!' Paul wrote to them because they had forgotten that all they had was ultimately received as a gift from God (1 Corinthians 4:8).

The Corinthians were not ready to share their financial wealth willingly with others. Paul had to defend his and Barnabas' right to food and drink as apostles and their decision not to make use of this right (1 Corinthians 9:12). Paul had to spend two chapters in 2 Corinthians (8—9) explaining why the Corinthians should go ahead and give to the starving church in Jerusalem!

Yet, simultaneously, the Corinthians were ready to donate to the 'false apostles', who demanded payment as their right (11:7–13). Jesus had taught his disciples that 'labourers deserve their food' (Matthew 10:10; Luke 10:7). The 'super-apostles' were among the first false believers who took advantage of the right for those who provide spiritually to be repaid materially (1 Corinthians 9:11).

Spending but not weighing down

Paul thus received donations from the Macedonian churches and not from Corinth (11:8–9; 12:13–14). Paul uses two Greek verbs to describe the relationship he does not want—'burden' (*katanarkao*, 12:13, 14; and *katabareo*, v. 16). In contrast, he uses two verbs to describe the relationship he does want—'spend' (*dapanao*) and 'be spent' (*ekdapanao*, v. 15). *Katanarkao* consists of the prefix *kata* ('down') and *narkao* ('become numb'). When the angel touched

Jacob's thigh, he made it numb (*narkao*, Genesis 32:25, Septuagint). The prefix intensifies the verb. Thus, Paul will not be someone who makes the Corinthians really 'numb'. He will not weigh heavily upon them.

Katabareo has the same prefix (*kata*, 'down') combined with the verb *bareo* ('weigh down'). Paul's opponents used the noun *barus*, 'heavy', to describe Paul's letters (10:10), but for Paul 'heavy' does not have positive connotations. 'Heavy' describes the effect of living with difficulties (1:8; 5:4). Paul does not want to 'overload' the Corinthians (v. 16). Would not weighing people heavily be a more apt description of the super-apostles (11:20) and the 'pagan' type of leadership (Mark 10:42)?

Instead Paul wants to 'spend' for the Corinthians (v. 15). *Dapanao*, elsewhere in the New Testament, is used quite literally: the woman who haemorrhaged for twelve years and the prodigal son 'spent' all they had (Mark 5:26; Luke 15:14). *Ekdapanao* (literally, 'to spend out') is to exhaust one's finances. Paul wants 'gladly' to give of his whole self for the Corinthians' lives (v. 15). Who has ever thought of full-time ministry as analogous to 'spending money' in love for others? Because of his love, Paul will do all he can to win the Corinthians over to Christ. Similarly, to the Thessalonians he writes that he, Silvanus and Timothy, like 'child-rearers', gave their 'own lives' because the Thessalonians had become 'beloved' to them (1 Thessalonians 2:7–8, my translation). Paul reminds the Corinthians of a truth from life: 'Children ought not to lay up for their parents, but parents for their children' (v. 14). In 1 Timothy 5:4, Paul writes about children and grandchildren giving to elderly widows, parents who have no means of financial support, whereas in 2 Corinthians, Paul as 'parent' has financial solvency. The Philippians could donate to Paul because they no longer had a child–parent relationship with him. They had matured into Paul's equals, at least in regard to their view of money (8:13–14).

PRAYER

My Parent in heaven, help me to be a parent to others,
seeking their best as your children.

PAUL DEFENDS THEIR HONESTY

Unfortunately, many Christian leaders have indeed wanted 'what is yours' (12:14)! Whether prominent TV evangelists or lesser-known church treasurers, few things undercut Christ's good news more than someone who in Christ's name robs another. The Jewish sages used to describe a saintly person as saying, 'What is mine is thine and what is thine is thine own' but a wicked person as saying: 'What is thine is mine, and what is mine is mine own' (*Mishnah, Aboth* 5:10). Robbery is a type of abuse, where the safety and privacy of a person are invaded and ransacked.

The bait is uncovered

Some critics at Corinth had been calling Paul such a robber (v. 16). The very same word Paul used to describe the super-apostles ('takes advantage of', 11:20) was used to describe Paul ('took in', *lambano*, v. 16)! It can be used for fishing, to take a fish unawares. Paul had compared the super-apostles to the serpent who deceived Eve by its 'cunning' (11:3) and now we learn that some people had also accused Paul of being 'crafty' (v. 16). Who is the real deceitful robber?

'Deceit' is the bait used to catch the 'fish'. In the garden of Eden, the serpent first raised doubt in Eve's mind as to what exactly God had said, then questioned God's character, motive and truthfulness (Genesis 3:1, 4–5). Eventually, it had Eve dwelling on the positive attributes of what God prohibited: 'The tree was good for food, and that it was a delight to the eyes, and that the tree was to be desired to make one wise' (Genesis 3:6). Only when Eve's attitude changed did she then act.

Paul responds to these false charges. Doubt is replaced by truth, character is reassessed (vv. 17–18) and misleading enticements are replaced with authentic enticements (12:19). First, Paul brings the accusations out to the open, restating to the Corinthians exactly what their charges imply: his very nature is one of craftiness (v. 16), not honesty (12:19; 4:2)! He has already told them that (for this very reason) he did not accept money as wages from them (12:14, 16), and probably neither did his co-workers (1 Corinthians 4:9, 11–12; 2 Corinthians 6:4–5).

After reminding them that he could never have stolen money from them since the Corinthians gave him no money (12:13–16), Paul then defends his associates. He raises four questions (vv. 17–18), the first two expecting negative answers, the last two positive answers. 'Did any of those whom I sent to you, through any one, did I take advantage of you?' (v. 17, my translation). Paul begins in a general way. He is fully confident of all his co-workers. 'To take advantage', literally, is 'to have more' than one's due, to be greedy. That was the problem of the rich farmer who built larger barns when he had more crops. He should have given the extra away (Luke 12:16–20). But Paul can confidently say of himself and his team: 'We have taken advantage of no one' (7:2) because they wanted 'you' (the Corinthians), not 'yours' (their belongings) (12:14).

Titus and another Christian had originally gone to Corinth (8:6) to help the Corinthians begin the process of saving for their donation (1 Corinthians 16:1). Paul now asks them directly: did Titus take advantage of you (v. 18)? Apparently, Titus is so honourable that the mere mention of his name would clear any fog of accusation.

The co-workers walk similarly

Paul then concludes (v. 18), reminding the Corinthians that Titus' co-workers are himself and Timothy. 'Conduct', literally, is to 'walk up and down', 'walk about'. People can have characteristic walks: some of us stoop over, others lean to one side, bounce up and down, drag our feet. Even today 'walk' is a metaphor for 'live'. Paul's opponents had accused Paul's team of walking 'according to the flesh' (10:2), but Paul responded that they walked 'in the flesh' (literally, 10:3). In verse 18 Paul reminds the Corinthians that their conduct or way of walking was similar to Titus'. They took the 'same steps' in the same 'walk'. Sometimes ancient cities would have footprints in the sidewalk to indicate to tourists how to get to a particular building. Paul, Titus, Timothy and the other co-workers all stepped on to footprints which followed Christ, the crucified Messiah (1 Peter 2:21). This was their common walk, their way (1 Corinthians 4:15–17).

MEDITATION

How can you be more satisfied with God's gifts to you so that you seek to love people, not what they own?

PAUL'S DEFENCE?

Paul now summarizes his letter (12:19—13:11). Verses 12:19 and 13:8–9 remind the Corinthians of chapters 1—5, Paul's defence of his team's behaviour: they behaved sincerely with pure motives in God's grace (1:3—2:17) and their competence comes from God (3:1—5:21). What has preceded has been intended to prepare the Corinthians to receive Paul. Have they been lulled by his apology into supposing that he has entered into some kind of public oratorical debate to impress the pseudo-apostles, while vying for the loyalty of the Corinthians? Paul denies that this has been his aim. What he has been doing is conducting a conversation in God's presence to help the Corinthians mature, preparing them for his visit.

A defence before God

Exactly what kind of letter is 2 Corinthians? Has it been a defence (v. 19)? *Apologeo* is a technical term, meaning to speak in one's own defence, especially before judges. Jesus warns his disciples that they will have to 'defend' their faith in him before synagogues, rulers and authorities, but not to fear, because the Holy Spirit will teach them what to say (Luke 12:11–12). Paul himself uses *apologeo* (the verb) and *apologe* (noun) to describe his talks before rulers Felix (Acts 24:10), Festus (Acts 25:8) and Agrippa (Acts 26:1–2). He also used *apologeo* to describe his defence before the authorities in Rome (Philippians 1:7, 16; 2 Timothy 4:16).

Aristotle classifies three general types of orations: 'deliberative', to persuade an assembly about the expediency or harmfulness of a future course of action; 'forensic', to convince judges about the justice or injustice of past events; and 'epideictic', to provide pleasure in the present, entertaining hearers by cleverly praising or attacking someone as worthy or not worthy of honour. The key for Aristotle is the hearer, the person to whom the speech is addressed. Hearers are members of the general assembly, 'a judge of things to come; the juror, of things past; the mere spectator, of the ability of the speaker' (*Rhetoric* i.iii). But who is Paul's hearer? Who is Paul's judge? All of 2 Corinthians does not clearly fit into any one of the above categories. It is not a defence before rulers or law courts. Paul certainly does not write simply to please his readers. His 'hearer' is God! Paul's judge and assembly is God! Moreover, rather than a formal defence (*apologeo*), Paul has conversations ('we are speaking') with God.

Paul repeats (v. 19) word for word the same phrases as in 2:17: 'before God in Christ we are speaking' (literally). Paul highlights how they speak, by placing the phrases 'before God' and 'in Christ' before the verb 'we are speaking'. What his team members state is done consciously before God as their witness in order to please God. Their words emanate from—and they live in—Christ's presence. From God they have received mercy, consolation (1:3–4; 4:1; 7:6), rescue (1:10; 4:14), anointing, the Spirit (1:21–22; 5:5), victory (2:14), competence (3:5), freedom (3:14), transformation (3:18), glorious knowledge, power (4:6–7; 6:7; 12:9), love (5:14), reconciliation (5:18–20), grace (9:14–15; 12:9), blessings (9:8), direction (10:13). Having received such wonderful things, having been sent out from God, logically Paul's team needs to work on behalf of their real audience, God.

Paul builds the temple

Therefore, because God is their real judge, Paul and his team can call the Corinthians 'beloved' and give of their all for 'building' them 'up' (v. 19). Love always builds up (1 Corinthians 8:1) and Paul has himself been loved and built up by the very God of love (1 John 4:7–8).

Paul was a tentmaker, and the greatest tent he could construct was God's living tabernacle (6:16). The Corinthians were 'God's building' (1 Corinthians 3:9). Paul has reminded the Corinthians that what he has done (1:23–24) and what he is doing (v. 19) and what he will do (13:10) is all to help them become more truly God's temple, set apart for God. One early Christian described God as 'constructing out of [Christians] a great and kingly house, glowing and full of light within and without, in that not only their heart and mind, but their body too, has been gloriously enriched with the many-blossomed adornment of chastity and temperance' (Eusebius, *History* 10:4).

PRAYER

You are great, O Lord God; for there is no one like you, and there is no God besides you.

David's prayer after learning that God would allow Solomon to build a temple, 2 Samuel 7:22

PRACTICES AFFECT EXPECTATIONS

If 12:19 and 13:8–9 refer back to Paul's defence in chapters 1—5, then 12:20—13:7 and 13:10–11 hearken back to chapters 6—12, where Paul entreats the Corinthians to change. Like poisonous weeds, the false apostles had flourished at Corinth because of the sinful environment already there. Like a good gardener, Paul will come and root these toxic growths out of his field; but, of more concern to him, he will till that field, filling it full of good nourishment that will allow healthy spiritual fruit to flourish (12:19). Paul wants the Corinthians to repent (v. 21), but if they do not do so, they will not be pleased with Paul. An analogy can be drawn to the alcoholic who hates parties where others do not drink. Such parties are not oriented to the most important practice in their lives—serious drinking. So, too, unrepentant Corinthians were orienting their lives toward 'works of the flesh' (Galatians 5:19–21), following the disguised angel, Satan (11:3, 14).

Some sins incite greater sins

The eight sins listed in verse 20 can be found in many an organization. 'Quarrelling' is strife. Like the goddess, Discord, who excites people to war, the Corinthians had formed themselves into 'combative' parties (1 Corinthians 1:11–12; 3:3). 'Jealousy' can be a positive trait if it protects people (7:11; 9:2; 11:2), but negative when it destroys them (v. 20).

The god Hades represented unbridled nature or 'anger' (v. 20) when he violently snatched Persephone. When Jesus told his hometown synagogue at Nazareth that Gentiles had more faith than they, they were filled with 'rage' and, ignoring legal means, sought to hurl Jesus off the cliff (Luke 4:28–29). 'Selfishness' is 'dispute, selfish or factious ambition, party squabbles'. Some adversarial believers at Rome were part of a 'party squabble' who did not think Paul should be in prison, increasing Paul's suffering in his imprisonment (Philippians 1:15–17).

'Slander' (katalalia) is to 'talk down' at someone. 'Gossip' (psithurismos) is 'whispering'. Katalalia might be an evil report announced before a person, while psithurismos may be stated behind a person's back. 'Conceit' (phusiosis) or 'inflation' is related to phusa, 'a pair of bellows' or 'wind'. Paul had warned the Corinthians already of the danger of being 'puffed up'. Some people had been acting that way in Corinth (1 Corinthians 4:6, 18–19), being 'puffed up' about the 'freedom' one believer exhibited in committing sexual immorality (1 Corinthians 5:2). Love, in contrast, 'builds up' (1 Corinthians 8:1; 13:4).

All these sins may appear insignificant, but the end result is horrific, producing 'disorder', which ultimately comes from Satan (James 3:14–16). 'Disorders', literally, are 'riots' (6:5) and 'insurrections' (Luke 21:9), as opposed to peace (1 Corinthians 14:33).

Other sins disown inheritors

The final three sins (v. 21) also flow out from the depths of one's being (Mark 7:21–22). 'Impurity', a general word, refers to an unclean, festering sore. In the old covenant it is a ceremonial impurity (Leviticus 15:3), like dead, mouldering bones (Matthew 23:27–28). Paul had warned the Corinthians not to associate with the 'unclean' (6:17).

'Sexual immorality' signifies any sexual acts done in a way not pleasing to God. It includes sexual intimacy apart from one's spouse, which was a major problem at Corinth (1 Corinthians 5:1; 6:15—7:2), a centre for sexual immorality in the ancient world. It also includes pornography (Matthew 5:27–28). 'Licentiousness' is 'unbridled lust', often associated with pagans and drunkenness (Ephesians 4:17–19; 1 Peter 4:3).

Unrepentant 'impurity' and 'sexual immorality' are included among sins which prevent us from inheriting God's reign (1 Corinthians 6:9; Ephesians 5:5). Sexual immorality also destroys Christ's temple (1 Corinthians 6:18). No wonder Paul mourned when people would not turn away from these sins in order to follow the living God (v. 21; 6:16)!

MEDITATION

Are you guilty of committing any of these sins,
of which you can repent?

CHARGES MUST BE BACKED UP

Paul states definitively what he has already previously announced (12:14): he will soon make his third visit to Corinth (v. 1). If Paul had not specified 'third', we would never know he made a second visit to Corinth. Paul's first visit to Corinth is recorded in Acts 18:1–18. Since it occurred during the office of proconsul Lucius Junius Gallio (Acts 18:12), the date of Paul's stay in Corinth (AD50–51) is one of the more definite New Testament dates.

Paul's second visit to Corinth is mentioned only in his letters. He left Ephesus to make what ended up as a brief 'painful visit' (2:1), apparently to deal with some 'arrogant' people (1 Corinthians 4:19). Paul's third visit to Corinth (following the reception of the letter 2 Corinthians) is described in Acts as a visit to 'Greece, where [Paul] stayed for three months' (Acts 20:2–3). Luke briefly mentions what must have been quite an emotionally laden visit.

Powerful testimony

Paul has heard of complaints about himself and charges by the Corinthians against one another. We know from 1 Corinthians 6:1 that they were taking each other to the Roman courts. Having been told (presumably by Titus), Paul prepares for grievances to occur again. Since 'slander' and 'gossip' are occurring in Corinth (12:20), truth will be needed to clear up false witnesses. Paul states first the basis on which the truth of grievances is established (v. 1), then he warns the Corinthians to be prepared (vv. 2–3). He quotes Jesus, who had explained that if we suspect a Christian of sinning against us, we need to go and indicate this sin privately between ourselves, with the hope that the other Christian hears us. If the matter is not resolved, then we need to return with two or three witnesses (Matthew 18: 15–16). Paul assumes the Corinthians have completed this first stage and discusses only the unresolved grievances. This principle of two or three witnesses goes back to the covenant God established through Moses. God prescribed the commandment that 'you shall not bear false witness against your neighbour' (Exodus 20:16). One way to prevent a false witness from establishing his or her deceit (Proverbs 12:17) was to require at least two or three witnesses to agree (Deuteronomy 19:15). Paul applies Jesus' teachings in Matthew 18:16 also to complaints against elders (1 Timothy 5:19) and to having fully representative teaching in church gatherings (1 Corinthians 14:27, 29).

A face-to-face witness is best

Multiple witnesses are, therefore, one guard for truth. In addition, the principle of two or three witnesses also highlights the importance of the verbal testimony: 'by mouths of two witnesses and three, every word will be made to stand' (literally, v. 1). We sometimes ask, 'Will this stand up in court?' The verb to 'stand' reaches back to biblical times. It personifies the word itself as a witness who stands up to speak. When Jesus first describes this principle, he uses the subjunctive, the mood of intention: 'so that every word might be made to stand' (Matthew 18:16). Paul uses the future, the mood of deliberation: 'every word will be made to stand' (v. 1), suggesting that Paul will definitely follow this principle.

Paul has uncovered his loving heart throughout 2 Corinthians. But if the Corinthians want a forceful presence (v. 3; 10:10–11), they will get it this time, but they will not like it. So Paul has warned them and continues to warn them (v. 2) to be prepared. Not everyone has committed 'impurity, sexual immorality, and licentiousness' (12:21; 13:2). But all will feel Paul's change of demeanour.

Now, 2000 years later, we cannot imagine that the Corinthians might have doubted that Christ was speaking through Paul (v. 3; 10:7). But the 'super-apostles' had undermined Paul's testimony as an apostle, by encouraging the Corinthians' doubts and replacing a gentle leadership style with an abusive, comfort-seeking one (10:1–2; 11:20–23). God is Paul's witness (1:23; 11:31; Galatians 1:12) that what he teaches and lives is commensurate with Christ's teachings.

PRAYER

Lord, let me be a faithful witness to you and to your people.

GOD'S POWER GIVES LIFE

Again Paul picks up the word 'weakness' that has been hurled in accusation against him. How does what Paul declared in 13:3–4 relate to his previous definitions of weakness? In relation to sin, in dealing with the Corinthians, Paul and Timothy are 'strong'. In their lifestyle they are 'weak'. Like Christ who was crucified in weakness, they live out of the strength of God.

Weakness leads to life

In verse 4, Paul summarizes his reinterpretation of 'weak'. In suffering for others, Christ is 'weak'. Christ is the ultimate model for Paul's team. Christ lived a life of difficulties, dangers, persecutions, insults, calamities. He was frequently near death. Yet God empowered him continually, even to a glorious resurrection (4:14). Therefore, Christ's followers need to live through difficulties for his sake, because God's strength will also empower them.

Paul wants the Corinthians to understand a marvellous paradox. Even as Jesus taught that only the seed which gets buried in the ground will grow (John 12:24–26), so too only the life given over to God will live (v. 4; 5:15). When Jesus was being crucified, of all people he appeared most pitiable. Thus, both the Roman and Jewish leaders and soldiers ridiculed and demeaned him (Luke 22:63; 23:10–11). But Jesus, for the 'weak', had become weak that he might win them (1 Corinthians 9:22). And God's omnipotent 'power' ('force' or 'strength') was what brought Jesus back to life (v. 4; 1 Corinthians 6:14).

'Power' in its relation to 'weakness' is an important theme for Paul. Paul never says that God is not powerful. God's power is phenomenal (4:7)! However, God's phenomenal power sometimes looks like foolishness to those people whose backs are presented to God and whose faces gaze toward the world (1 Corinthians 1:18). Even witnessing powerful miracles in themselves will not last as the basis for a victorious Christian walk (1 Corinthians 1:22). Rather, perseverance is enabled by loving and obeying and relying on Christ who is himself 'the power of God and the wisdom of God' (1 Corinthians 1:24).

Christian leaders follow Christ

Paul's team's own analogy to Christ has striking similarities and differences. Jesus, at a specific past point in time, 'was crucified' (v. 4). He no longer continues to be crucified. For the Jews, this was a disappointing event because many expected the Messiah to overthrow the Romans politically (Acts 1:6). For the Gentiles, crucifixion was a shameful death (1 Corinthians 1:23, 27–28). 'Weakness' was the basis from which the crucifixion happened. Jesus allowed himself to be 'weak', in other words, arrested and killed, in order to redeem the 'weak', sinful humanity (v. 4; 5:19).

But Jesus now lives continuously. He was resurrected and he remains resurrected. 'God's power' was the basis. Meanwhile, Paul and his team are now continuously 'weak', enduring difficulties for Christ's sake. And in the process they identify with Christ's sufferings ('weak in him', v. 4). Paul's team do not 'live' now, but they look forward both literally and symbolically to a future rebirth. This 'life' is the final resurrection, a future literal event. Glorious commendation from God is a future, not a present, event for genuine Christians.

This future life is modified by three phrases: 'with him', 'from God's power', 'to you' (v. 4, literally). By enduring the same tribulations as Christ did ('in him'), they will be sure to be resurrected 'with' Jesus. The community of suffering will be continued in a community of victory. The same source of power, God, that resurrected Jesus will resurrect Paul, Timothy, Titus and others. Because Paul and his co-workers are willing to limit gratification to the future, they then can be Corinthian-focused.

Vibia Perpetua of Africa was brought to the arena to be killed (AD203). Looking forward to being with the resurrected Christ, even in the midst of her suffering she could be focused toward others, teaching, 'Remain strong in your faith and love one another. Do not let our excruciating suffering become a stumbling block for you' (*Martyrdom of Perpetua* 19).

MEDITATION

What are your gut-level feelings about 'strength' and 'weakness'?
How can you more rely on God's resuscitating power?

TESTS *of* ALL KINDS

Test yourselves against Christ's example, Paul counsels (13:4–6). 'You' is plural. Christ's model is imitated where at least two or three are present (13:1). Paul wants the Corinthians to do good (v. 7). While they may fail to imitate Christ, he hopes that they will recognize that he and his co-workers have not failed. That proof of the presence of Christ that was challenged by Paul's accusers is displayed in a life withstanding the sufferings Christ endured, and through them experiencing the power of God that Christ manifested. Why does Paul undergo such suffering? Has not Jesus' death been sufficient, so that Christians do not have to suffer? Paul's purpose is didactic. We are the only Jesus that many people will ever see. Christ-in-us is the ministry that models Jesus' example for the world. Model on me, Paul once counselled the Corinthians, as I model on Christ (1 Corinthians 4:16; 11:1).

Paul responds to tests

Suddenly Paul appears to discuss a lot of 'tests': 'examine yourselves', 'test yourselves', 'fail to meet the test', 'failed', 'met the test' (vv. 5–7). Sometimes students are attracted to teachers who boast about being 'rigorous' as if the class were a necessary race toward achieving academic maturity. Some students barely crawl over the hurdles to completion and others crash against the hurdles devastated. Paul appears to repeat the imagery of 'tests', probably because the super-apostles had flaunted their claims to be 'super', 'preeminent' achievers as 'apostles'.

Since the point at issue is evidence of Christ's authority, Paul reminds the Corinthians who Christ is and what Christ is like. Christ is the one who was crucified, whom Paul and his team imitate (13:4). Therefore, Paul begins verse 5 with the object: 'yourselves—examine'. The Corinthians should test themselves! In reminding them of Christ's character, Paul shows that they are the ones who are using the wrong criteria. 'Examine' (*peirazo*) has mainly negative connotations in the New Testament. *Peirazo* can refer to an experiment or exploration, as opposed to a spontaneous or accidental act. Satan 'tempts' because he experiments on people, intending them to fail (for example, 1 Corinthians 7:5). Some religious leaders tried to test Jesus, hoping he would fail their tests (see, for example, Matthew 16:1; 19:3; 22:18, 35). Similarily, Paul recommends that the Corinthians, who want to conduct a test with the intent that Paul fail, can take that test themselves!

'Test yourselves' (v. 5; 'proof', v. 3, *dokimazo*), which is mainly positive in 2 Corinthians, means 'examine for authenticity before giving approval, verify'. Luke and the Macedonian churches are such 'verified' believers (8:2, 22). *Dokime* signifies the verification of an elected candidate or the examination of metal. Thus, the Corinthians should establish their own authenticity before Paul.

Finally, Paul raises a question for the Corinthians: are they themselves in doubt about whether 'Christ is in' them (v. 5)? Are they thoroughly confident of Christ's presence among them? Or, are they afraid that they themselves may not be qualified? 'Fail to meet the test' means 'worthless', 'dross' removed from silver (Proverbs 25:4), a runner 'disqualified' from receiving the trophy (1 Corinthians 9:27). In other words, are these Corinthian doubts about Paul in reality projections, on to Paul and his co-workers, of fears about themselves (v. 5)?

Paul prays for their success

In verse 6 Paul makes a transition from the Corinthian expectations to his own expectations. His goal ('hope') for the Corinthians is that they will come to learn (through his letter and his co-workers) that he and his team are not disqualified. Paul's prayer to God (v. 7) on their behalf has several parts, all of which make one point: we want you to do well. First, they do not pray that the Corinthians 'do anything wrong'. Moreover, they do not want the Corinthians to see themselves in competition with Paul. Thus, Paul's main concern is not that he and his co-workers are approved. He might even be willing for his team to look as if they are disqualified. His main concern is that the Corinthians do 'right'. Paul wants the Corinthians to become purified gold.

PRAYER

Prove me, O Lord, and try me; test my heart and mind. For your steadfast love is before my eyes, and I walk in faithfulness to you.

Psalm 26:2–3

COMMUNITY LIVING

After explaining his own expectations for the Corinthians (13:6–7), Paul repeats the key principles behind his team's actions (vv. 8–9), the main reason he wrote the letter (v. 10) and his summary of exhortations to the Corinthians (v. 11).

Paul works for truth

Love 'rejoices in the truth', Paul had taught (1 Corinthians 13:6). Therefore, in one letter Paul could express both his love for the Christians (for example, 12:15) and his desire that they do good (13:7–8). At first glance, verse 9 might be mistaken as a final ironic shot by Paul: 'We rejoice when we are weak and you are strong.' But nothing surrounding this verse is ironic. Instead, Paul is revealing that he has modelled Christ for them so that they might enjoy the power of God (13:4). All of his actions, even his receipt of authority, have been for the purpose of building up the saints (v. 10). How truly he has emulated the suffering servant, displaying the greatest love that is possible in his willingness to give his life for the churches.

'That you may become perfect' (*katartisis*, v. 9) and 'put things in order' (*katarizo*, v. 11) have the basic sense of maturing, restoring, as in 'mending' a net (Matthew 4:21). The Corinthians are a 'ripped net' which needs to be 'mended'. Paul prays for their 'mending' (v. 9) and then commands the Corinthians to 'be mended' (v. 11), a two-pronged balance between prayer and action.

In verse 10 Paul explicitly expresses the purpose of the whole letter—a warning before punishment. God told Ezekiel, 'I have no pleasure in the death of the wicked, but that the wicked turn from their ways and live' (Ezekiel 33:11). The Lord also taught Peter that the Lord 'is patient with you, not wanting any to perish, but all to come to repentance' (2 Peter 3:9). Thus we, too, need to warn those under our own authority, not once but repeatedly, persuasively and clearly before enacting any punishment, because our goal is to build up others into God's marvellous living pillars (1 Peter 2:5; 2 Corinthians 13:10).

Paul advises siblings

Paul summarizes his exhortations to his beloved 'brothers and sisters' with five verbs of command (v. 11). 'Farewell' can also be translated 'rejoice' (NRSV).

'Joy' and 'grace' (the noun forms of 'rejoice') remind the reader that God's grace—that which affords joy, pleasure and delight—works through difficulties. Paul's team relies on God's grace (1:12). Humans who rely on God's grace then pass on that grace to others (1:15; 4:15; 8:1). Afterwards, 'grace' is returned to God as 'thanks' (2:14; 8:16; 9:15). Thus, the first step in change is gladness, rejoicing because God is at work providing so many interrelated gifts. And a positive attitude will bring out the best in all.

'Put things in order' is next because the Corinthians need to end wrongdoing in an attempt to mend themselves both individually and corporately. 'Listen to my appeal' or, more literally, 'encourage for yourself', now suggests positive action. God encourages us so that we can encourage others. The Corinthians need to become others-oriented, once they have mended themselves.

Then they will be ready to 'agree with one another' (v. 11). Paul wants the Corinthians to have the same purpose, which is to imitate Christ who 'was crucified in weakness, but lives by the power of God' (13:4).

Finally, the Corinthians are to 'live in peace'. 'Grace' and 'peace' are two key attributes of God (1:2). Literally, on a personal level, 'peace' is complete physical wholeness, being without injury. On a national or community level, it is freedom from war. The church in Corinth has been a place of war—'quarrelling, jealousy, anger, selfishness, slander, gossip, conceit, and disorder' (12:20). If they move through this progression of positive attitude, reparation, advocacy and unity of purpose, they will end up working together for each other's well-being.

James says, 'Draw near to God' and God 'will draw near to you' (James 4:8). If the Corinthians became more godly, then the God who is the source of love and peace would accompany them (v. 11).

MEDITATION

How is your church doing in the areas of rejoicing, mending, advocating, unifying and doing justice?

THREE CIRCLES *of* LOVING PEACE

As Paul closes this letter, he expands the concept of 'love and peace' (13:11) with greater and greater concentric circles: the local congregation, the church as a whole, God.

Loving peace is between Christians

The first circle begins in the immediate; that is, from one Christian to a neighbouring Christian. Paul urges, 'Greet one another with a holy kiss' (v. 12). Some cultures still practise the kiss on the cheek as a personal symbol of welcome. A kiss should be a sign of love (1 Peter 5:14). Thus, Judas' kiss to betray Jesus was like death drawn from a means of life (Luke 22:47–48). 'Affection' can express many different types of love, but this one is 'holy', dedicated to God, an outward sign for believers who have been justified by God ('the saints', 1:1) and who are striving to become pure in practice (7:1). Thus, this kiss represents welcome, communion, peace, God's love and holiness. In the early Church it became a part of every service. Before the Lord's Supper, the kiss indicated peace or reconciliation between members of the congregation (Justin Martyr, *First Apology* 65). Thus, when Paul urged, 'Greet one another with a holy kiss', he was entreating that they be reconciled to one another and that they indicate it by the sign of reconciliation. This, then, is the first circle—that the Corinthians be reconciled one with another.

The next circle expands out with the next phrase, 'All the saints greet you' (v. 12). Paul has sounded again and again his theme of economic family interdependence among the churches. Now he reminds the churches one last time that there are other Christians around them who take an interest in them. Which saints specifically does he have in mind? No doubt Paul means the Macedonians with whom he has just been ministering and whose example he has held up continually before the Corinthians, some of whom he will bring with him to receive the Corinthian collection. 'All the saints greet you' reminds the Corinthians that they are but one part of a unifying whole, and they ought to contribute to the good of that whole.

God gives loving peace

Finally, Paul ends with the greatest circle of all, the one in which we live and move and have our being, as he reminded the Athenians (Acts 17:28): 'The grace of the Lord Jesus Christ and the love of God and the communion of the Holy Spirit be with all of you' (literally, v. 13). The great divine family, the unified Trinity, the God who is three-in-one, is in relationship with all of the Corinthians.

The Bible does not always refer to God the Trinity in the order of Father and Son and Holy Spirit (Matthew 28:19). Here the sequence is Jesus and God and Holy Spirit, possibly because Paul's letter has focused on the 'grace' of Jesus Christ who gave joyfully of himself (13:13, 4; 8:9; 5:14–21; 1:5). In Paul's first letter, as he highlighted the work of the Holy Spirit, Paul listed the sequence as Spirit, Lord, God (1 Corinthians 12:4–6). The qualities of 'grace', 'love' and 'communion' are true of all persons of the Trinity.

Grace, love and communion (partnership) are three concepts Paul has highlighted in this letter as necessary especially for the Corinthians. God, who is 'love' (1 John 4:8), loves the cheerful giver (9:7) and is the source for the mutual love between Christians (2:4, 8; 8:24; 11:11; 12:15). The Spirit, who searches everything (1 Corinthians 2:10), then brings genuine 'partnership' to the church, Christians sharing with one another in suffering, advocacy and material gifts (v. 13; 1:7; 8:4; 9:13).

From single believers, to the Church of all believers, to the great engulfing, surrounding love of the triune Godhead, Paul draws a powerful picture of the connecting bonds of love that embrace the Corinthians. 2 Corinthians has been a masterpiece of persuasive literature—poignant, passionate, compelling. How could the Corinthians not respond to such a powerful portrait of their true status?

PRAYER

May we be like rain that falls on the mown grass, like showers that water the earth. In our days may righteousness flourish and peace abound, until the moon is no more.

Paraphrase of the prayer for Solomon, Psalm 72:6–7

NOTES

NOTES

NOTES

NOTES

NOTES

NOTES

NOTES

THE PEOPLE'S BIBLE COMMENTARY

VOUCHER SCHEME

The People's Bible Commentary (PBC) provides a range of readable, accessible commentaries that will grow into a library covering the whole Bible.

To help you build your PBC library, we have a voucher scheme that works as follows: a voucher is printed on the last page of each People's Bible Commentary volume (as above). These vouchers count towards free copies of other books in the series.

For every four purchases of PBC volumes you are entitled to a further volume FREE.

Please find the coupon for the PBC voucher scheme overleaf.

All you need do:

- Cut out the vouchers from the last page of the PBCs you have purchased and attach them to the coupon.

- Complete your name and address details, and indicate your choice of free book from the list on the coupon.

- Take the coupon to your local Christian bookshop who will exchange it for your free PBC book; or send the coupon straight to BRF who will send you your free book direct. Please allow 28 days for delivery.

Please note that PBC volumes provided under the voucher scheme are subject to availability. If your first choice is not available, you may be sent your second choice of book.

THE PEOPLE'S BIBLE COMMENTARY
VOUCHER SCHEME COUPON

```
┌─────────────┐  ┌─────────────┐
│             │  │             │
│             │  │             │
│             │  │             │
│             │  │             │
└─────────────┘  └─────────────┘

┌─────────────┐  ┌─────────────┐
│             │  │             │
│             │  │             │
│             │  │             │
│             │  │             │
└─────────────┘  └─────────────┘
```

TO BE COMPLETED BY THE CUSTOMER

My choice of free PBC volume is
(please indicate your first and
second choice, as all volumes are
supplied subject to availability):

❑ 1 and 2 Samuel

❑ 1 and 2 Kings

❑ Chronicles to Nehemiah

❑ Psalms 1—72

❑ Psalms 73—150

❑ Proverbs

❑ Nahum to Malachi

❑ Mark

❑ Luke

❑ John

❑ Romans

❑ 1 Corinthians

❑ 2 Corinthians

❑ Galatians and Thessalonians

❑ Timothy, Titus and Hebrews

❑ James to Jude

❑ Revelation

Name: . . . .

Address: . . . .

. . . .

Postcode: . . . .

TO BE COMPLETED BY THE BOOKSELLER

(Please complete the following.
Coupons redeemed will be
credited to your account for the value
of the book(s) supplied as indicated
above. Please note that only coupons
correctly completed with original
vouchers will be accepted for credit.):

Name: . . . .

Address: . . . .

. . . .

Postcode: . . . .

Account Number: . . . .

Completed coupons should be
sent to: BRF, PBC Voucher Scheme,
First Floor, Elsfield Hall, 15–17
Elsfield Way, OXFORD OX2 8EP

Tel 01865 319700
Fax 01865 319701
Registered Charity No. 233280

THIS OFFER IS AVAILABLE IN THE UK ONLY
PLEASE NOTE: ALL VOUCHERS ATTACHED TO THIS COUPON MUST BE ORIGINAL COPIES.